CAROL CARTER

Majoring in the Rest of Your Life

Carol Carter is her own best success story.
She became Prentice Hall's director of marketing by age twenty-six
and is now vice president and publisher of Student Success and
Career Development at Prentice Hall. She lives in Denver, Colorado.

Majoring in the Rest of Your Life

Career Secrets for College Students

Carol Carter

FARRAR, STRAUS AND GIROUX
NEW YORK

Farrar, Straus and Giroux
19 Union Square West, New York 10003

Copyright © 1990, 1995, 1999 by Carol Carter
Afterword copyright © 1999 by Carol Carter
All rights reserved

Distributed in Canada by Douglas & McIntyre Ltd.

Printed in the United States of America

Designed by H. Roberts Design
Illustrations by Howard Roberts

First published in 1990 by The Noonday Press/Farrar, Straus and Giroux
Revised edition, 1995
Third edition, 1999

Library of Congress Cataloging-in-Publication Data

Carter, Carol.
    Majoring in the rest of your life : career secrets for college
students / Carol Carter. — Rev. ed.
        p.   cm.
    ISBN 0-374-52602-8 (alk. paper)
    1. Vocational guidance—United States.   2. College students—
Employment—United States.
    HF5382.5.U5C37   1999
    650.14—dc21   98-46504

See pages 287–288 for permissions.

*For my parents, John and Mary,
and my brothers, David, Scott, Craig, and Kent,
who have always provided the balance between
being demanding and being supportive*

Contents

APPENDICES

Majoring in the Rest of Your Life

Introduction

"Dear Freshman..."

Majoring in the Rest of Your Life can help you choose a career and give you specific suggestions to get you from your freshman to your senior year and on to the job of your dreams. It makes no difference whether you've already selected a career. Just keep your mind open. All that's necessary, really, is for you to commit yourself to getting a good education, setting career goals and then working to reach them.

For Example?

Mark Garrety graduated from the University of Washington with a history degree and a 3.9 grade average. Four months later he still hadn't found a job.

Sharon Heider partied through four years at the University of Georgia. She was a marketing major with mediocre grades. Everybody loved her. Now she's a bank teller. People still love her. But she's unhappy and thinks a degree should be bankable for more than $19,000 a year.

José Rodríguez is a senior at Northwestern. He's made good grades, worked part-time in the library, and served as campus coordinator for the United Way. What will he do after graduation? José has no clue. Law school, maybe.

Then there's you. You're browsing through these pages wondering why you should read this book. Will it really help you get a job once you're out of school?

Yes. It will help you analyze your interests and decide what you do and don't like in and out of school, and it will give you advice on how to get from your first freshman class to your first job.

By reading this book and taking action, you'll be one giant step closer to the job you want. The job that stimulates you, motivates you, challenges you, inspires the best in you. The job that is invigorating as well as rewarding.

But that's what everybody wants, you say. True, but it's not what everybody gets. Why?

Because most of us are ill-prepared in two areas: self-awareness and planning. Put simply, you must first know what you want and then devise a strategy that will enable you to get it. These skills aren't typically taught in college. They are secrets of common sense that one learns readily on the job. But they *can* be learned in school. In fact, if you learn them early, you'll have an enormous advantage once you're out working.

Second, few people in college bother to get good advice. They fail to realize that there are all kinds of people whose perspective on college, jobs, and life can greatly benefit them. This book gives you lots of examples of how people in college and at work continue their education, build their skills, and enjoy themselves. You'll see that there are many different methods to achieve success. And you'll learn how to develop relationships with people: how to get help from them and how to give help yourself.

Third, this book will show you not only how to recognize opportunity but how to *act* on it. Seizing the moment is as important as thinking things through. You'll learn how to make your pipe dreams real.

Most important, you will learn to recognize your own unique potential. This is not a way of looking at the world that puts you at the top by placing everybody else at the bottom. On the contrary. It is a way to understand that everyone can succeed.

You will take this knowledge and experience and put it to work for you. You will learn to overcome the fears and doubts that limit your ability to go after what you want. Bottom line: you will learn to tap your own internal resources and talents.

So remember, the only person you have to compete with is you. You know the dialogue between your ego and alter ego: one says "Go for it!" while the other screams "No way, I'm scared!" You'll learn to bring these two sides into line so that YOU can really work for YOU.

Okay, you say. I'm ready. But maybe I don't know what I want to do.

No problem. This book will help you define your skills and interests so you can choose a career. Maybe you screwed up in high school. Okay, college is a clean slate. Maybe academics aren't your strong suit. Well, you can strengthen your weak suit and finesse your strong ones into a winning hand. (The classroom isn't the only proving ground.) Maybe you've never held a job or joined a club. All right, you can start now.

You'll use this book throughout your college career. So the earlier you read it, the better. If you're a freshman, great. If you're a senior, that's fine too. It will teach you valuable business lessons that will help you in your first job.

How can *Majoring in the Rest of Your Life* best serve you? Read it from cover to cover the summer before or during your freshman year. That will give you a broad overview. As you go from one year to the next, you can refer to the book as necessary. In your freshman year you'll have little need for the information on landing a job, but it is useful to know at the outset what kinds of things you'll have to prepare for down the road. After reading this book once, keep it on your reference shelf next to your dictionary and textbooks.

Life Skills

Each chapter in *Majoring in the Rest of Your Life* will help you both in college and out. The "tools" for success are categorized below, but you will learn their true meaning in the context of real-life situations in school, and later at work. For now, just take note of each skill.

If you master these skills in college, chances are you will have a greater chance of succeeding scholastically. Think of the categories below as life skills. Though few people are adept at all of them, becoming good at some of them is a significant accomplishment. Decide which skills you have. Then think about the ones you want to work on and develop over the next few years.

1. *Write Your Own Success Story*
- **Planning/Organizing.** The ability to define specific points of action for yourself and others, which will allow you to set priorities and get a job— or goal—completed successfully.

2. *Discover Who You Are*
- **Problem-Solving/Analytical Skills.** The ability to analyze and identify problems, determine their causes, and make suggestions for resolving them. The ability to take positive action.

3. *Futures and Options*
- **Creativity/Innovativeness.** The ability to let your mind wander; to discern larger patterns and relationships, to see the overall as well as the detail-filled picture.

4. *Take the Plunge*
- **Drive/Energy.** The sheer energy to get the most out of your courses and your professors while balancing your work and activities. The ability to be productive over long hours; to go above and beyond what's required.

5. *Being on Your Own*
- **Continuous Improvement.** The ability to commit yourself to lifelong education and continuous personal improvement through stretching your mind, learning new skills, and embracing change.

6. *Stand Up and Be Counted*
- **Teamwork.** The ability to work with others toward a common goal; to be supportive of their ideas and to focus on the goals of the group.
- **People Management.** The ability to work with a group by helping each member to set and define personal and group goals; to delegate responsibility and to give constant credit to those who participate.
- **Leadership.** The ability to influence others in a positive, motivating way; to command attention and respect.

7. *The Real World*
- **Commonsense Smarts.** The ability to know how things work in the "real world"; to know instinctively what to do in different kinds of situations.

8. *Intern We Trust*
- **Independence/Tenacity.** The ability to be unconventional; to take a stand on something you firmly believe in, but which may be unpopular with a larger group.

9. *Windows on the World*
- **Personal Adaptability.** The ability to adjust quickly to any situation, group of people, or environment; to use past experiences to measure new ones and to respond nondefensively to criticism.

10. *Networking*

- **Communication.** The ability to articulate your thoughts well, both on paper and orally; to speak effectively one-on-one as well as in groups.

11. *Paperwork*

- **Marketing Yourself.** The ability to make a clear and convincing presentation to those whom you want to persuade.

12. *Your Third Degree*

- **Interpersonal Skills.** The ability to talk openly and freely with others; to put them at ease with you and to exude confidence and enthusiasm.

13. *You're Hired!*

- **Stress Tolerance.** The ability to cope in stressful or discouraging situations; to keep things in perspective.

14. *Outlooks and Insights*

- **Results/Remaining Goal-Oriented.** The ability to set measurable and attainable goals and to be motivated by the challenge of achieving them.

At the end of each year, refer to this list. Where have you made progress? Where do you need to improve? Which specific goals will you set to help you improve?

1

Write Your Own Success Story

Planning Ahead

I find that the harder I work, the more luck I seem to have.
Thomas Jefferson

We have an extraordinary leverage and influence—individually, professionally, and institutionally—if we can only get a clear sense, a clear conception, a clear vision of the road ahead.
John Naisbitt, in Megatrends

Who am I to talk to high school graduates and college freshmen about planning? As a high school student in Tucson, Arizona, I never planned. I just coasted along, letting things happen to me. Sure, I was spontaneous. I spent weeknights talking on the phone and studied only when I felt like it—i.e., seldom. On weekends my friends and I roamed shopping malls and partied in the mountains. The typical irresponsible high school student.

And then, BOOM. The ax fell. The ax was not some accident, scandal, or divine intervention. It was simply a conversation with my older brother Craig during the first week of my senior year in high school. Our talk changed the course of my life.

At seventeen I was intimidated by my four older brothers. I saw them as bright, motivated, and respected achievers—the opposite of me. Whenever one of them asked me about what I was doing or thinking, I'd answer with a one-liner and hope he'd soon leave me alone.

This conversation with Craig was different. He didn't give up after five minutes, despite my curt, vague responses.

"Carol, what are you interested in?"

"I dunno."

"What do you think about all day?"

"I dunno."

"What do you want to do with your life?"

"I'll just let things happen."

Craig persisted. His voice grew indignant. He criticized me for talking on the phone, for spending too much time at pep rallies and rock concerts, for not studying, for not challenging myself. He pointed out that I hadn't read an unassigned book in three years. He asked if I intended to approach college the way I'd approached high school—as one continuous party. If so, he warned, I'd better start thinking of a career flipping burgers at the local hamburger stand, because no respectable employer would ever take me seriously. He asked me if that was what I wanted to do with my life. He cautioned me that out of laziness and lack of planning, I would limit my options so narrowly that I would never be able to get a real job. I had wasted three years of high school, he said. College was a new start, since employers and graduate schools seldom check as far back as high school for records. So he advised me to quit making excuses, decide what I wanted, and plan how to achieve it. My only limitations would be self-imposed.

Craig then left my room, sermon completed. I didn't speak to him before he flew back to New York that afternoon to finish his senior year at Columbia.

I hated him for interfering with my life. He made me dissatisfied with myself. I was scared he was right. For the first time, I realized that "typical" was not necessarily what I wanted to be.

The next day, still outraged but determined to do something, I went to the library and checked out six classics: *Pride and Prejudice* by Jane Austen; *The Great Gatsby* by F. Scott Fitzgerald; *A Farewell to Arms* and *For Whom the Bell Tolls* by Ernest Hemingway; *A Portrait of the Artist as a Young Man* by James Joyce; and *Sister Carrie* by Theodore Dreiser. Then I wrote down in a notebook a few goals that I wanted to accomplish. They all seemed boldly unattainable: Earn straight A's (previously I had made B's and C's); study every week, including one weekend night; keep reading classics on my own. If I couldn't make it in my senior year of high school, why should I waste time and money on college? I'd beat fate to the door and begin my career at the hamburger stand immediately.

Three weeks later, I got a letter from Craig. He knew how angry I was with him. He told me that our conversation hadn't been easy for him either, but that if he hadn't cared, he wouldn't have bothered to say anything. He was right. I'd needed that sermon. If I didn't come to terms with my problems, I would never be able to move from making excuses to making things happen.

I worked hard and got results. The second semester of my senior year, I made all A's (except for a B in physics). I finished the six classics, and others as well. I started reading newspapers and magazines. I had to move the *Vogue* on my nightstand to make room for *Time, Harper's*, and *Fortune*. I found that I could set goals and attain them, and I started to realize that I wasn't so different from my brothers after all.

To my utter astonishment, I discovered that for the first time, I enjoyed learning. My world seemed to open up just because I knew more about different kinds of people, ways of thinking, and ways of interpreting what I had previously assumed to be black-and-white. (If you are a shy person, joining a club and getting to know—and actually like—a few people whom you had originally perceived as unfriendly or uninteresting may astonish you as much as my newfound appreciation for learning astonished me.)

The summer before college, I thought about what I wanted to do with my life, but couldn't decide on a direction. I had no notion of what I wanted to major in. What to do . . . what to do?

I turned to Craig, a phone call away in New York City. He told me not to spend my first year of college worrying about what I wanted to do. The main priority was to learn as much as I could. College, he told me, was my golden opportunity to investigate all kinds of things—biology, psychology, accounting, philosophy. He told me I'd become good at writing and critical-thinking techniques—skills that would help me learn any job after graduation. And though I could continue to expand my educational horizons throughout life, college was the best opportunity to expose myself to the greatest minds and movements of our civilization.

Craig also warned me that being a scholar, though important, wouldn't be enough. (He had just graduated from Columbia as a Phi Beta Kappa, but since he hadn't gained any real-world experience in college, it took him several months to find his first job.) To maximize my options upon graduation, I would have to do three things:

1. Learn as much as possible from classes, books, professors, and other people
2. Participate in extracurricular activities
3. Get *real-world* experience by working part-time and landing summer internships

If I did these three things reasonably well, Craig assured me, I could choose from a number of career opportunities at the end of my senior year. And even if I only did two of the three full-force and one half-speed, I'd still be in good shape. Making an effort in each area and having a modest outcome were attainable goals. That way I could balance my college experience and open options for the future.

Craig advised me to look ahead and develop a plan of action for each of my four years of college. He told me that foresight—the ability to consider the bigger picture beyond short-term challenges and intermediary goals—is invaluable in most jobs; it distinguishes outstanding people from the rest of the pack.

This book is designed to be for you what Craig was for me—my adviser during college. The following chapters will provide you with guidelines for success by asking you to examine yourself, set goals, and believe in your ability to achieve them. It will give you specific examples of how to get things done. It will also introduce you to all kinds of people, all of whom followed their own varying, yet similar, paths toward their goals. Most important, you'll learn that everyone—including YOU—has his or her own set of skills, abilities, passions, and talents to tap. Finding the career and lifestyle that allows you to cultivate and nurture them is one of the most important secrets of success.

So Take Action!

A good way to start is to assess your shortcomings and strengths. As I've already told you, one of my shortcomings in high school was not learning all I could from my classes and teachers. Your shortcoming may have been that you focused entirely on your studies without developing many outside interests. Someone else may feel that he concentrated so much on an outside activity—such as training for a particular sport—that he had no time for studies or friends. What was your major shortcoming in high school?

Now think about three things:

1. What pleased you in high school?
2. What could you have done better?
3. What do you want to improve upon in the future?

Identifying these areas will help you strike a good balance during college. Once you get in the habit of analyzing past experiences, you will have a clearer notion of what you do and don't want in the future. That's important.

As a high school senior, a college freshman, or a college senior, the next thing you must do is decide to take action. Don't worry if you don't know what you want to do. Just commit yourself to the process. If you do, you'll eventually find out which careers might be best for you and how you could best prepare for them.

To recap, here are the priorities:

1. Gain knowledge
2. Participate in activities
3. Get *real-world* experience

Making It Happen

"Luck is the residue of design," said Branch Rickey, known as the Mahatma for his strategic methods as a team owner and general manager in baseball. He developed the farm system in which the minor leagues are organized. His plans of action took a handful of disjointed teams in faraway cities and banded them into an organization that has left its mark on American culture.

Nothing happens magically. If you want to be a success, you are going to have to take personal responsibility for your life. Why do some graduates get twenty job offers while others receive none?

Although successful people may appear lucky, in fact they illustrate the maxim "Luck favors the prepared mind."

Joe Cirulli agrees. He is the owner of the successful Gainesville Health and Fitness Center in Florida. Early on in his life, exercise was a priority, an essential part of his day. So he followed his interests and put his talents to work by starting his own health club. While many other clubs have folded around him, he has experienced enormous success—his membership continues to grow, and he is able to keep his club filled with the best equipment and the most knowledgeable professionals.

When Joe was twenty, he worked as an assistant manager and sales representative for a health club. One of his responsibilities was to train new sales representatives for the club. He worked hard to prepare them for their jobs only to have to compete with them once they were trained.

He remembers talking with the vice president of the company about his frustration. The vice president, a person Joe respected, advised him to keep on putting his best efforts into his work. "Right now you may not see the benefit of your hard work, but one day you will."

Joe followed his advice. Less than five years later, his skill at training people in the health club industry paid off—he was able to put his expertise to work in his own health club. "Knowing how to motivate employees to do their best, to care about the quality of their work and to care about our customers, has had an enormous impact on the success of my own company."

Joe believes the secret to his success is giving 100 percent of himself in everything he does. "Success is the culmination of all your efforts. There are thousands of opportunities for people who give their all."

How do you arrange to have the most options when you leave college? Plan, develop foresight, and take charge of your life and you will become one of the lucky ones. Most important, decide that you want to succeed—and believe it.

Charles Garfield, a clinical psychologist who has spent his career studying what motivates people to superior effort, says that the drive to excel comes primarily from within. Can "peak performances" be learned? Yes, says Garfield. High achievers are not extraordinarily gifted superhumans. What they have in common is the ability to cultivate what the German writer Johann Wolfgang von Goethe termed "the genius, power, and magic" that exists in all of us. These achievers increase the odds in their favor through simple techniques that anyone can cultivate:

- Envision a mission
- Be result-oriented
- Tap your internal resources
- Enlist team spirit
- Treat setbacks as stepping-stones

These are skills that this book is going to teach you.

First Things First

The first thing to keep in mind when planning: Accept the world the way it is. Your plans should be based on a realistic assessment of how things are, not on some starry-eyed vision of how they should be. You can dream, but there's a happy medium between cold reality and pie in the sky. That's why you must be open to opportunity. Indeed, you must create it. Although you can't change the hand you were dealt, you can play it as wisely as possible. That's what this book is about.

So start today. Start now.

The more questions you ask now, the better prepared you'll be in four years. You don't want to be stuck in a boring job or wondering why you can't find work.

Are you going to make mistakes? I hope so, unless you're not of the human species. Making mistakes is the process by which we learn. And whenever we're disappointed by the outcome, we have to maintain a positive attitude, log the information—and keep going. The key is to learn from mistakes without letting them slow us down.

2

Discover Who You Are

Defining Your Interests, Abilities, and Goals

Know thyself.
Inscription, Temple of Delphi

To thine own self be true.
Shakespeare

Y ou've been told that it pays to find out everything you can about the colleges you're thinking of attending and the jobs they might lead to. But it's also worthwhile to do some serious research into the subject that can make or break your college experience: *yourself*.

Phil was a pre-law freshman. After spending six months talking to law students and attorneys, he made a great discovery: he realized that he didn't want to be a lawyer. No area of law intrigued him. He disliked spending hours in solitary research, and law didn't accommodate his strong suits—working with groups and developing programs. So Jeff switched his major to English and his minor to history. Today he's in business for himself as an international marketing consultant. And he loves his work.

If you don't know yourself, you'll make uninformed decisions. My college friend Mary was an accounting major because she knew she'd be employable. She was right. However, after graduating, she discovered that she hated working with numbers, and after just two years, she quit accounting. So long, general ledger.

I recently had dinner with Mary. She's living in New York and writing for a food-and-wine magazine. We talked about the internal struggles that had prompted her to make a career change. Now she's crazy about her job and only regrets that she didn't invest the time and energy in college to determine her interests. "College students shouldn't opt for a career because it will be easy to find a job," Mary says. " 'Easy' can equal 'uninteresting' and 'unfulfilling' if you don't have passion and interest for the work itself. Pursue what will be rewarding in the short term *and* the long term."

Cathy Hudnall agrees. After five years as a secretary at Wells Fargo Bank in San Francisco, she was invited to join the bank's junior officer training program. Realizing she had a true interest in and aptitude for banking, she enrolled in the American Graduate School of International Management. "Find out while you're in college what makes you tick," says Cathy, who is now a senior manager and vice president at the Bank of Canada.

"Nothing great was ever achieved without enthusiasm," said Ralph Waldo Emerson. You want to be enthusiastic about your job so that you will do it well and enjoy it. In order to do that, you must first take some time to analyze what it is you like to do.

An honest and complete self-appraisal is your first step toward choosing the right career. By asking yourself critical questions, you'll be way ahead of most of your classmates—leagues, fathoms, kilometers squared. *Way* ahead.

The Three D's

Which of the following describes you best?

- **Drifter.** Life just happens to you, often in ways decidedly unfriendly or random.
- **Dreamer.** You have wonderful plans for the future but can't al-

ways realize your dreams. Your favorite line is borrowed from Scarlett O'Hara, of *Gone with the Wind* fame: "I can't think about it now. I'll think about it tomorrow."

- **Doer.** You have the confidence, the vision, and the persistence to make your goals come together. You plan, act, and achieve.

Most people are some combination of the above. Maybe you've been a *Drifter*. In this chapter, you will be able to graduate to *Dreamer* as you explore your interests, abilities, and passions. The rest of this book is devoted to your becoming a *Doer*.

Does this mean that drifting and dreaming are not important? On the contrary. One of my best friends, Madeline, aptly reminded me that a balance of drifting and dreaming is necessary. "All doing squashes the learning, pain, and growth that dreaming and drifting inspire," she wrote. "Success is balance. It is reading well, thinking deeply; having the wisdom to see the broader picture; knowing the importance of friends and family; taking the time to marvel at a sunset, a small child, or an older person."

Finding a Balance

A balance of drifting, dreaming, and doing will help you define and achieve what you determine is most important in college, in work, and in life. So how might you go about "discovering" yourself further? Here are four suggestions:

1. Keep a journal
2. Survey yourself
3. Keep asking questions
4. Overcome obstacles

1. ❒ *Keep a Journal*

Throughout college, keep track of your plans, deeds, fears, and dreams. Write down goals for yourself and then reread them after six months. Which have you achieved? Which do you want to pursue now?

Your journal is your secret companion. Write in it every day, through good times and bad. Share your expectations and aspirations, your disappointments and fears. Write about the world as you see it. Be blunt and blatantly honest. After a month, begin rereading your journal. It will reveal interesting patterns. You'll see a definite progression, and that's rewarding.

Pam Zemper, vice president and director of marketing at Security Pacific Executive Professional Services, says that she has always kept lists—they are her form of journal writing. Her lists remind her of activities she wants to try, subjects she wants to learn, ways she wants to grow. "As I go back and review my lists over the years, I can see how certain dreams tie together. My lists give me a framework out of which I formulate my goals and then my plans."

2. ❒ *Survey Yourself*

Answer the following questions as honestly as you can. After all, no one else is going to see your answers unless you want them to. These questions should help you evaluate your high school experience and define your college goals. It will also help you get a handle on your strengths and weaknesses, key elements in the process of self-discovery.

Periodically, throughout your life, you'll find it helpful to look back at what you've done so that you can get perspective on what you want to do as you go forward. Later in the book, you'll have a chance to look ahead and dream about what kinds of things you want to do. Now look back and reflect for a moment.

HOW I SEE MYSELF

1. In high school, I felt most proud that I _____

_____ .

2. I feel most disappointed that I did not _____

_____ .

3. The most important thing I learned in high school was _____

_____ .

4. I developed confidence by_____

_____ .

5. The teacher who had the greatest positive influence on me was

_____, who taught me _____ .

6. In high school, I was motivated by _____

_____ .

7. The five things I enjoyed most were _____

_____ .

8. The five things I enjoyed least were_____

_____ .

9. The five things I find most interesting are _____

_____ .

10. My biggest disappointment was _____

_____ .

11. My greatest success was_____

_____ .

12. The most difficult thing I've had to do is _____

_____ .

13. In high school, I considered myself_____

_____ .

14. My friends would describe me as _____

_____ .

15. If I could change one thing in my life, it would be _____

_____ .

16. I am angered by_____

_____ .

17. I would describe myself as the kind of person who_____

_____ .

18. The thing I would most like to change about myself is _____

_____.

19. My philosophy of life is _____

_____.

20. One thing I would like to improve is_____

_____.

MYSELF AMONG OTHERS

1. The kind of people I most like to be with are _____

_____.

2. I most admire my fellow students and teachers who_____

_____.

3. The kind of people I find it most difficult to be around are _____

_____.

4. The person who has had most the most influence on my life has

been _____ because _____

_____.

5. The character traits I most like in people are_____

_____.

6. The ones I dislike most are _____

_____.

7. Given a choice between being with others or being by myself, I usually

choose to _____ because _____

_____ .

Keep in mind that self-discovery requires continual re-examination. As your perspective and ideas change, you'll find yourself revising your earlier lists. With each revision you will move closer to your goals, both in the short and long term. Don't worry if you can't answer all of these questions now. You'll have plenty of time in the next few years to explore several different areas that interest you. These answers will serve as your information base when the time comes to evaluate your career path.

3. ❐ *Keep Asking Questions*

Don't be complacent, and don't accept everything you read and hear. Find out if things make sense. We've all read the slogan QUESTION AUTHORITY. Let it serve as a gentle reminder.

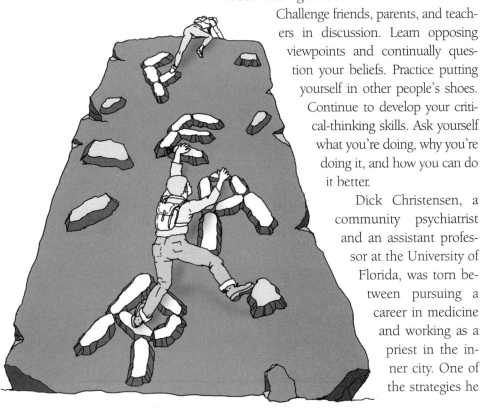

Challenge friends, parents, and teachers in discussion. Learn opposing viewpoints and continually question your beliefs. Practice putting yourself in other people's shoes. Continue to develop your critical-thinking skills. Ask yourself what you're doing, why you're doing it, and how you can do it better.

Dick Christensen, a community psychiatrist and an assistant professor at the University of Florida, was torn between pursuing a career in medicine and working as a priest in the inner city. One of the strategies he used to help him make a decision was to talk with people and ask them questions.

"Perhaps the most valuable experiences of my college years were the opportunities I found to spend time with people who were doing what I was considering," he explains. "I spent time with people who had returned from the Peace Corps; I listened to physicians talk about their experiences in medicine; and I saw firsthand what it was like for a person to live and work in the inner city as a priest. My college years afforded me the luxury of time, even in the midst of academic demands, to approach others with life questions that could only be answered by life experiences."

4. ❏ *Overcome Obstacles*

Everyone has insecurities and shortcomings. It's a fact of life. However, we don't like to explore our dark sides. We usually keep them locked up tightly inside. Left unattended, our insecurities are manifested as fear; and the more you try to run from fear, the more it will dominate your life. Think of the dilemma as an intellectual puzzle to be solved. Turn the puzzle around in your mind, looking at it from as many angles as possible. Be comforted by the fact that you do have a choice: you can be courageous and deal effectively with your fears.

The first step toward overcoming your fears is identifying them. Complete the following statements honestly.

WHAT ARE YOU AFRAID OF?

1. Very few people realize that I am afraid of _____

_____ .

2. When I am alone, the thing that frightens me most is _____

_____ .

3. When I am with other people, the thing that frightens me most

is _____

_____ .

4. I'm embarrassed when_____

_____ .

5. My greatest fear about college is _____

_____ .

The next step is for you to accept these fears. That's right. In order to overcome fears, it helps to embrace them. Here's an exercise that will help you do just that. Imagine that each of the five situations above came true and that you were forced to confront your fears. Answer the following questions for each:

1. Describe the scene in detail_____

_____ .

2. What happened? _____

_____ .

3. What did it feel like? _____

_____ .

4. What were you thinking?_____

_____ .

5. What could you have done to make the anxiety more tolerable?_____

_____ .

Aside from fears, other obstacles will surely get in your way. Maybe you think you're not smart enough because of that IQ test you took in fourth grade. You were having a bad day; it happens. Maybe you believe that you're incompetent because you didn't ace the SAT's. Relax. Remember, even Einstein flunked at least one critical exam.

Einstein is not unique, at least not on that score. Robert Sternberg, a Yale psychologist, has done extensive research on IQ tests and intelligence. He has noted that intelligence is a composite of several factors. Many of these—including motivation and the capacity to adjust to change—are difficult to measure accurately with a written test. If you do score well on aptitude tests, don't rest on your laurels. Your brain is not a bank. It cannot pay the rent, nor can it pay for the Himalayan odyssey you're hoping will get you away from home for the summer. Stretch your natural talents by coupling your intellect with determination and a commitment to action.

Winning Against All Odds

There are other obstacles much more formidable than genius or the lack of it. Jackie Fitzgerald, the national sales manager for Sunlover Clothing Products, supported her family while attending Villanova University in Pennsylvania. She had begun college as a pre-med student because her mother had always wanted her to be a doctor.

"I didn't have the financial support from my family that most students have," Jackie recalls. "After I decided I didn't want to be a doctor, I lost all emotional support from my mom." This, Jackie says, was the greatest obstacle she had to overcome.

She learned how to encourage herself when no one else was there to cheer her on. With her many commitments, Jackie learned time management and self-reliance. These skills enabled her to graduate with honors as a sociology major and psychology minor, and later on to be enormously successful in business. "It's better to graduate with a solid education in a field you love than to pursue a career in an area you're not passionate about."

For Jill Goldfarb, things were worse. During the first week of her freshman year at the University of Michigan, her mother died of a stroke. Jill dropped out of school for the fall semester, working at a department store before returning to school in the spring. In March, her father died suddenly of a heart attack.

"I survived because I had to," says Jill, who immersed herself in her studies and extracurricular activities. Her hard work and dedication were perhaps the greatest tributes she could pay to her parents. Remarkably, Jill graduated with a degree in management information systems with a 4.0 average.

If you're starting college under a difficult (or even tragic) circumstance, don't let a disadvantage deny you success. There is truth to the old adage that adversity breeds character. Learn the difference between situations that you can and can't control. Set your sights on a goal that you can achieve, and then go for it. Throughout life, each of us encounters obstacles and challenges on a regular basis. It's how we deal with these challenges, and what we make of them, that determines our true success.

3

Futures and Options
Matching Your Interests with a Career

I don't know what I'd like to do. That's what hurts the most. That's why I can't quit the job. I really don't know what talents I may have. And I don't know where to go to find out. I've been fostered so long by school and didn't have time to think about it.
  Chicago phone receptionist, quoted in Studs Terkel's Working

There is a job, and a future, waiting for you, as long as you really want to work. There are opportunities galore, as long as you make the effort to seek them out. There are tested ways to success in the job market.
  Robert O. Snelling, Sr., in The Right Job

Consider a typical freshman's nocturnal musings on what it means to use the career planning and placement center:

A career planning and placement center is a secret building in the middle of campus where seniors are escorted at night, blindfolded, for initiation into inescapable careers. Jobs are assigned on the basis of Alphabetical Synergy, a scientific technique developed in California during the mid-seventies. Alphabetical Synergy pairs career and candidate by matching the first letter of the student's last name with the first letter of a career. For example:

Michael Crosby: double major in economics and physics
Career Selected by Alphabetical Synergy: Coffey . . .
co . . . CHEF . . . co . . . CRAPS PLAYER . . . No, wait a minute—
*********CONTRACTOR**********
!!!!!!!!!!!!!!!!!!!!!!!!!!!!!!!

Still blindfolded, Michael is given a burlap sack containing the tools of the trade: hammer, nails, hard hat, and keys to the trailer that will be his new headquarters, along with a map specifying its exact location at a construction site in Death Valley, California.

Then he wakes up, screaming.

The moral of this nightmare? Simple. Don't be afraid of your career center. It won't hurt you in the light of day. Don't wait until three days before graduation and expect to nail down the perfect job. Go early—during your freshman and sophomore years—to gather information about the fields that interest you. Career centers have a wealth of materials, including books, company files, videos, and names of contacts. Trained career counselors are a valuable resource; they can help you get that summer internship, help you write your résumé and prepare for the interview, or lend an ear as you talk through job possibilities. Take advantage of this service.

Most placement centers offer interest surveys. Take them. These inventories are a good place to begin figuring out what you want to do.

One such test, the Strong-Campbell Interest Inventory, compares the responses of the test taker to those of professionals in various occupations. Students get an idea of the careers people with similar interests have chosen, pointing them toward jobs they may not have considered. The inventory also helps you identify your natural learning style, which can be a good thing to know before you spend years and thousands of dollars on a program that may not fit your style. If Strong-Campbell results tell you that you are more of a practical learner, for example, you'll want a short program focused on specific skills. That way, you'll be able to walk away with a degree you can use immediately to further your career. On the other hand, if you find you are more of an academic type, one who loves theory and abstraction, you may be happier in a longer course of study. (Even if you risk becoming an Eternal Student!) In any case, it's important that you meet with a career counselor who can help you interpret the results of any tests you take.

"But don't rely solely on standardized tests," says Tim Dalton, a senior at Columbia University. "Many students who seek career guidance think they can just fill in the boxes, stick numbers into a computer, and then get a printout on the career they should pursue. The tests are a starting place; you must look within yourself for the answers."

Sometimes these tests can be off target. Anne, a friend of mine who is an editor, completed a survey that indicated that she could be a dental hygienist—a job in which she has no interest! Like a hygienist, however, Anne does enjoy working quietly by herself and with a small group of people. This is precisely what she does as an editor. The moral? Consider the broader interest profile as well as the specific job suggestions.

Cyrus Vesser, who worked for twelve years before returning to school to get his doctorate in history, says that brainstorming helped him choose his career. "The self-assessment tests and group discussions provided by my university were useful," says Cyrus. "Five years of wrong leads can be avoided by self-examination and experimentation in areas which spark your mind."

Many students fear they won't get a job after graduation. They consider only a few of the thousands of possible professions from which to choose. Students who don't know what they want to do frequently accept jobs they hate, or for which they're unsuited.

That's not how you want to spend your career—or your life. You can do better than that. Use your imagination! *There are thousands of jobs available*.

Your first step? *Relax*. You are going to get a job in the career of your choice, even if you now have no idea of what you want to do.

Your second step? *Explore* the careers available to you—by reading, interviewing people, investigating your career center. Realize how many options you really have.

Your third step? *Commit yourself* to the process of discovering what you want to do.

Your fourth step? *Chart* your career path(s) by listing

1. *What you have done* (your previous volunteer and work experiences, such as having a part-time salesclerk position at the Gap clothing store)
2. *Where you are now* (your current volunteer and work experiences, such as doing summer volunteer work for the Humane Society)
3. *Where you want to be* (other experiences you need to plan for now, such as preparing to interview with an honorary society on your college campus for the purpose of developing your leadership skills)

Your fifth step? *Take action*.

Chapter 2 dealt with those characteristics that are unique to you. It asked you to identify both your strengths and your weaknesses and encouraged you to conduct an introspective look at yourself. Now let's focus on what you can do with your newfound understanding of yourself in the professional world. In your journal, label a section "Personal Inventory Assessment" and devote at least one page to each of the following categories: interests; talents; skills; likes and dislikes; goals, values, and ambitions. Be sure to fill everything in. Don't worry if some of it doesn't make sense. Many of your thoughts will develop after you have a chance to reflect on your initial responses.

Interests
- I am curious about _____.

- I question _____.

- I'm concerned about _____.

- I'm fascinated by _____.

- I like to think/read/write about _____.

Talents
- I am good at these kinds of activities (physical, intellectual, creative, social, religious, etc.):_____.

- People compliment me on _____.

- People encourage me to _____.

Skills
- Specific skills (such as public speaking, car maintenance, word processing, etc.) I have: _____.

- Skills I want to learn: _____.

_____.

Likes and Dislikes

- About people—their character, habits, shortcomings, influence, etc.:

Likes	Dislikes

- About working environment—indoors or out, with people or alone, small company or large, etc.):

Likes	Dislikes

Goals, Values, and Ambitions

• I like _____.

• I want to accomplish _____.

• When I die, I want to be remembered for _____.

• In life, I value these things most: _____.

• Contributions I want to make to the world: _____.

• Things that give me peace of mind: _____.

Survey Your Qualities

Below are some essential characteristics every career seeker needs, regardless of what the inventory says. Take stock. Which characteristics best describe you? Which least describe you? How might you improve your weak areas before you graduate? If you analyze these things yourself, you'll be well prepared for your first salary review when your manager tells you what you've done well and where you stand to improve. You can't become better at something if you don't know where you need to improve.

• Supportive
• Decisive
• Follow up
• Organized
• Ethical
• Sets and keeps high standards
• Confident, but not cocky
• Fair
• Honest
• Sets goals
• Keeps promises
• Has long-term vision
• Sense of humor
• Winning attitude
• Ability to separate the trivial from the important
• Pays attention to detail
• Able to manage stress
• Even-tempered
• Works well with all kinds of people

Take the Next Step

After you've completed your self-assessment inventory, analyze your responses. What are you learning about yourself? Is a pattern of what you'd like to do beginning to emerge? You don't have to draw any permanent con-clusions now. The important thing is that you've identified your skills and interests.

What's so important about that? You are not easily convinced. What's im-portant is that you can use this knowledge to select your career options. Many people spend years in unrewarding careers before they realize that their jobs do not utilize their skills and interests. Consider the frequency of the midlife crisis as evidence. You are learning a different path—and you haven't even graduated from college yet.

Ask the Right Questions

You have surveyed your skills and interests. Now it's time to examine the specific characteristics of different career options. Turn to Appendix 6 (pages 270–283) and look at "The World of Work: A Sampler" from *What Color Is Your Parachute?* by Richard Bolles. You'll notice that the chart is grouped ac-cording to profession. Three categories—"Job Requirements," "Work Envi-ronment," and "Occupational Characteristics"—are listed across the top.

Look first at the "Job Requirements" category and select the character-istics that best describe you. Find the professions that require these charac-teristics to see which interest you. Then let this chart trigger questions such as the following:

1. What training would I need in the next four years to prepare myself for the types of jobs that interest me?
2. Under the "Work Environment" category, which of the conditions ap-peal to you? If you're not sure, then you might want to visit a few differ-ent workplaces and get a feel for the atmosphere.
3. What about the occupational characteristics? Are there plenty of jobs in your areas of interest? Will the industries that interest you grow over the next few years?

These are important questions. Finding out the answers will help you make informed decisions. So keep these questions in mind as you read the chart. Remember, you don't have to know all the answers right now. The purpose of the chart is simply to jump-start your thinking about career pos-sibilities. For now, all you need to do is keep a running list of four or five ar-eas you might be interested in. Over the next few years you'll explore these interests, narrow your focus, and eventually choose a career.

Learn to Reason

Why do we accept what we believe? Reasoning provides an answer. To reason is to understand the underlying motives and logic of our beliefs. Lex Kaplan began college thinking that he wanted to be a lawyer. Originally from Englewood, New Jersey, Lex majored in journalism. As president of his college political magazine, he fell in love with reporting and writing. He enjoyed them so much that when he graduated, he freelanced for *The Phoenix*, a Boston periodical. He used his writing experience there to help him land a job at *The New Yorker*, fact-checking and writing "Talk of the Town" pieces. But after a year there, he started to fear that being a journalist would make him a dilettante—a writer without a specialty. So, without reasoning, he reverted to his pre-freshman beliefs and enrolled in law school. He quickly realized his mistake. While he was a hard worker, he discovered something about himself at law school.

"I found out I wasn't a fighter," he says. Competition on campus for corporate jobs was fierce. Lex found himself disliking both the competition and the idea of corporate law, which to him "seemed like a form of death." This time, Lex used his experiences in considering his next career move. He knew he wouldn't be happy as an attorney after all. So he turned down a job with a law firm in New York and decided to combine all his skills by starting up his own magazine.

Throughout your college and working careers, you will continually have to (1) come up with your own ideas and (2) convince others of their validity. Once you've reached a decision, opinion, or point of view, get used to defending it both orally and in writing. You will feel more confident, even among your toughest critics, when you can back up your claims.

You probably have ample opportunity to practice that skill now. For example, let's say your parents do not approve of the major you've chosen; they don't think you will make enough money from it to earn a living. When you have carefully thought through the decision yourself, you can more clearly articulate why you chose as you did. Even though your parents still may not agree with you, at least they will respect the reasoning behind your judgment.

Lex gave a star performance in the art of persuasion when he came up with a novel idea for a magazine that would fill a void in the market. He gave a seven-page proposal to an acquaintance he knew was interested in investing in the arts, and the man gave him $50,000. During the year that followed, Lex enthusiastically pitched his concept to writers, friends, and investors. Within the year, he had (1) convinced some of his former colleagues at *The New Yorker* to work for his magazine, called *Wigwag*; (2) contracted articles from a number of known authors, including Alice McDermott, Ralph Ellison, and Richard Ford; and (3) raised $3 million. All this he did from his two-bedroom apartment in New York City, making the most of his "cold" phone calls and "blind" visits. Because Lex Kaplan believed in his project, so did many others.

Do the Right Things for the Right Reasons

You come to college with a certain set of preconceptions, and you are also probably very aware of your parents' expectations. It is important to understand how these influences affect your decisions and to evaluate what is important to you—what really interests you. "Don't let somebody else persuade you to enter a career based on *their* idea of what's right, or practical, or something that 'you can always fall back on,' " advises Nancy Wingate, a journalist and freelance writer who majored in English in college. She knew she didn't want to teach, but she wasn't sure exactly what she would do with an English degree. She did know that if she worked hard and kept pursuing her interests, she would find work that satisfied her. "Everyone kept asking me, 'But what are you going to *do* with a degree in English?' I would just smile and say, 'I don't know, but I know I'll find something.' Sure enough, my first job (still during college) was as a part-time editorial assistant; my first full-time job was as a television producer—both jobs I absolutely loved!"

Steve Fort, an engineering supervisor at a Lockheed space facility in Florida who graduated from college ten years ago, was motivated by money. "Quite frankly, my biggest goal in college was to get a well-paying job. I was rather single-minded in my pursuit of money because I thought money would lead to the good life. Now I wish I had spent more time considering what it was that I enjoyed rather than what would make me the most money."

"Too often, freshmen lean toward whatever will bring in the most money right after graduation," muses Mary Hopkins, a graduate student and editor of *The Daily Texan*, the student newspaper at the University of Texas. "The job market fluctuates more than it used to; top-paying jobs one year may drop out of sight the next. And at the end of a life, what does it matter how much something paid compared to how much you were able to contribute to the world?"

Mary makes an important point, namely, that people are motivated by different things. For some people, money isn't nearly as important as finding fulfillment in their work. It's not that they don't want money altogether. It's just that if they must choose between a career that promises a good salary but isn't work they care about and a lower-paying job that promises work they love, they'll choose the latter. In fact, there's a trend in this country called "voluntary simplicity," meaning that folks are scaling down their lifestyles and "getting back to the basics." That's why discovering what matters to you now is so key. You aren't only choosing a major, you're choosing a lifestyle.

Even after you are established in your career, you will periodically need to evaluate what is motivating you and decide if your work is taking you in directions that are important to you. Cruce Stark was a professor in the English department at the University of Delaware. His career was moving along as he planned. He was doing all the "right" things—writing solid scholarly articles and getting published. On a year-long sabbatical in Latin America, he realized that what he really wanted to do at that point was to write a novel.

"During that trip I started asking questions about what I really wanted, about what I'd think about my life when nobody would be there except me to think about it; or when it truly wasn't going to matter what anybody else thought. Would I be happier when I was looking back at seventy if I'd been a success in my profession, with a string of highly regarded critical works, or would I like myself better if I'd tried to write fiction and failed? But of course I knew I wouldn't fail. If I worked as hard as I intended to, I'd have to succeed."

Cruce worked on his fiction-writing for years before he got his first novel published. During that time, the senior people in his department at the university kept suggesting that he return to doing what he knew how to do. When his novel *Chasing Uncle Charley* was published, it received rave reviews from *The New York Times* and *Publishers Weekly*. As a result, he was promoted and was assigned to teach courses and lead workshops in creative writing.

"My basic realization was that, for better or for worse, I was stuck with myself—so that's what I'd better get in touch with. Trying to satisfy anything or anybody else was going to leave a very important part of me very empty. Most of us spend too many years worrying what our lives will look like from the outside, as though it were some kind of movie for somebody else to see. It may come with age, but sometimes it finally breaks through—nobody's standing in line buying tickets to watch."

Dream On

Now that you've defined your interests, skills, and goals, it's time to focus on the job that will incorporate them. What would you like to do if you could do anything? Really, truly, outlandishly . . . *anything*. Imagine the sheer delight of finding the career that taps your passion and allows you the privilege of being paid for doing it!

Francie Berger's childhood dream was to build Lego models for a living. Being a practical child, she assumed that no one would pay her to play, so she decided to become an architect. When Francie entered Virginia Tech's

architecture program prepared to pursue a career in architecture, she had no idea that her childhood fantasies were about to come true.

During her freshman year, a toy designer gave a guest lecture in one of her classes. After hearing him speak, she decided to approach him about interning for him. Through her internship, she developed a mentoring relationship with the toy designer, who encouraged her to approach Lego about creating a model design department in the United States. At that point Lego had a manufacturing and sales plant in the United States, but all the models and designs were made in Denmark.

For her senior project, Francie designed a model Lego farm that included fourteen buildings and vehicles—she drew up the plans and projected the costs. She then presented her project to the director of special events at Lego. "I never doubted that I would persuade them to create this job for me—my dream was going to come true. As a kid, I didn't think this kind of job existed. Once I knew the possibility, I knew I had to get this job."

It took her months of following up, calling her contact at Lego at least once every month, before she was given a job. Three months after Francie graduated from architecture school, upon her return from an extended vacation traveling around the United States, Lego called and offered her a job designing large Lego model displays for

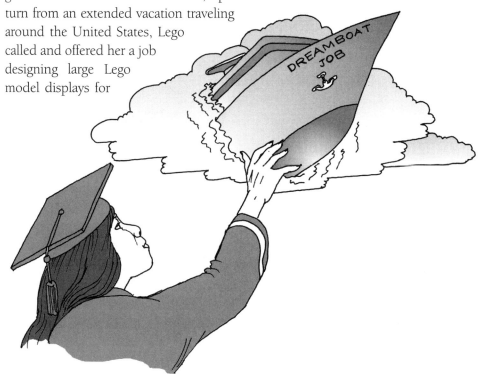

places like F. A. O. Schwartz and the National Toy Fair in New York City. The Lego design department has since grown from three people to forty-eight people as of 1990. Francie supervises five designers responsible for envisioning the models, and she has been featured in *The New Yorker*, on the Discovery Channel, and in a PBS children's series.

Francie's story is a good example of how it is possible to find work that really matches your interests. In order to do this, though, you sometimes have to allow yourself to dream BIG and to think beyond the immediate possibilities. Once you've found your vision, then it often takes ingenuity, creativity and perseverance to see your dreams come to fruition.

Now you are going to do just that. Using the insights you've gained from the inventory, you are going to design your possible success stories. Include everything that the perfect job entails. Where do you work? What is the work environment? Does your job include travel? What is an average day like? What is your compensation (does this include your quarterly bonus)? Describe your position in detail. The goal is to make it real. Try to taste it, hear it, feel it. Do not hold back. No holds barred. *Write it down.*

DREAMBOAT JOB/STELLAR ACHIEVEMENT NUMBER 1

DREAMBOAT JOB/STELLAR ACHIEVEMENT NUMBER 2

_____

_____

_____

_____

_____

_____

_____

DREAMBOAT JOB/STELLAR ACHIEVEMENT NUMBER 3

_____

_____

_____

_____

_____

_____

_____

Now it's time to take your head out of the clouds and focus on planning strategies that will make these dreams become reality.

The Narrowing Process

Once you've analyzed the bigger picture, pick two or three areas of interest and begin developing career strategies for each. You can write them down below. (If you don't know what to choose yet, come back to this after you've had more time to think.)

_____

_____

_____

_____

_____

_____

_____

Using What You Know

The key to choosing career options is a willingness to explore. You could convert the basics of the "dreamboat job" approach to fit any possible path: that of poet, advertising copywriter, stockbroker, farmer, cowboy, or corporate psychic. Remember, you're interested in these careers (all of them) because you think they would be fun. So have fun finding out about them!

And while you're out pioneering, continue to ask yourself questions that will help to refine your career goals:

1. How can I gather more information about those careers that interest me?
2. Do I know any people in this field? (If you don't know anyone, do some research.) What can they tell me about the pros and cons of the work? What is needed to succeed?

3. What else can I do each week and each month to prepare myself? How can I get more experience? (Remember: experience leads to intelligent decisions.)

Life Goals

It is crucial to think about what kinds of goals you have for your life as a whole. Pam Zemper of Security Pacific Executive Professional Services, advises people to think about what their goals are in four areas—social, material, professional, and personal growth. "Once you have an idea of what you want in each of these areas, it's easier to choose a career."

"Your job becomes your lifestyle," says Tony Ponturo, director of media services for Anheuser Busch. "So you'd better like what you're doing."

Tony is right. Know what you want, even if you don't know how to get it right now. The path to a really interesting career is often circuitous.

After college, Tony identified the three areas he loved most—business, sports, and television. He moved to New York City and got a job as a page for NBC, hoping to get a foot in the door of NBC Sports. This approach didn't work. So he took an alternative route and went into advertising, working for three successive advertising agencies as a media buyer. His work on a Coca-Cola campaign earned him a shot at his firm's Anheuser-Busch account. Anheuser-Busch was so impressed with his work that they lured him away from the agency and created a position for him in their home office in St. Louis. Since Busch promotes heavily during sports telecasts, Tony finds himself working in all three of the areas he enjoys: business, sports, and television.

Larry Maslon acquired his job through a similarly circuitous route. Larry is the dramaturge for the prestigious Arena Stage in Washington, D.C. His various responsibilities include helping to choose the season's repertoire, interpreting the plays, researching their historical background, and editing the theater's publications. But when he started out, Larry knew nothing of dramaturgy—he only knew his interests. A lover of stage directing and Renaissance literature, he majored in both in college. For his thesis in theater arts, he directed Shakespeare's *Tempest*, and then he wrote a paper on the play for his Renaissance literature thesis.

"Unbeknownst to me," says Larry, "by both critically examining and producing a play, I was doing a dramaturge's work." Later, intending to become a theater director, he enrolled in a master's program in theater arts at Stanford. He was disappointed that the program primarily focused on the academic side of theater, so he directed some plays on his own time.

"Again, unbeknownst to me, I was becoming exquisitely prepared to be a dramaturge" he says. He now possesses something that is extremely rare: a challenging steady job in the theater. He strongly believes that every student should pursue what he or she loves. He says he has benefited from following his heart, from doing what he's done "in spite of myself."

Malcolm Forbes, the late publisher of *Forbes* magazine, was quoted in *The Achievement Factors*, by B. Eugene Griessman, as saying: "I think the foremost quality—there's no success without it—is really loving what you do. If you love it, you will do it well."

"You've got to have fire in the gut," says Milton Pedraza, a Colgate (the company, not the college) recruiter and marketer. "You have to be committed to your job once you land it, but in college you must commit yourself to becoming well-educated and as well prepared as possible, even if you don't yet know what kind of work interests you." If you don't develop a burning passion to get things done in college, Milton says, it will be hard for you to motivate yourself on the job.

Get Going!

Your senior year of college, though it seems like a long way off, is just around the corner. The trick to not being caught off guard by its arrival is balance: balancing the long-term agenda with current agendas for the month, the week, the day, the moment. For now (this moment), set some career goals. Don't worry about revising them. That will come later. Time is very forgiving to those who act, which is what you're doing right now by committing to a career direction . . . however tentative.

"As you begin to discover what you truly enjoy, try to picture yourself two, five, or ten years after college, involved in that interest," advises Bob Kinstle, a computer consultant for a large New York bank. "Imagine what your typical day might look like; then re-examine your current activities to see if they are helping you achieve that dream," he says. "College is a time for growth and adventure. You are building the foundation and honing the skills that will determine your success and happiness in the years ahead. Find out what your school has to offer—academically, socially, culturally, athletically—and try to sample as much as possible."

Turning Your Dreams into Reality

Someone once said, "If you aim at nothing, you'll hit it every time." For our purposes, think of your target as being your goals, dreams, and ambitions. Consequently, the arrows are your plans. Stock your quiver full of them——your plans—and you're bound to hit the bull's-eye eventually.

Former college professor Lynn Troyka suggests a planning strategy that a friend shared with her years ago. The formula goes like this: "Envision where you want to be, then establish steps toward that vision." Notice that this formula has two distinct parts: a *projection phase* (envisioning) and a *planning phase* (establishing steps toward that vision).

The Projection Phase

The projection phase usually comes first. It entails thinking and dreaming about what you want (i.e., your vision). This includes the soon-to-be-realized fantasy of your acceptance speech in Stockholm when you humbly receive that long-deserved Nobel Prize (you are thirty-three before the committee finally comes to its stuffed-up senses and has the decency and vision to recognize you). Envisioning the goal is where projection comes in, and that's important. But it's not enough. Lots of people have a dream; few turn it into a reality.

The Planning Phase

The second phase, planning, involves work that is more long-term. Once you've visualized the epic ending, you have to figure out how to get there. You do this by establishing the *steps* that lead you toward the goal. The "how" part of the formula requires creativity, tenacity and—most difficult of all—discipline. Living your dream means maintaining your focus on a goal and refusing to allow distractions to divert you from the time and effort needed to accomplish it. This may sound simple, but for many people, aligning their dreams with their life habits isn't simple at all. Turning your vision into a reality entails weathering hard times, sometimes over long periods. You will not magically become a CEO overnight, no matter how potent your powers of fantasy. Achieving your dream takes 1 percent inspiration and vision coupled with 99 percent perspiration and hard work.

Dr. Michael DeBakey, a pioneer in cardiovascular surgery, including artificial-heart research, and the driving force behind the establishment of the Medical Center in Houston, Texas, believes that dedication, self-discipline, and a clear direction and purpose are the keys to human achievement. "Success is the result of focusing your energies and efforts in a specific direction and exploiting your skills and capabilities to the fullest," he says. He advises students to master whatever it is they are studying. "Apply yourself fully. Once you have devoted your efforts totally to one project, you will be able to transfer those skills and habits to every other project."

It is your task to map out the road to the corner office, or the mid-office cubicle, or the outdoor post—from college classes, internships, work experience, and appropriate role models. Remember to take it one step at a time. One hundred thousand planned steps will go by much more quickly than one hundred thousand unplanned steps.

Following is a list of broad goals a student might realistically expect to accomplish in four years of college. Look at the list closely. See how these activities begin to build on each other? For example, a summer job will help you learn the basic skills of managing responsibility, a key qualification for securing an internship. (See Chapter 8 for a discussion of the importance of internships.) Internships are usually offered only to those students who can prove from their past job experience that they are trustworthy. That's the idea: one year's accomplishments (such as a favorable reference letter from your summer employer) increase the next year's options (e.g., getting an internship).

If this agenda doesn't fit your own projections and plans, fine. Come up with one that does. As your career adviser, I only make suggestions. You make the decisions.

COLLEGE GOALS

Freshman-Year Objectives

- Assess your study skills and habits. Improve on them if they need work.
- Get off to a good start academically.
- Apply for a second-semester or summer part-time job.
- Join at least one extracurricular activity.
- Adjust to the responsibility of your new environment.
- Have fun.

Sophomore-Year Objectives

- Apply for a summer internship (apply for more than one).
- Begin planning for a summer, semester, or junior year abroad.
- Make at least one career contact.
- Join one or two clubs or special-interest groups.
- Continue to make good grades and get the most out of your classes.
- Cultivate mentors (see Chapter 8 if you are stumped on the meaning of the word *mentor*).
- Visit the career center.
- Have fun.

Junior-Year Objectives

- Spend the summer, semester, or entire year abroad.
- Plan for an internship between your junior and senior years.
- Join another activity or honorary society.
- Mail out preliminary job inquiry letters.
- Become a leader of one of the organizations you belong to.
- Prepare a résumé.
- Take some classes that don't pertain to your major but will make you a well-qualified job applicant and a more interesting person.
- Have fun.

Senior-Year Objectives

- Wage a full-fledged job search in the early fall.
- Make many business contacts; gather information.
- Send out at least twenty-five cover letters with résumés.
- Research the companies with which you wish to interview.
- Hold mock interviews to prepare for the real thing.
- Land the job, negotiate your salary, and start taking home the paycheck.
- Have fun.

Should you aim to do all these things? Probably not. Choose the activities that suit you best, and be proud of yourself for trying new things and having the vision to see and plan for the bigger picture. Don't forget the common thread that ties each year together—*having fun!*

As you make projections and devise a plan on behalf of your noble destiny, keep in mind the three key areas you'll need to develop: academic, extracurricular, and work experience. Strive for balance. Keep this triangle in focus—maybe it won't be equilateral, but just make sure it's got three sides.

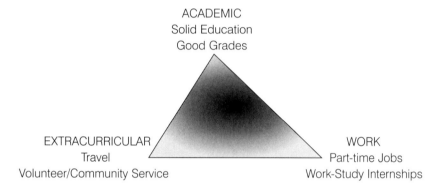

ACADEMIC
Solid Education
Good Grades

EXTRACURRICULAR
Travel
Volunteer/Community Service

WORK
Part-time Jobs
Work-Study Internships

In the spaces below, list the specific steps you think you'll have to take in order to get from where you are to where you want to be. The rest of this book will help you take the steps . . . one at a time.

YOUR OBJECTIVES

Freshman Year

_____

_____

_____

_____

_____

Sophomore Year

_____

_____

_____

_____

_____

Junior Year

_____

_____

_____

_____

_____

Senior Year

_____

_____

_____

_____

_____

Your First Five Steps

Below are five steps designed to assure achievement wherever it is you want to go. Keep them handy for encouragement and as a gentle reminder.

1. ❐ *Strike a Balance*

"The most valuable experience I had in college was learning that it was a microcosm of life, with opportunities to grow broadly in several areas," remembers David Glenn, who was a division manager at Chevron for thirty years. "Too often people focus on one area, to the exclusion of others, with the idea that they will develop after they finish college and get a job."

Kip Berry, assistant professor of veterinary medicine at North Carolina State University, spent most of his time in college doing academic work. "I believe this hurt me. In retrospect, I should have diversified my curriculum and educational experiences instead of focusing only on the hard-core academic work."

In college, you'll have to balance your academic, personal, and real-world experience. Make good grades, but realize that good grades alone are usually not enough. Even if you want to be an astrophysicist, you don't want to be a lonely astrophysicist. Therefore, you also need to make room in your life for the other essentials: extracurricular activities, sports, socializing, and work.

Denise Chamblee, a pediatric ophthalmologist, remembers her college years: "I worked hard academically, but I made a distinct pact with myself not to lose sight of social and extracurricular activities. I think that has helped me tremendously in keeping my sanity through the long road of medical training. It has been an even bigger help in relating well to patients."

2. ❐ *Set Goals*

Learn to set specific goals and have a plan by which to achieve them.

José Galvez not only balanced his schoolwork with a part-time job as a copy boy for his local paper, but also set concrete goals for himself. After eight years with his hometown paper, José is now a photojournalist for the *Los Angeles Times*.

"Identify concrete goals," Jose advises. "Get as much out of the smaller places as you can—then run with it from there. Shoot for the stars."

3. ❑ *Be Decisive*

A wrong decision is better than no decision at all. If you spend a year as a pre-med student, loathe it, and then switch to French, you haven't wasted a year. You've learned something valuable—what you like and what you don't, or, to put it another way, what you'd be good at and what you'd be *not* so good at. And you've acted accordingly. Bravo for self-assertion.

Anthea Coster, a space physicist who tracks satellites at MIT, was struck by the words of one of her philosophy professors. "He said that there is probably more than one right choice. What is important is not necessarily the choice itself, but, once you make the choice, what you do with it. This has probably been one of the guiding principles of my life."

Supreme Court Justice Sandra Day O'Connor learned about decision-making early in her career as a trial judge. "I put all the time and effort in at the front end, trying to decide a case correctly in the first place and do the best I can. Then I don't look back and I don't agonize over it. I may have to live with the consequences, but I'm going to live with them without regrets, because I made the best decision I could at the time."

Learn to analyze your options and then make your move quickly. Don't dilly-dally in thermodynamics if Neo-Impressionism is what you love. Decisiveness goes a long way toward a glorious destiny.

In the words of Steve Fort, the Lockheed engineering supervisor, "Boldness has genius, power, and magic in it. Whatever you do or dream, begin it now."

4. ❑ *Believe in Yourself*

Know that you can succeed. The only difference between *You* and *Them* is that you've got the motivation to get the job done.

Jim Cochran developed self-confidence while attending the University of California, Davis. He had a part-time job for three years as a basketball referee for the intramural sports program. During his third year, he was the head student official.

"When making a call, it's all in the manner in which you carry yourself. If you blow the whistle and hesitate, wringing your hands and gnashing your teeth, people may pick up on your indecision. The fans and players will jump all over you, grabbing you by the collar and chanting 'Blood! Blood! Blood!' "

Gordon Bock, a Columbia graduate, was a UPI reporter when he heard that a *U.S. News and World Report* editor was coming to town. In a "Jobs" file, Gordon had kept a 1977 newsletter that quoted the editor as saying he would hire as many students from journalism schools as he could. Gordon sent a letter to the editor reminding him of this promise, adding, "I'm volunteering to help you in this lofty goal." The editor hired Gordon. "I think he was impressed that I took that statement and threw it back at him, instead of begging for a job," Gordon says.

5. ❏ *Go for It*

Lauren Ward, a brand marketing manager with Pepsi in Purchase, New York, says getting a job as resident assistant during her junior year was one of the most valuable "business lessons" she learned during college.

When Lauren applied for the RA job at the end of her sophomore year, she was refused an application because she had never lived in a dorm before. Since Lauren had transferred from another college during her sophomore year, it had been impossible for her to gain admission to the dorms, which had waiting lists. Still, the interviewing board would make no exception: there were too many people applying for the RA positions, and rules are rules.

Lauren was determined to get a fair shot. Believing in her own competence as an applicant, Lauren went up the hierarchy to the director of housing to ask for some rule-bending so that she could be considered with other applicants. She listed all of her qualifications, showed her keen interest in and enthusiasm for the dorms and the women who lived there, and diplomatically presented her case. The director of housing bent the rules and allowed her to be interviewed.

Out of forty-four applicants, Lauren was the only one to score a perfect 10 with each of the six interviewers. She was accepted as an RA.

The business lesson? As Lauren succinctly put it, "no" does not necessarily mean "no." People will always resist change—in school, in business, at home. Count on it. Action-takers don't take "no" for an answer; they can't, if they want to get anything done. If you believe in what you're doing, whether it be yourself, your product, your ideas or somebody else's, be prepared to utilize creative strategies to combat the stonewalling you'll find yourself up against time and time again.

Lauren, like Jim, believed in herself and convinced others of her abilities. If Lauren hadn't been 100 percent confident when she had her appointment with the director of housing, she would have been cooked. But once her foot was in the door and she had the interview, she had no problem convincing the panel of interviewers that she had potential.

Now it's your turn. Take the ball and start running.

4

Take the Plunge

Managing Your Time and Study Habits

Education has really
only one basic
factor . . . one must
want it.
G. E. Woodbury

The direction in
which education starts a man
determines his future life.
Plato

While writing this book,
I gave a few seminars
in the New York area to
seniors in high school preparing for
success in college. At the beginning of each seminar, I distributed a questionnaire to get the students thinking about what really scared, bothered, excited, thrilled, bored, or disgusted them when they thought about college. The opener was: What do you fear most about starting college? Here are some of the responses from students in one seminar:

- "I fear failing my freshman year."
- "I fear the extra work that I will actually have to do."
- "I fear loneliness, being stuck at a college that I hate, and failing out."
- "I fear studying all day and night."
- "I fear that college will be a letdown from what I've imagined."
- "I fear not having a good time."
- "I fear getting lost."
- "I fear not making friends or finding my classes."

- "I fear too much pressure and too much work."
- "I fear not doing well academically."
- "I fear not fitting in."
- "I fear that I will become so socially active that I will not pay attention to my classes."
- "I fear not being able to compete, work, and do well."
- "I fear the responsibility."
- "I fear I will not be able to work my way through school and support my-self."
- "I fear not finding a date."
- "I fear I won't like my roommates. I'm afraid of leaving home and trying to meet new friends."
- "I fear being on my own."
- "I fear that I won't have a good time."
- "I fear that I won't succeed."
- "I fear the academic load."
- "I fear not 'getting something' from my education."
- "I fear that I will over-sleep."
- "I fear not doing well in class, having problems with roommates, and running out of money."
- "I fear not being able to com-plete, understand, or do well on tests."
- "I fear academic difficulties and no free time."
- "I fear too much work and not enough discipline."

Notice any pattern? Al-most everyone is nervous about starting college. They fear that they will be unable to keep up with the academic challenges that college poses. That's understandable. It's a big transition from high school. But it's like the first day of school in first grade. It only seems like a big deal until the second day, after which you know what to expect.

The key is to convert your fears into positive actions that will help you conquer your academic weaknesses and master the skills needed for success in college. Once you've learned how to manage your time and develop your study skills, you will be up to the challenge.

"I never studied in high school," says Jon Jannes, a former high school basketball star who became an education major at Northern Illinois University. "It took me two years of college to learn to study effectively." Jon spent those first two years at Black Hawk Community College.

Unlike Jon, Matt Jacobson was a top student at Alleman Catholic High School. He was on the honor roll, captain of the football team, and class valedictorian.

"I didn't study much in high school—I just made sure I was ahead of everyone else," says Matt, a pre-law freshman at Northwestern University. "But college was a lot different. I was so overwhelmed and excited about being away from home for the first time that I didn't study much my first semester. As a result, I didn't do very well. Since I'm on scholarship, I'll have to do better next semester." One of the challenges Matt faces is improving his grades while honoring his extracurricular commitments—as a fraternity pledge, a member of the pre-law association, and an assistant at the campus library.

Succeeding scholastically in college is very similar to succeeding in every other area of your life: first make an honest self-appraisal of your strengths and weaknesses; then develop a game plan to achieve your goals.

Selecting a Major

Some college students know from Day One that they want to major in chemistry to become doctors, or major in business or a particular field of engineering. For these students, there is generally a set curriculum defined by the college, with some latitude for elective courses.

However, if you are like many college freshmen, and you haven't decided on a major, you may want to stick to a broad general curriculum for your first year, until you can narrow down your true interests. (I didn't declare a major until the end of my sophomore year.)

As a freshman, you will be required to take general courses that are required for any four-year degree. These courses are usually referred to as the *core curriculum*. For most universities, it takes approximately your first four semesters of school to complete your core. This places you at the end of your sophomore year—the time at which your major takes a front seat. The last two years of your undergraduate studies are geared specifically to your major; therefore, it is before you begin your junior year that you absolutely have to have decided on your major course of study. Don't fret if you don't know what you want to major in as a freshman—you've got plenty of time to decide. Your best bet is to find those classes that are offered within the core (there are generally choices rather than a rigid list) that appeal to your tastes. From there,  you may begin to get a feel for where your interests lie.

As a peer adviser, Julie Balovich speaks with many freshmen who simply aren't sure what they want to study and what career they want to pursue. "What you learn from not picking a major in your first year, and being open to new things, is that there is a lot more out there than you originally thought. Even if you do decide what you want to do, there are ways to experience more than just English or mechanical engineering. By making a point of taking at least one really random nonrequired class every semester, I found out to my surprise that I was very interested in evangelical Protestantism, the politics of developing nations, and the genre of autobiography. I also found out that I was not interested in deconstructionism or bureaucracy in government. I feel like my wide range of interests will give me more to offer law schools in the way of diversity when application time comes around. Instead of saying 'I'm Undecided,' I think we should say 'I'm Discovering' or 'I'm Exploring.' "

Suzanne Babinsky believes it is important to choose the more challenging courses, even when they aren't required. "The harder classes kept me on my toes. They held my interest because I had to focus harder on the material. And when I decided after teaching high school science that I wanted to go to medical school, I had no problem getting in because I had taken the rigorous prerequisites."

Employers often urge students who are undecided on a major to gain a broad liberal arts or business education. "I believe that businesses should go back to basics in recruiting, should forget about the business schools and recruit the best young liberal arts students we can find," says Felix Rohatyn, a senior partner at one of New York's largest investment firms.

Darren Walker, an investment banker in New York City, agrees. "Resist the temptation to specialize in anything. In the long run, what will benefit you most are good writing skills, good reasoning skills, and people skills. My greatest disappointment was realizing that law was an unfulfilling profession for me. However, because of the wide breadth of my academic background and extracurricular activities, I was well positioned to move into a number of different professions."

Here's a recap:

1. Take at least one elective each semester you are in school.
2. Remember to say, *to others as well as yourself*, "I'm exploring" instead of "I'm undecided."
3. At least in your first two years, resist specializing. Take a broad range of courses.

When Steven Harwood began his college career, there was a demand for professors. So he decided to get a doctorate in biochemistry and get an academic job. When he graduated, however, the job market was dry. He then decided to go on to medical school and eventually specialized in nuclear medicine.

He advises students to find out what the real job situation is. "Also, take a wide variety of courses and get as much enrichment experience as possible. Be flexible, and be prepared to change. The job situation may be different by the time you finish four years later."

Arnold Popinsky, a potter and former art professor, remembers, "Concern over good performance and a safe curriculum were too dominant in my mind . . . It kept me from seeking adventure in my college experience." He advises students to take risks and to enroll in courses outside their majors.

Colleen Smith, a counselor who runs a program for women over fifty returning to school, has the following recommendation: "Study what you love. Don't think you have to have it all figured out in advance, because life takes amazing twists and turns."

Jesse Keller, a junior at Yale University, originally decided to major in computer science because he felt the subject would be broad enough to allow him to participate in whatever field he chose after college. But after several semesters, he realized that the standard computer science curriculum was not meeting his needs.

"I arrived at the idea of an interdisciplinary major—'The Impact of Information Technology on Society.' With this trendy title, I approached the sociology department and suddenly had a new major. My course requirements are drawn from the sociology, computer science, and engineering departments. As a senior, I will write a thesis dealing with some aspect of the impact that all of our progress has had on our day-to-day lives. I am looking forward to doing the research—it's my own version of computer science."

THE FIRST-YEAR SCHEDULE: SOME IDEAS

Sample A

FIRST SEMESTER	UNITS	SECOND SEMESTER	UNITS
Freshman Composition	3	Freshman Composition	3
Algebra (or Calculus)	3	American Government	3
Introduction to Psychology	3	Astronomy	4
French I	4	French II	4
Economics	3	Art History	3
Total	16	Total	17

Sample B

FIRST SEMESTER	UNITS	SECOND SEMESTER	UNITS
Freshman Composition	3	Freshman Composition	3
Biology	4	Calculus	3
American History	3	Music Appreciation	3
Spanish I	4	Spanish II	4
Racquetball	1	Anthropology	3
Total	15	Total	16

Consult your school catalog or a counselor for more information on courses and majors.

General advice: Take fewer, not more, courses your first semester. You'll have many adjustments to make, so it's best to be underextended, rather than overextended. If you take fifteen or sixteen units, you'll be in good shape. Also, work as little as possible during your first semester to give yourself time to get used to school.

A good scholastic start should be your first concern. The knowledge you gain in college—and the grades you earn to show for it—don't assure job success but it will make you more attractive to a prospective employer. Good students are organized and responsible; top marks show you're able to learn and willing to work and apply yourself. Aside from helping you get the job, a sound education will open all kinds of other doors for you. An educated mind is your most valuable asset.

Improving Your Ability to Learn

Frank Landy, an industrial organizational psychologist at Penn State, teaches introductory psychology on a regular basis. "My first class each semester is on study tips," says Landy. He discusses different methods of learning, taking notes, and preparing for various exams. "If students learn basic habits of discipline and time management early, they will do best over the long haul," says Landy.

"I plunge into the material at the beginning of the semester, so I expect students to know what they're doing," says Doug Finnemore, who teaches the calculus-based physics course for engineers at Iowa State. Finnemore expects students to hit the ground running once he starts class, but if they need help, he encourages them to seek him out, or to ask any of the teaching assistants who lead discussion sections. "The people who do well in my course come to class and work throughout the semester, while the ones who do poorly show up once in a while."

If you're not a great student, don't be overwhelmed by past failure. There are certain tips that work well for all kinds of people—those who are common-sense smart, those who have high IQ's, and those who may be infinitely wise. Consider the skills that all good students have, regardless of their particular learning aptitude:

- Critical thinking
- Active learning

- Good study and test-taking habits
- Time management
- Priority setting
- Effective note-taking

Learn to Think Critically

The first step to successful studying is being a good student. College is more challenging than high school. Rote memorization of facts won't cut it—you'll need to learn to think critically. "Learning to think is the most important thing you can learn in college," says Bobbie Katz, who attended McGill University in Canada. Bobbie, now a lawyer with Milbank, Tweed, Hadley, & McCloy, a Wall Street firm, wanted to be a gym teacher when he started college. The more he found out about his future profession, however, the less well suited to it he felt he was. Ultimately, he opted not to pursue physical education. But because he had a broad liberal arts education, he learned to make good use of his mind, disciplining himself to think in increasingly complex ways.

Become an Active Learner

Since one of the primary goals of college is to learn *how* to learn, you must become an *active learner*. How? Well, one way is to finish your assigned reading (or at least skim it) before you attend the lectures. That way, the professor's comments become a review for you—not an introduction.

But don't think you can do the reading and skip the class. That's what Jason Moore tried to do in his first semester at the University of Washington. What he discovered, much to his dismay, was that some of the material covered on exams came from lectures.

If your professor's lectures are supplemented by discussion groups led by graduate teaching assistants, attend them. "Go to class, take notes and reflect on what you've learned," recommends Gigi David, a curriculum coordinator for a private elementary school.

Develop Good Study Habits

Nimbleness of mind is nurtured by developing good study habits. Below are several basic learning principles endorsed by memory experts.

Resist the Urge to Cram. The brain operates best when you feed it information repeatedly, over a period of time rather than all at once. Therefore, plan to study a certain amount of time every day. Before a test, reread your notes several times over the course of two weeks and you'll have better recall.

Take Study Breaks. Your brain can only pay close attention to one thing for so long. You begin learning with a high attention span, but after a while, it drops off. Research shows that jumping from one activity to another, however, increases your mind's ability to retain material. For instance, read for twenty minutes; then play an instrument, exercise, or call someone on the phone. Then come back to your studies. Of course, if a learning period is going well and you're at a good pace, don't make yourself stop. You may lose valuable momentum. But such instances are rare. It's much more common to have lost attention and not be aware of it.

Set Up Your Ideal Study Environment. When you are studying, do you like it quiet, with few or no distractions, or does a little background music and having other people around actually help you concentrate? Discover your optimal learning environment, then create that atmosphere for yourself.

Pick Your Best Time for Learning. As a college student, you will probably be able to determine your class schedule. Use that flexibility to your advantage. "I work best late at night," says Karen McMillen. "So my best semesters were those where I had no taxing classes earlier than nine or ten a.m. I hit a slump right after lunch, so I found that giving myself two to three hours in the middle of the day worked well. "I could focus better on my classes if they were scheduled during my 'peak brain function' times."

Jill Ruvidich, a computer technical specialist, could tell in her first five minutes of studying if her time was being spent effectively or not. If it wasn't, she went running or accomplished something else on her "To Do" list. "Don't sit around putting in hours if you're not absorbing," she says. "Make sure your study time is quality time."

Give Your Brain a Workout. Memory experts say crossword puzzles are one of the best forms of brain work. Begin with simple ones, then progress to ones that are more difficult. Here are a few other suggestions for developing your mental prowess. Pick one or two that you don't normally do; that way you'll be adding variety to your thinking processes. The goal of these exercises is to stimulate your brain to think in new ways.

- Build something—a birdhouse, a model airplane, etc.
- Repair something—fix a broken bicycle chain, the latch to your door, or, if you feel inclined, take a stab at your car's engine!
- Grow a garden; herbs are especially popular right now and window boxes are suitable for dorm rooms and other cozy living quarters.
- Work on a cube puzzle and other kinds of "brain teasers."
- Talk with someone else about what you are learning.
- Practice visualization. Think of a personal challenge you face. Perhaps you need to talk with your roommate about a problem in your relationship, or maybe you need to take an important test. Picture the steps that will move you closer to the desired outcome. Play around mentally by imagining several approaches you could take to meet the challenge.

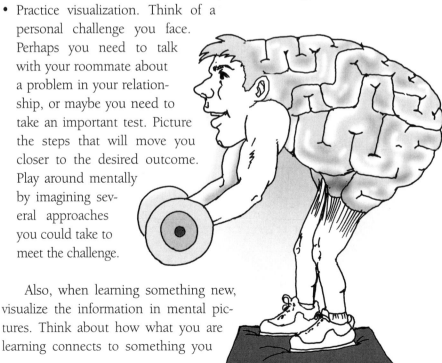

Also, when learning something new, visualize the information in mental pictures. Think about how what you are learning connects to something you already know. Try new methods of note-taking that incorporate visual images. For example, draw a diagram of the information you receive in a lecture or during your study time.

Engage your auditory senses as well. For example, repeat what you are reading aloud; this study technique might help ingrain the material in your mind.

Manage Your Time

Time is money, so why not budget it? Even a billionaire's calendar has just twelve months. As a student, you have many different classes, and if you're going to pursue the extracurricular activities or part-time work that will help you to become well-rounded, you're going to have to make a time budget and then stick to it. There's no other way. It doesn't have to be elaborate. Consider Benjamin Franklin's typical schedule:

        5 a.m.: Wake up, wash, and dress. Plan the day; breakfast
        8 a.m.: Work
       12 noon: Lunch; read
        2 p.m.: Work
        6 p.m.: Relax; dine; review the day
       10 p.m.: Sleep

It's simple enough, and yet this daily schedule served Benjamin Franklin well for over sixty years.

In his autobiography, Lee Iacocca, the former president of Ford, writes, "The ability to concentrate and use your time wisely is everything if you want to succeed in business—or almost anywhere else for that matter." As an engineering major at Lehigh University, Iacocca had to balance his studies, his job at the school newspaper, and his other extracurricular activities. "You've got to know what's important and then give it all you've got," says Iacocca. "Anyone who wants to become a problem solver in business has to learn fairly early how to establish priorities."

Why is writing down your schedule so important? For one thing, writing things down commits you to action. If you just keep your priorities in your head, you may or may not remember what you have to do. Second, writing down your schedule helps you to determine which things are most important. The "do or die" things you have to do each day take priority over things you should do if you can find time. Third, crossing things off your list at the end of each day gives you a sense of accomplishment. You

---

H O W   T O   T E S T   B E S T

1. *Know the structure of the exam.* Do the easiest questions come first? If so, do all questions count the same, no matter what their level of difficulty? Will the questions be multiple-choice or essay, or a combination of both? Find out ahead of time so you can study accordingly.

2. *Be prepared.* Sharpen pencils and bring an extra pen. You might also want to bring a book or your Walkman so that you can chill out during breaks rather than listening to everyone else talk about what they do and don't know.

3. *Get a good night's sleep.* If necessary, spend a week getting on a sleep schedule so you don't come in bleary-eyed.

4. *Eat a healthy snack.* An empty stomach is a distraction.

5. *Don't cram.* Instead, review relevant material several times over the course of a few days instead of just the night before.

6. *Don't stress.* If a question seems hard for you, it probably is hard for everyone else taking the test too. Skip that question and move on to the other questions, then come back to it.

(Adapted from Kaplan Staff/Newsweek "Tipsheet," 1999 edition)

---

realize that you are getting from one point to the next and that you are setting the agenda. Creating a schedule enables you to be in control. Following are some sample schedules from college freshmen.

Let's be realistic. You may not want your schedule to be this detailed. But you'll accomplish more by having a daily game plan.

Set Priorities

Francis Bacon probably said it best: "To choose time is to save time." You won't waste time on things that don't matter if you identify your priorities. But before you can decide which task to tackle first each day, you have to set goals. Take time in the next few days to set long-term (life), intermediate (five to ten years), and short-term (daily) goals in each of these areas: spiritual, educational, health, cultural/social, and financial. Then make a list of

Sample Schedule No. 1

Monday		To do today:

Monday

6:30	Wake up, breakfast
7:15	Read history assignment
9:00	Calculus
10:00	Freshman composition reading before class tomorrow
11:00	Astronomy
12:00	Lunch
1:00	Library time
1–2	Calculus homework
2–3	Finish rough draft of paper on Hemingway's *Farewell to Arms*
3–4	Read Chapter 4 of astronomy text; review and highlight class notes
4:00	Visit Julia Plant, composition instructor; review rough draft; make notes for revision
5:00	Golf class
6:30	Dinner
8:00	Revise composition paper; double-check calculus homework
9:30	Madeline's surprise birthday party in the dorm
10:30	Sleep

To do today:

1. Buy Madeline's birthday card
2. Bring Eric to coalition meeting
3. Finish history assignment
4. Double-check calculus homework
5. Finish draft of paper

Sample Schedule No. 2

Monday

8:30	Wake up
9:30	Management Information Systems
10:30	Computer Center—run program
11:00	Begin reading *The Odyssey*
12:00	Introduction to the Humanities
1:00	Lunch
2:00	Accounting
3:00	Marketing Club meeting—bring advertising plans
4:00	Library time
4–5	Accounting homework
5–6	French lab work
6–7	Read at least to page 100 of *The Odyssey*
7:00	Dinner at Student Union with Cynthia and Alex
8–9	Write rough draft for composition assignment on Keats's *Ode on a Grecian Urn*
10:00	Watch the news, read the newspaper
11:00	Review French for tomorrow's test
11–12	Organize/write schedule for tomorrow

To do today:

1. Finish French assignment
2. Run program
3. Begin reading *The Odyssey*
4. Meet with Marketing Club
5. Double-check accounting homework

tasks that need to get done. As you study your list, ask yourself these five questions to help you order the list from high- to low-priority goals:

1. What important things must I accomplish first today?
2. What are the consequences if I don't accomplish each task today?
3. If necessary, what can wait until tomorrow?
4. What on my list is helping me move toward my long-term or intermediate goals?
5. What, in the long run, produces the highest rewards?*

Throughout the day, keep asking yourself: "What is the best use of my time right now?" It will only be a matter of time before you notice that your world is more ordered and purposeful. Taking charge of your time will help you with the one lifelong goal—that of achieving your personal best.

Take Effective Notes

Frank Landy, the professor from Penn State, once found the notebook of one of his students. "Since I had just given what I thought was a particularly clear, well-delivered lecture, I opened the book to see what kind of notes the student took. To my dismay and surprise, the student had written down only the anecdotes and stories that described the main points. The real meat of the lecture was scribbled in the margins as an afterthought."

Professors will often use stories or real-life examples to explain a concept or term. "The bones," says Landy, "are the theory, while the flesh is the story." To truly learn the subject matter, you must listen for and grasp both.

To take good notes you must go to class. Don't kid yourself. You need the material your professors give you in their lectures no matter how well you've read and retained the information in the texts.

Most professors will organize their lectures around several controlling points. Obviously, you can't write everything down, but the main ideas—which your professor may write on the board or summarize at the end of each lecture—are the ones you want to record on paper and commit to memory. Some students organize their lecture notes in outline form. Others write in more of a prose style, which they can highlight later on. Find a style that's comfortable for you and stick to it.

Keep your notes organized and in one place. Date each set of notes so

*Reprinted from *Manage Your Time, Your Work, Yourself* copyright © 1993 by Merrill E. Douglass and Donna N. Douglass. Reprinted by permission of AMACOM, a division of American Management Association International, New York, NY. All rights reserved. http://www.amanet.org.

that you can easily match the lecture up with the corresponding text chapter. If necessary, go back and rewrite your notes after the lecture. Or sit down with your professor during his or her office hours and make sure you are grasping the information.

Review your notes. In the same way that you must continually review the summaries after every chapter, you must continually review your class notes. If you keep up with the material along the way, studying for exams will be a whole lot easier. You can't cram for life, so start your good planning habits now. You'll be prepared for the long haul.

Achieving Your Personal Best

In the first half of this chapter, you learned about how to become a better student. Among other things, you now know how to set priorities and how to take effective notes. To achieve your personal best, however, you will also want to add a few additional skills. In the second part of this chapter, you will learn more about how to develop your potential.

Get to Know Your Professors

When John Diaz was a reporter for the *Denver Post*, he also served as part of a panel on a weekly discussion program on a PBS affiliate that dealt with issues central to the state of Colorado. During the summer, John taught a newswriting course at Colorado State University.

"I was amazed at how few students sought me out," he said. "The ones who went the extra nine yards to ask me outside of class how they could improve benefited the most from the course."

John was surprised that one of his students, a journalism major, said she didn't have time to read the newspaper.

"That's like an aspiring doctor who doesn't have time to be with sick people," John says. John was able to help this student organize her time so that she could read the paper every day, and he helped her brainstorm about other career avenues so that she could be sure that journalism was what she truly wanted to pursue. John was both a teacher and a mentor to her.

Few college students bother to get to know their professors. They don't take advantage of office hours unless they fail a test or miss a class. They don't realize that college professors are an invaluable resource.

Margie Oemero, an honors student at the University of Texas, agrees. "A lot of students are intimidated by their professors. They worry that the professor will feel bothered if they seek him out. My experience is that it is worth it to build that mentoring relationship." During her sophomore year, Margie took an honors seminar on marriage taught by a prominent researcher. She enjoyed the material and took the time to get to know the professor. "Now I work for him, have taken graduate courses with him, will do my senior thesis with him and possibly write an article with him. Deciding on a graduate school will be so much easier with the help of a professor who knows which departments and professors are reputable."

Colleen Smith felt extremely intimidated by one of the psychology professors in her graduate program. "I was sure he had evaluated all of my faults and decided that I was unfit for the profession. During a staff meeting, I was describing a new client who needed to be assigned to a counselor. As I spoke, the professor started scowling— I felt like I would either start to cry or laugh hysterically any minute. So I made a joke about how he was scowling. Everyone laughed, including him. It turned out he was trying to figure out who would be the best counselor for the client. He was not thinking negatively about me. In fact, I soon found out he thought I was a talented counselor. That experience reminded me that teachers and employers are human—they are much easier to work with if we take them off the pedestals we put them on. This man has turned out to be of great assistance to me in my career, encouraging me and sending leads my way."

Diana Cuddeback, a hospice social worker, believes finding a mentor was one of the most important experiences of her college career. During her sophomore year at Sacramento State, she took the required abnormal psychology course. Over the course of the term she sought out her professor for questions and advice. The following year, he offered her a position as teaching assistant for the course (she was still an undergraduate student). Through the experience of being a TA, she got first-hand training in leading discussion groups, grading papers, and supporting students. Her professor was also able to see how she handled the responsibility.

During Diana's senior year, this professor nominated her for the Most Outstanding Senior award, which she won. He encouraged her to attend graduate school. "He provided opportunities for me to grow and learn about myself. He also introduced me to other faculty members. His friendship and encouragement helped build my confidence and self-esteem. Under his guidance, I began to see myself as a professional, as someone who had natural abilities to develop."

Start to visit your professors' offices during the first few weeks of school. Go over your class notes with them to make sure you properly understand key concepts. Let them know that you are truly interested in learning their material. They will be impressed by your diligence and your willingness to go above and beyond what is expected. If you have good rapport with a professor, he or she will probably give you the benefit of the doubt if your grade is on the border between an A and a B. If you are trying harder than anyone else to learn the material, chances are your professors will recognize and admire your tenacity.

What about aloof professors who would rather spend time doing research than talking with undergrads? Well, you're going to meet them. So instead of giving up and assuming that all professors are like that, go to the ones who are willing to help. And remember: you are the consumer. You are paying for your education and you deserve your professors' attention. Each semester you'll probably have at least one professor who becomes your favorite. Pursue the aloof ones too. This will build your confidence, and it will prepare you for the aloof people you will need to build relationships with in business.

Think of professors as "senior advisors." They can ask you questions regarding your major, start the wheels in your head turning, inspire you to superior effort, and give you insights on how to learn, think more broadly, and achieve your goals. The best professors you will have in college are quite similar to the best managers you will have in the business world. Learning from them will go a long way toward teaching you what being the best means—as a manager or as a teacher.

The cynic in you may say that this sounds like the behavior of a brownnoser. Resist the impulse to believe this. Many "brownnosers" who work hard and build successful relationships with peers and professors make the best grades, get the best recommendations, and go on to get top jobs.

Kevin Dellsperger, a cardiologist and professor of medicine at the University of Iowa, believes the mentoring relationship was one of the most valuable and enjoyable experiences of his college career. The relationship with his mentor turned into a lifelong friendship and professional relationship.

During his freshman year at Tulane, Kevin heard a lecture given by David Wieting at a meeting of the Biomedical Engineering Society. The lecture was about prosthetic heart valves. "After his lecture, I was excited and remember telling my friends and family about Dr. Wieting. I also thought I wanted to work with him during my time at Tulane. I actually made an appointment to talk with him about working in his lab. Unfortunately, at that time he had nothing available, but he put me in contact with another faculty member.

"During my junior year, I took Dr. Wieting's physiology course, and he rekindled my great interest in prosthetic heart-valve work. This time he did have a position in his lab . . . Without a doubt, those last two years were the happiest in my undergraduate years. I must have seemed like a child of four or five, constantly asking him questions about heart valves and bioengineering principles.

"He may tell you otherwise, but I would not be where I am without his guidance. In our program, we were to do research as part of our curriculum. I remember during the summer of my junior year asking David for advice about prosthetic heart valves and their complications. After two or three weeks, I told him I wanted to design a new valve. He had a smile on his face and asked me what it should look like. I told him I didn't know. He told me to think about it and bring him a design. Well, several weeks later I had a 'brilliant' idea. I took it in to David, and the look on his face was one of shock. He went to a locked file cabinet, took out a book of his personal ideas, and showed me a nearly identical thought. I believe it was at this time that our relationship was changed from student-teacher to student-friend-teacher.

"The next year, working on the valve and in the lab with him, was wonderful. I was having such great fun that in March or April I strongly considered delaying medical school for a year to get a master's degree. It was at this time that David was the best mentor I could have had. He told me emphatically that since I had always wanted to go into medicine, I should not delay my training. He said other research opportunities would come to my attention and that I could jump on the bandwagon.

"We kept in touch after I graduated. When he left Tulane, he joined Mitral Medical (a heart-valve company) and asked me to come out during the summer to help set up the lab and do some testing. His job as a mentor was not over, as he directed the research portion of my Ph.D. work. Now I believe that I can scientifically contribute as an equal partner for the first time. His efforts at Tulane and Mitral Medical lit a fire of questioning that is critical for success in research. While my emphasis these days is not primarily heart-valve prostheses, I am still active in that area, with collaborative efforts with David. He is like a big brother to me. I value his advice and care deeply about him."

Master Your Communication Skills

"No higher-level job can be obtained without a good command of the language," says Steven Harwood, chief of nuclear medicine at the Veterans Administration hospital in Bay Pines, Florida. "Writing skills are the most important skills you can develop—especially for obtaining higher-management-level jobs. You must be able to clearly communicate your ideas to others."

Mick McCormick, a Nike sales director, believes written and oral communication skills are essential for success in the workplace. "I have seen qualified, gifted people passed over for top promotions because they could not communicate their ideas effectively. Corporations value verbal skills."

"Look for examples of great writers so that you can have the best models for your own work," says Greg McCaslin, who has taught students from kindergarten to college. "Read the newspaper, ask your teachers to let you see the work of some of the best writers in your class, and seek styles which vary from your own." Greg, who taught for fifteen years and became director of the New York Foundation for the Arts, says that with writing, as with learning anything else, the determination to improve and a nondefensive response to criticism will overcome any lack of aptitude.

Freshman composition may be one of the most important classes you take in college. Even if it's not required, try to take a writing class during your first semester. Learning to become a good writer means learning to communicate—to refine and develop your thoughts—so that what you mean to say, or what you think, is clear to others. If you learn to be a good writer as a freshman, you will be successful in your sophomore, junior, and senior-level courses, where you will be required to write research papers and do special assignments. Also, beyond the freshman level, essay exams become the norm.

In the business world, good writing is essential. Throughout your career, you'll be writing memos, business letters to clients, reports, strategic and planning proposals, persuasive or informative speeches, and more. If you can communicate effectively on paper and orally, you'll have an advantage in business over those who know how to manipulate numbers, but know little about expressing themselves or their work.

"I try to make it fun," says David Plane, who teaches geography at a large state university. He helps his students understand their audience by asking them to write from the point of view of someone in the field. "I ask them to write on a topic and pretend that they are an urban planner. What questions would that person ask? How would they best explain and communicate their ideas to a reviewing committee or to their managers?" The following week he might ask them to write a paper from a manager's point of view, presenting the urban planner's proposal.

Becoming a good writer means becoming good at revising your thoughts and observations. Writing, like thinking, is a process. Working on several drafts means distilling your ideas. So get comfortable with rewriting, crossing things out, and throwing away some of your initial thoughts. That's part of the fun of writing.

Among the many composition books available, I think *The Simon & Schuster Handbook for Writers* by Lynn Troyka stands out. It explains how to become a good—even a great—writer. It also contains everything you need to know about the rules for writing. After your freshman year, you'll use it to write research papers for your higher-level courses.

Here's an excerpt from the book that should help clarify how you (and everybody else) can master the art of writing:

> Many people assume that a real writer can pick up a pen (or sit at a type-writer or a word processor) and magically write a finished product word by perfect word. Experienced writers know better. They know that writing is a process, a series of activities that start the moment they begin thinking about a subject and end when they complete a final draft. Experienced writers know, also, that good writing is rewriting. Their drafts are filled with additions, deletions, rearrangements, and rewordings.

So remember that good writing means practicing. And be patient with yourself. You're embarking on many new things at once.

Understand Technology

In addition to mastering your communication skills, you will also need to keep up with computer technology and the ways in which it can help you

TIPS FOR BECOMING A BETTER WRITER

1. Keep up your journal. You'll be able to look back over your entries to see if your thoughts are coherent. Do your sentences make sense? What style do you use?

2. Write letters. Instead of picking up the phone to call your friends or parents, try writing. Do your thoughts flow easily? If they don't at first, don't worry. And remember that you are going to improve with practice (as well as lower your phone bill!).

3. Read magazines and the newspaper. Analyze the writing of columnists and reporters. What is clear and crisp about their writing? How could you apply the same techniques?

4. Have a friend look at and comment on your writing. Your teacher is not the only resource for feedback. Meet with a friend or two outside of your composition class and do some peer editing. Analyze their writing and ask them to give you constructive criticism of your own work.

5. Write your thoughts down on lists that you can refine later. Jotting things down before you have to write—or think—them out will help you crystallize your original thoughts.

during college and in your career. Computer technology touches every possible field and job.

Although technology has made life easier for many people, it's also the source of a lot of anxiety for others. More to the point, some people are afraid of their computers. In a 1994 MCI-Gallup survey, almost half of the white-collar workers (people employed in office jobs) identified themselves as "cyberphobic."

In today's information age, however, avoiding computers is no longer an option. Since 1984, the percentage of jobs that require knowing how to use a com-

TIPS FOR BECOMING A BETTER SPEAKER

1. Contribute to class discussion as often as possible. As you begin to share your ideas and ask questions, you will become more comfortable speaking in public and articulating your thoughts in front of groups of people.

2. Assume leadership positions in your extracurricular organizations. Whether you are the president or a committee leader, you will have many opportunities to practice communicating your ideas in a group.

3. When you have formal presentations to prepare, practice your speech in front of a friend. Ask your friend to give you feedback. Did you enunciate your words clearly? Were your ideas interestingly presented? Did you speak too fast? Too slow? Too quietly?

4. Enroll in a class on public speaking or debate where you can hone your speaking skills. Not only do communication classes teach you specific tips, they also give you plenty of chances to practice.

5. Find out if your college has a student chapter of Toastmasters, an organization that is specifically designed to help you become comfortable and skillful in public speaking.

---

puter has risen from 25 to 46 percent. More than 70 percent of all management positions now demand computer literacy. Becoming competent with computers is easier than you might think. Experts suggest taking these steps to overcome your fears:

1. *Don't be snowed by terminology.* When you shop for a computer, decide what you'd like to do with it and list those goals, advises Kris Jamsa, author of *Welcome to Personal Computers.* Then, if a salesperson asks an obscure question—such as "How many megahertz do you want?"—respond: "I don't know. You tell me what I need to accomplish my goals, which are . . ." The salesperson should be able to answer in plain English.

2. *Dive right in.* You don't need to know the technical details of your computer any more than you need to understand the technology behind your microwave oven. "Don't get bogged down in a hefty computer manual," advises Joe Kraynak, author of *The Complete Idiot's Guide to PCs.* "Go ahead and flip the switch, click and move the mouse." For some people, the biggest obstacle to pressing that first key is the fear of hitting the wrong one. Don't worry about your mistakes. Your computer won't remember how many wrong keys you press—unless you ask it to. And don't worry about losing information. Most computer programs have a feature that can retrieve lost data or undo the previous command. According to Kris Jamsa, if you master just three specific tasks—saving and printing a document, sending and receiving E-mail, and browsing the World Wide Web—you'll be as computer-proficient as most of the population.

3. *Ask for help.* Most schools require students to take computer courses. Many schools also have computer resource centers on campus, complete with computers for students to use and a staff to assist them. Tell someone that you need help getting started. A fellow classmate who navigates the computer easily might be glad to help you get started.

Overcoming your apprehension of computers may enrich your life in ways you'd never imagined. Computers today can be invaluable in helping you research topics and compose papers. They can also be useful in helping you balance your checkbook and keep track of your daily responsibilities. And with the explosion of on-line services, you have a wealth of information at your fingertips.

While terminology changes rapidly, here are a few buzzwords that you should know now:

- The *Internet* is a worldwide electronic superhighway that carries electronic mail and information services from a variety of sources. It connects all kinds of computers and computer systems, regardless of size or program. Many college professors now put their syllabi, lecture notes, and tests on the Internet. Some schools are hooking each dorm room up to a campus network, which in turn allows students access to the Internet.

- *On-line services* such as America Online, Prodigy, Netscape, and CompuServe are available by subscription and provide a wide variety of information in an easy-to-use format. They operate through a modem

hooked to your phone line. These services have an incredible array of information, available anytime you need it, on topics such as current events, investment opportunities, technology news, and advice on purchasing computers or other software. On-line services also allow you to "talk" with other subscribers about issues that interest you. You can browse through the system and find bulletin boards that feature discussions on specific topics, or you can send E-mail to friends. The on-line service can also provide access to periodicals you might need for researching papers.

• *E-mail* is mail sent from one personal computer to another through an on-line service. A recent special issue of *Time* magazine, "Focus on Technology," describes one way E-mail is used at MIT: "A student who wants to talk about a particular problem at 2 a.m. doesn't have to wander the dormitory halls looking for slits of light under doorways. Instead, the student posts a message on Zephyr, MIT's instant-message system devoted to specific topics—many of them classroom-related—where similarly stumped students are likely to be discussing precisely that problem."

• A *CD-ROM drive* allows your personal computer to deliver complex and expanded programs contained on compact discs. If you loaded these kinds of programs onto your hard drive, your computer's memory would be crammed with information in no time at all. So you need to have the CD in the disk drive in order to run the program. Sarah Lyman Kravits, a writer in New York City, uses her CD-ROM drive to run programs such as Bookshelf and Encarta. "Bookshelf gives me instant access to a dictionary, thesaurus, quotation reference, condensed encyclopedia, atlas, chronology, and almanac. When I am using my word-processing program, the icons appear at the top of the screen, so whenever I need to look something up, I slide my mouse up there and click. That's all it takes. Then I have a whole library to browse through."

Technology is rapidly changing the ways companies function—how managers manage and how employees communicate with one another and their supervisors. Many businesspeople find it is necessary to return to school periodically to update their skills in order to continue to be valuable to their companies. If you take advantage of the services computers provide now and learn how to keep abreast of changes and developments while you are in college, you'll have learned an invaluable skill for whatever career you choose.

Asking for Help

If you find out early that you're having problems reading, writing, or understanding class material, get help fast. There are plenty of people available to help you in these areas. You can hire a professional, or you can go to one of the tutors your campus may provide. If you need to take off a semester to refine your study skills, do it. It will be well worth your time and energy in the long run. It is better to make mediocre grades for one semester than for four years.

Christina Bernstein felt "unmotivated" during her sophomore year in college. She was especially challenged by the language requirement, which called for four semesters of a foreign language. After taking the first semester of her junior year off and living with a family in Bogatá, Colombia, Chris was able to return to school speaking Spanish fluently. She not only finished up her language classes, she also had new enthusiasm for the rest of her studies.

To get you started focusing in on your study skills, fill in the academic evaluation chart below:

Academic Strengths   **Academic Weaknesses**

1._____   1._____

2._____   2._____

3._____   3._____

If at First You Don't Succeed...

You may fall short of some of the goals you set for your freshman year. Maybe you won't achieve a 3.0 average or become captain of the women's soccer team. Instead of dwelling on your defeats, think about ways to improve next year. Can you sharpen your study skills? Manage your time better? Better apply yourself to your studies until you improve? Whatever your problem, see what can be done during the summer before your sophomore year begins. You may want to spend part of the summer taking reading and writing courses so that you'll have better study skills as a sophomore. You may want to take a year off to attend a community college where you can refine your basic study skills. Whatever your reasons for not meeting your goals may be, analyze what happened and develop a strategy for remedying the situation.

Maybe you gave it your best shot and you've come to the conclusion that you're just not cut out for college. Okay, it's not the end of the world. It does mean, however, that you'll have a somewhat different path, which may lead you to something equally as rewarding as the college-grad path.

Jack Naughton never graduated from high school. He sold Fuller brushes and La-Z-Boy recliners until he had a brainstorm one day: a reclining chair that dentists could use to treat their patients more effectively. He patented the idea internationally and made his life's fortune from that one idea. The original chair, by the way, is now in the Smithsonian.

However, unless you have the unbridled ambition and fortitude to forego a traditional education, you're better off staying in school. You may never be on the dean's list or make Phi Beta Kappa. That's okay. The most you can do is try, learn as much as you can, and go forward. Most people improve with time.

5

Being on Your Own

Balancing the Demands of Your World

Freedom is not worth having if it does not connote freedom to err.
Mahatma Gandhi

Responsibility educates.
Wendell Phillips

L eaving home to attend college was really my first experience of being on my own," remembers Ingrid Damiani. "All of a sudden, it was completely up to me to decide when and how much I studied, how late I stayed out, and how I spent my money."

The freedom you experience as a freshman can be thrilling. The responsibilities that come with it, however, can be overwhelming. "How you face decisions in college can determine whether your college experience is filled with challenges you master or a series of crises that drain you," says Ingrid's husband, Tim Damiani, a psychiatrist who has counseled college students. "Many of the personal habits you establish during your college years will follow you through your life."

Residence-Hall Life Versus Life Off Campus

Living in a residence hall is one way you can make the transition from your parents' home to being on your own easier. Residence halls are usually less expensive than living on your own; most provide meal plans so that you don't have to worry about grocery shopping and meal preparation during your first year. Residence halls also come with built-in support systems.

In addition to being a source of many new friends, they offer the help and support of resident assistants.

Amir Abolfolthe, a biomedical engineer and product manager, believes that living in a residence hall during his first two years of college was an important part of his adjustment to college life. "Many of the people in the residence hall are new and have the same anxieties you do. The residence hall also helps you to keep a balance between your social and academic life. When you want to play, there are always people who are ready to go out. When you need to study, you can always find someone to go to the library with. And when you are having trouble with a tricky calculus problem or are feeling blocked on your term paper, there are always other students around who are taking the same classes to brainstorm with. In my residence hall we supported each other and looked out for each other. We were like a big family."

As a foreign student, Amir found that living in the residence hall helped him to form friendships with American students. "Many of my Iranian friends lived at home and stuck to themselves on campus. I felt fortunate to be able to interact comfortably with everyone."

Juggling Your Finances

My brother Craig was the first person to sit down and have a talk with me about finances. Although I was making the minimum wage, he explained how important it was to save at least 10 percent of what I made.

"If you get in the habit of saving now, you'll have a decent cushion of savings all your life. It is one of the most important disciplines you can impose on yourself," he said. "You never know what is going to happen to you. You may want to quit your job someday, or you may lose your job. You could get sick. You could decide you want to take six months off and travel the world. If you have learned to save, you will have more options as you get older."

Craig helped me open my first investment account with Merrill Lynch, in a money-market mutual fund. At the time, the account was yielding about 9 percent, which was far better than a standard checking or savings rate. Now that the market conditions have changed, money-market funds are not as good as bonds or stocks. Several years ago, I made a switch from the money-market fund we opened when I was in college to a more diversified investment plan, which is a much better deal for where I am at this point in my life. A good financial adviser can help you make the best decisions about investing and saving your money.

That initial sum of money has really grown over the fourteen years since I began college. And what is more important is that I have been strict about saving. Craig was right. The more you learn to save, the more options you will have later when those inevitable unforeseen circumstances arise.

Tim and Ingrid Damiani handled their money very differently before they got married. Tim knew exactly where he spent his money and carefully budgeted his income. During college, he passed over some things he wanted, but he graduated with no debt and had saved enough to put a large down payment on a car he had been dreaming about. Ingrid spent money more impulsively. She didn't spend a lot at once, but she never knew just where her money was going. "I felt like I was living on the edge financially. I was never sure I'd have enough to cover all my bills."

During the year before they got married, Tim and Ingrid earned about the same amount of money. When they got married, Tim deposited several thousand dollars he had saved into their joint savings account, and Ingrid contributed several thousand dollars in credit card debt.

"We quickly agreed on a budget. It was rough at first, but now that we've set one and stayed on it, I love it," says Ingrid. "It's such a good feeling to have a plan for our money. When we spend money, we enjoy it and do so without guilt or worry because we know it's in the budget. We can save for specific goals in the future. It is a more peaceful way to live."

When you are in control of what you spend, you can feel good about what you buy. Being confident that you've got enough to cover each bill allows you to feel secure and to pursue other interests without money worries hanging over your head. Further, if you budget, you will be able to save money that can be used toward special worthwhile goals, such as traveling.

Establishing a Budget

Whether your education is being paid for by your parents, a scholarship, a loan, or your own hard work, you will be managing your own expenses. Money problems are stressful, but avoidable. If you can get a handle on the amount of money available to you and develop a plan of how you will spend that money, you will avoid wasting your valuable time.

The first step is to determine the amount of money you need to cover the essentials—rent or mortgage payments, utility bills (electricity, gas, phone, water), transportation, tuition and books, food and toiletries, insurance (car, health, renters'), and clothes. After you have determined the amount that these basic needs will cost, you will know how much you have left over for saving and spending on entertainment (eating out, movies, concerts), gifts, and other fun purchases.

There are now computer software programs that help consumers establish budgets and track spending habits. Check with your local computer store for budgeting software.

Financial aid counselors also provide budget advice. Contact your school's financial aid office for information. There are also private financial counselors who can help you establish a budget, but they will charge a fee for this service. Examine your options and determine what will work best for you.

Smart Ways to Use Credit Cards

Credit cards can be very helpful if you use them shrewdly. Many credit card companies make their cards easily available to college students. When choosing a card, pay attention to the annual fee and interest rates; they vary from card to card. Pick one with a low interest rate, and try to find one with no annual fee.

Using credit cards modestly and paying them off every month will help you establish a good credit history. Credit cards can also help you in an emergency and provide a clear statement of how you've spent your money. However, a word of caution: avoid paying your tuition on a credit card.

When Joe Wieting was in college, he did not have enough money to pay for everything he needed. "When I was short of cash, I charged what I needed, reasoning that I would be able to pay off my debt quickly when I

L E A R N I N G   T O   B U D G E T

SAMPLE COLLEGE STUDENT MONTHLY BUDGET

INCOME:

Parental support	$2,000.00
Student loan ($2,500/year)	283.00
Part-time job (20 hours/week)	640.00
Total Income	$2,923.00

EXPENDITURES:

Tuition ($15,000/year)	$1,600.00 (9-month payment plan)
Transportation (car payments, gas, insurance, repairs)	350.00
Phone	30.00
Utilities (electricity, water, gas)	30.00
Groceries and necessities	150.00
Rent	400.00
Taxes	160.00
Entertainment	50.00
Total Expenditures	$2,770.00
Amount left over for savings	*$153.00*

YOUR PERSONAL BUDGET

INCOME:

Parental support _____

Student loan _____

Part-time job _____

   Total Income _____

EXPENDITURES:

Tuition _____

Transportation (car payment, gas, insurance, repairs) _____

Phone _____

Utilities (electricity, water, gas) _____

Groceries and necessities _____

Rent _____

Taxes _____

Entertainment _____

   Total Expenditures _____

Amount left for savings _____

got my first job after graduation. I was always careful to pay the minimum amount due each month so that my credit history would be acceptable. What I didn't realize was how fast the interest charges would build up. By the time I graduated, I had a hefty debt that was not easy to pay off. Now I wish that I had taken out a bank loan—the lower interest rate would have made it much easier to pay off, and I would have had the piece of mind of knowing I had enough money to cover my expenses." Be careful to keep track of how much you are spending on your credit cards. Some people make notes on their check register so they can make sure they aren't overspending.

If you are spending more than you are able to pay off at the end of the month, you will be incurring further debt because interest rates are always high. If you miss a payment or make a late payment, your credit rating will be lowered. Bad credit ratings can prevent you from securing a bank loan for a car or a new home, and prospective employers often check credit ratings to get a sense of how responsible the applicant is. The way you use a credit card says a great deal about whether or not you are responsible, so use it wisely. Leo Murphy, a financial specialist at the Chicago Board of Trade, offers the following guidelines:

- *Create a budget and stick to it.* Doing so will help you accomplish three objectives:
  1. To control your spending;
  2. To know where your money is going; and
  3. To help you meet your immediate needs (necessities) and future plans (priorities).
- *Avoid impulse buying.* If you see something you want, always ask yourself the question "Do I really *need* this?" Also, don't buy anything on the spot. Instead, wait at least a day or two before making a purchase. The wait will help you determine whether you really need the item or not.
- *Prioritize your spending.* This guideline involves defining your life goals. Sometimes it's wise to spend money; your colledge education, for example, is an investment in yourself. Therefore, prioritize your spending on the basis of these three categories:
  1. Necessities—food, housing, medical care;
  2. Priorities—your hopes; things that show appreciable growth. Example: your education; and
  3. Luxuries—things you may want but don't need and that can hurt your present and future. Live in the present while keeping your eyes on the future.

• *Limit credit card spending.* Remember that advertisements will entice you to spend money with slogans like "Buy now with no money down." See these ads for what they are: they want your money.

As Murphy says, "The lack of money doesn't prevent people from achieving their goals as much as mismanagement of it." Therefore, begin to establish good financial habits now and you'll have one of life's major responsibilities in check.

The Dating Game

College offers many opportunities to meet different kinds of people and to find out what sort of people you enjoy being with. I'm not an expert on dating during college, since I had only one serious boyfriend in college, and that was during my senior year. Before I met him, I was frankly more interested in my studies and my friends than anything else. But I was clearly the exception. Most of my friends had boyfriends from the start of their freshman year.

Pam Zemper, an RA (resident assistant) who worked in a women's residence hall at the University of Texas, found that many freshmen are confused about how to handle relationships from high school. "These students

are so excited about college. They want to meet new people and to enjoy all the new, interesting things college has to offer. But they also want to maintain the same level of closeness with their boyfriends from home. I always advised the girls on my floor to establish new ground rules with their boyfriends. If they talked every night on the phone in high school and their boyfriends want to continue this, it will hold the girls back from activities they want to try. They need to discuss their expectations about how often they will see and talk to each other. And if they are attending different schools, they probably need to talk about dating other people."

Jeanne Stark, who began dating someone seriously in the middle of her freshman year, remembers opportunities she let slip by because she was in a relationship. "He was an English major like me—he was poetic, charming, and distinctly unambitious. At the time, I found him attractive and enjoyed his company. What I didn't realize was that my involvement with him was keeping me from pursuing other activities and friends I was genuinely interested in. After my sophomore year, he graduated and spent the next few months traveling around Europe. While he was gone, I became a reporter and eventually the copy editor for the school yearbook, and I began working on an honors tutorial with one of my English professors. All of a sudden, all of these doors and opportunities started to open up! What an eye-opener! I realized that I was wasting my time with someone who did not share my goals or values. A few years later, I met the man I eventually married. He has shown me that the best partner is someone who shares your interests and dreams, challenges you, and cheers you on to greater successes."

This doesn't mean that it is wise to date a clone of yourself, or that college is the end of your high school romance. What it does mean is that it's important for you to take stock of yourself—to know what you want from your time in college and what goals you have for your life, and to spend time with people who support you rather than distract you. Even if the person you are dating is the person of your dreams, you still need to make sure you are allowing yourself time to get to know yourself.

Toward the end of college, many of my friends were engaged or starting to think seriously about marriage. Some of them seemed to be using marriage as an escape from the demands of academic work and graduation. Obviously, the decision to get married is personal and the right time for marriage is different for everyone. I'm a slowpoke. I just got back from my ten-year college reunion, and only five of us weren't married. I felt really out of it when people were passing around pictures of their kids. And yet, I'm

D A T I N G   V I O L E N C E

Dating relationships should be fun, enriching experiences. Unfortunately, statistics reveal that sometimes they become the exact opposite. The National Crime Survey from 1997, conducted by the U.S. Department of Justice, shows that as many as one-third of teenagers and young adults, people aged 15 to 21, experience violence in an intimate relationship during their high school or college years. In addition, studies have shown that 67 percent of young women reporting rape were raped by dating partners. Even more alarming is the fact that every abusive relationship has the potential to end in murder. The FBI reports that 20 percent of all female homicide victims are between the ages of 15 and 24, and that one-third of female homicide victims are killed by a male partner.

Anyone can end up in an abusive relationship, but you have to be strong to get out of it. Young men and women often become emotionally involved with their partners before they really know them. They think they love their partners (and maybe they do), and because they are in love, they think they can and should tolerate anything their partners do, say, or prefer. Abusive relationships revolve around this kind of power and control.

Experts say the cycle of violence often begins with small things like name-calling and then builds to an explosion that often results in physical or sexual aggression. Being alert to the warning signs that trigger the cycle will make you less vulnerable to unhealthy dating patterns. Below are questions for you to think about and maybe talk over with your friends, student counselors, or parents.

WARNING SIGNS OF DATING VIOLENCE

The following list is provided by the National Domestic Violence Hotline. If you answer "yes" to two or more of these questions, your partner is likely to be abusive.

- Does your partner verbally put you down or call you names that hurt your feelings?
- When your partner gets angry, are you afraid?
- Does your partner drink or take drugs?

(continued)

- Did your partner grow up in a violent family?
- Does your partner always expect you to follow his orders or advice?
- Does your partner ridicule you for being stupid or for characteristics that he thinks are "typical of women"?
- Has your partner ever bragged about intimidating or hurting other people?
- Is your partner jealous of you and your friends?
- Do you like yourself less than usual when you're with your partner?

If you are in an abusive relationship, take immediate steps to get out of it. If you think your partner might freak out and try to hurt you (a classic response of abusers when their partners try to leave them), break up with him in a public place and arrange for family or friends to take you home.

Also, be alert to your partner's response. If he says anything like "You're not going to leave me," be sure to tell someone (your parents, a roommate). The more people who know, the safer you are. For more information, call the National Domestic Violence Hotline at 1-800-799-7233. Trained counselors are there twenty-four hours a day. The Hotline provides help, not only for the victim, but for the abuser as well. If you have a hearing disability, call the Hotline at 1-800-787-3224 (TDD).

HEALTHY DATING RELATIONSHIPS

Just as unhealthy dating relationships are marked by certain characteristics, so are healthy ones. Healthy intimacy is based on cooperation and equality. Here are the characteristics of mature, nonviolent relationships:

- *Negotiation and fairness.* Seeking mutually satisfying resolutions to conflict, which includes a willingness to accept change and to compromise.
- *Nonthreatening behavior.* Talking and acting so that you both feel safe and comfortable expressing yourselves and doing things.
- *Respect.* Listening to each other nonjudgmentally, being emotionally affirming and affirmed, understanding and valuing each other's opinions.

(continued)

- *Independence and autonomy.* Recognizing each other's interdependence, yet accepting "separateness" as nonmarried persons. Fostering individual identity.
- *Trust and support.* Supporting each other's life goals. Respecting each other's rights to have personal feelings, friends, activities, and opinions. Overcoming issues of envy and resentment.

Of all the demands you encounter in college, developing healthy dating relationships is one of the most critical. Every dating relationship is serious because it plays a part in defining who you are. How you relate to your dating partners, and how they relate to you, are key to your well-being. Establishing equality in your dating patterns now will help ensure a lifetime of close, supportive relationships.

not making one of the biggest decisions of my life unless it is for the right person. Why compromise?

Ingrid Damiani married her husband three years after she graduated from college. "Having time to truly be on my own—to earn my own living and to feel like an adult in the working world—has been invaluable to me in my marriage. That time on my own helped me to define my goals and to learn about myself. Looking back, I can see I grew a lot in those first few years after college. For me, that growing happened better while I was single. It was important for me to know I could succeed on my own terms before I made a commitment to someone else."

Rachelle Shaw is a pediatric dentist in Albuquerque, New Mexico, and the mother of three children. She says, "You can always get married and have children. You won't always have the opportunity to go to school. Following your dreams and achieving goals allows you to subsequently focus on your family or others, enriching all."

Overcoming Obstacles

College students face challenges of all kinds—in academic work, health, finances, and in combatting prejudice. Whatever you are facing, there is probably a resource on campus to support you. You may feel as if you are the only one who is struggling with a problem, but chances are you aren't, and there are people on campus who can help.

Academic Challenges

Most colleges have a learning resource center to give students support with study habits, time management, writing, test anxiety, and other such matters. In addition, many departments offer study groups or tutoring sessions to assist students with particular subjects. Your professors will often be able to send you in the right direction to find these support systems.

Emotional/Psychological Problems

Most universities have counseling centers available specifically for students. These centers usually provide for a certain number of counseling sessions at no cost and then offer another set of sessions at affordable rates (way below the rates you would pay for a private therapist). Counselors can often provide the support and the resources you need to get through your problem.

There are also many groups in the community that can provide support for specific problems such as bulimia or anorexia, being the child of an alcoholic or suffering from alcoholism, and programs for people who have been abused. The counseling center at your school may offer these programs or be able to send you to the right place. If not, check one of the local churches—they often host support groups, and they can also usually provide the name and address of a support group near you.

Physical Disabilities

Cyrus Sarmadi, a junior at the University of California, Santa Barbara, is hearing-impaired and a foreign student. Has he let these challenges slow him down? Not on your life. So far, he has co-founded and supervised a computer club at his college, and he was a gold medalist on the Men's National Deaf Water Polo Team at the World Games in 1993. He is also in the planning stages of starting a Persian club at his school. "My advice is to take a deep breath and plunge. If you fall, get up and jump again."

Cyrus advises other students with challenges to "take advantage of all services that are available at the university, such as note-taking and tutoring services, or any other campus assistance."

Look in your school directory for an office designed to help students with special needs and take advantage of the help offered to you as a student. These offices usually have people who can solve problems quickly (such as finding you a reader, getting a ramp installed, etc.).

Alternative Routes

Dick Christensen, a psychiatrist, remembers beginning college "in a very rigorous premed program which was heavy on the sciences and light on the arts and letters. Not realizing at the time that there was much room for flexibility in the curriculum, I blindly accepted the overwhelming program as a given and proceeded to flunk one exam after the other. Desperate and panicked, I sought out an academic adviser. He allowed me to create my own curriculum, which not only was more manageable but eventually led to a dual major in biology and philosophy. I learned two lessons: each person has unique strengths and weaknesses, and there are always alternative routes to achieving the same goal."

Roadblock? Detours Are Allowed

If you have pursued every avenue for help and you still feel overwhelmed by a problem at college, you might consider taking some time off. Carla Summers, an archivist at the University of Florida, dropped out of school after her sophomore year and spent several semesters waiting tables. "Taking some time off was the best decision I could have made. Before I left, I

was unmotivated, underdirected, and making poor grades. When I returned to school, I had a clear sense of wanting to be there, and I was very focused. My grades reflected my new sense of direction."

Jesse Keller decided to take a year off between his junior and senior years at Yale. His detour was carefully planned to give him a variety of work experiences and to provide him with a refreshing break. For the first half of the year, he worked with a professor on a computer music-software development project. "I found this to be a satisfying situation. I lived in New Haven and kept in touch with my Yale friends, but worked full-time (and was financially independent) in a job that was both interesting and résumé-building." The second semester, Jesse worked at Microsoft as a software designer for a few months. Working at Microsoft gave him hands-on experience in his field. Finally, he spent six weeks traveling across the country before going back to school. According to Jesse, the year off provided "work experience from two different perspectives in the same field and a chance to see a whole bunch of possibilities as I traveled. It also gave me time to renew my academic enthusiasm."

Appreciating Your Diverse World

Unfortunately, equality is an ideal that this country has not always honored. Now, more than ever, we need to make a commitment to create an environment where all people have the opportunity to use their skills and to succeed regardless of race, religion, gender, or disability.

"We must cooperate to compete in a global marketplace," says George Fraser, an author and founder of Success Source, a company that publishes networking guides for African-Americans in various cities. "That means leveraging the collective resources of every single cultural group within our country."

As a recent issue of *Time* magazine devoted to diversity in the United States noted, "Immigrants are arriving at the rate of more than one million a year, mostly from Asia and the vast Hispanic world. The impact of these immigrants is literally remaking America. Today more than 20 million Americans were born in another country."

American companies are responding to this diversity by making sure their workplaces reflect the diversity in society. A recent issue of *Fortune* magazine, which featured an article on diversity in the workplace, noted that executives are starting to see positive results as they implement workforce diversity. "Says IBM chief Louis V. Gerstner, Jr.: 'Our marketplace is made up of all races, religions and sexual orientations, and therefore it is vital to our success that our work force also be diverse.' " Companies are finding that when the workforce is made up of people from different backgrounds, their teams are able to come up with more creative solutions.

Ted Smith, a video producer in Washington, D.C., worked as an RA in an off-campus apartment complex at Virginia Commonwealth University. One of the policies was to pair RAs from different backgrounds to solve problems. Usually a white RA would be paired with an African-American RA. "In addition to resolving residential disputes, we also prepared presentations about resolving racial conflicts. This job helped me to see some of the challenges of living in a diverse environment and showed me creative ways of resolving problems. I use these tools every day in the work I do."

Racist or prejudiced feelings, or disrespecting others because they differ from you, can be damaging to you as an individual as well as to those with whom you associate. These feelings can hinder you from advancing. If you learn to overcome your prejudices or feelings of discomfort with those who are different, you will be an asset to your future employer. In today's world, people value those who care about the advancement of others and who show through their actions an open mind toward people of all backgrounds.

Working with people whose backgrounds are different from yours takes practice and patience. College is an excellent opportunity for you to broaden your experience with other cultures. Through extracurricular activities, volunteering, and friendships, you can meet people who think and live differently from you. Many schools are now requiring students to take courses that help them understand multicultural issues. The University of California at Berkeley, for example, requires that its students take courses that focus on at least three ethnic groups (Asian, Latino, Native American, African-American, or European).

In the words of George Fraser: "Every cultural group is like an instrument in a symphony orchestra. Each instrument brings a different tonality and character—together, the instruments make powerful music."

When There's Resistance

In his book *Out of the Madness*, Jerrold Ladd, an award-winning journalist, tells his story—how he fought to succeed against the odds of growing up in the projects in Dallas surrounded by drugs, violence, and poverty.

He faced many discouraging setbacks in his attempts to gain an education and find meaningful work. At the height of his despair, he asked, "Where was the black man's wisdom and guidance to lead us around snares and guide us through tribulation?"

Since he had no role models in his life to turn to, he found them in the pages of history. He spent hours in the library "reading about black heroes, philosophers, and thinkers . . . My discovery of dead literary role models permanently cured my doubt and made me go back to the fundamental truth. Knowing the great accomplishments of my people, when they existed in their own civilizations, started a chain reaction that would change the foundation of my mind."

He goes on to say, "I felt that my entire life had been like that of a man who had wings of strength and splendor. From childhood this man had watched his brethren sweep the heavens and glide gracefully in the sunshine. But because his wings were a different color, he had been fooled into believing that he could not fly. He knew his wings looked the same, were built the same, flapped the same. But he never had proof. So he had never tried. Then he discovered in a remote cave, a cave that had been kept well hidden, pictures of men of his color flying in the clouds. And on this glorious day, in desperation, he jumped off a cliff, was swooped up in the winds of truth, flapped his damnedest and found he could fly above them all."

Maybe you have not experienced prejudice and poverty to the extreme that Jerrold Ladd did, but his experience of finding role models can benefit anyone trying to overcome an obstacle. We gain inspiration and encouragement from the stories of those who have succeeded before us.

"There are no magic solutions," says George Fraser. However, he too believes that education is critical in overcoming prejudice. His advice? "Read about people who have succeeded despite racism. Seek out mentors and role models and learn about yourself. Through education and knowledge of self, it is possible to overcome the obstacle of racism. Find ways over, around, and through it. Racism is a reality that many people have to face, but it is not a reason to fail."

Many schools have ethnic student centers (an African-American student center, a Hispanic student center, a Middle Eastern student center, etc.). These offices can provide support in many ways—they can help you obtain financial aid, they can intervene in problems you may be having with the administration or professors, and they can introduce you to students who may be facing similar challenges. Some of the centers also offer mentoring programs in which they pair you with a member of the community.

Women in traditionally male-dominated fields such as engineering or science often find an effective support system when they join women's organizations in their field. Rama Moorthy, an engineer in technical sales, says that belonging to the Society of Women Engineers puts her in touch with other women who deal with the same kinds of pressures she does.

When Anthea Coster was a graduate student in space physics at Rice University, she found that women friends in her field were a great support. "We studied together—more as a team than as a group competing against each other."

Being on your own can be scary, lonely, exciting, exhilarating, and sometimes plain uneventful. Balance the highs and lows by getting the rest, relaxation, and rejuvenation you need in order to feel inspired so that you can appreciate what is great in your surroundings and within yourself.

6

Stand Up and Be Counted

Extracurricular Activities

Is there any way of predicting the capacity to lead? The only way I know is to look at college records. If they were leaders during the ages of 18 to 22, the odds are that they will emerge as leaders in middle life.
   David Ogilvy

Y ou've got to make it happen," says John Garcia, who cites belonging to organizations as the best way not only to enjoy yourself but also to learn to relate to people. John, who was a civil engineering major, was hired by Sandia National Laboratories in Albuquerque, New

Mexico. Sandia sent John to Purdue to get a master's degree in structural engineering.

"Engineers are typically great theoreticians and scientists," says John, "but most of them have a hard time getting their ideas across." To balance his college experience, John worked part-time, skied, hiked, and was active in the honorary engineering society Beta Pi.

Lynne Ewing buried herself in her books during her freshman year at Notre Dame. "That was the worst semester I ever had," says Lynne, whose grades were far below the goals she had set for herself. "The next semester, I joined the choir, the school newspaper, and a religious group. My grades went way up. So did my morale, the number of friends I could count on, and my interest level. I kept busy, managed my time, and no longer had a reason to feel sorry for myself for being from out of state and away from my friends and family."

Dawn Pakluda began college at the University of Texas at Austin. She wishes she had joined extracurricular activities. "I could have had a lot more fun and met many more people during college," says Dawn. "Since I only studied and worked, I feel I don't have the strong friendships and rich experiences that college should provide."

My own extracurricular college activities included joining a sorority and several honorary societies, doing volunteer work at a hospice for cancer patients, and participating in the international student club's English-tutoring program for foreign students.

Although large group projects taught me leadership in a broad context, the one-on-one contacts I developed through my other activities helped me to "read" people in business. I learned to listen, to question, to analyze problems, and to motivate even the most unenthused people.

Join extracurricular activities to expand your world. You'll be more interesting, and you'll learn to work with people. By better understanding others, you'll better understand yourself.

To succeed in the workplace, you must be a "team player." Those who give beyond what's expected command the respect of their peers and supervisors. Chances are greater that they'll be promoted to positions where they manage and motivate others. Being valuable to an organization in college will teach you how to become valuable to a company.

Darren Walker, a New York investment banker, was president of several organizations. As a student board member for the University of Texas Student Union, he learned how different people competed to run the union. "When you work with successful people from diverse backgrounds, you have to learn to work toward consensus. I learned to be open to different people and different ideas. Through extracurricular activities, I learned a great deal about politics, group dynamics, and egos." Learning those skills now will give you an advantage when you start your first job.

Companies want to hire employees who will go above and beyond what is expected of them. If you balance work, school, and play, you'll be prepared to juggle your career and personal life. You'll learn to naturally think of new ideas and projects, and you'll learn to be the first person to volunteer for additional responsibility. The busiest people are often the ones who are most likely to take on new projects because they know how to manage their time.

What exactly does the college recruiter learn about you from your extracurricular activities?

- You are a self-starter.
- You've got your act together enough to balance classes with activities.
- You like people and get along with them; you can be a team player.
- You aren't a one-dimensional grind or some gnome buried in your books. You know there's a world beyond the classroom.
- You have sought out career-related experience.

Sometimes extracurricular activities can lead you straight into the business world. Bob Rogers, a pre-law student, says, "Working as the associate editor of the student newspaper prepares me for my long-term goals by teaching me to write, analyze political issues, and persuade readers. I have interviewed attorneys and criticized their arguments, studied how the battle for public opinion works, observed office politics within the paper, and seen the results of different management approaches."

During her freshman year in college, Jeannine DeLoche became a writer for Columbia University's *Course Guide,* a student publication that reviews most of the classes at the college. After writing more articles than the rest of the staff, she was promoted to the post of executive editor. When she needed extra money that year and decided to apply for a job, she interviewed for positions as an editorial assistant, banking on her *Course Guide* experiences. Her first interview was for the editorial page of *The Wall Street Journal*. Says Jeannine, "I remember the interviewer saying, 'You have real editing experience. That's unusual in someone your age.' He offered me the job right then!" Jeannine continued to work as an assistant to the editorial features editor of the *Journal* while at Columbia. She's considering staying there after graduation. "In addition to joining clubs just for fun, try to find extracurriculars which may match your career interests. That way, you can develop the necessary skills and see if you enjoy the work," Jeannine advises.

Participating

You may belong to the right organization, but unless you get involved, you won't have much to show for it. Joe Durrett, the chief executive officer of Broderbund Software in Novato, California, says that when he considers an applicant for his company, he looks for their record of accomplishment. If their record of accomplishment is more about having been at certain places than having done something there, this tips him off that the applicant probably won't work out.

Julie Balovich, a college senior at a large university, found that she had to be responsible for seeking out ways to become involved. "The first thing I learned about student organizations is that the best way to get involved and have people recognize you is to do the grungy work. During my freshman year, I participated in several functions of the student association, and in every one I stayed after and helped clean up. Each time, without fail, upper-division persons would approach me and introduce themselves."

In addition to college-affiliated organizations to join, keep your eyes and ears open for other groups that might intrigue you. Consult the campus counseling center for lists of activities. Read the school paper. Check bulletin boards. Then plunge in. If you don't like your first choice, get out. Remember: it's a numbers game. So try another. Once you find a group you like, participate fully. Volunteer to chair projects. Accept responsibility. Run for office. And if you don't get accepted by Kappa Psi Whatever or you get cut from the snorkeling squad, don't be discouraged. Try something else!

Developing Friendships

One of the greatest aspects of joining any organization is that you meet interesting people, some of whom will become your close friends. Campus organizations will also introduce you to other students who are focused on their goals. As Gregory Sapire, a law school graduate, recalls, "Working in student government put me in contact with a number of other ambitious students who challenged me to achieve my best. Through their experiences, they suggested opportunities—study abroad, summer enrichment programs, research positions—that I found interesting. If you hang out with people going places, you'll find yourself going places too." Another student advises, "Try to make friends with other students who are striving for excellence. They will inspire you to achieve more." That's excellent advice. Unless you're a social recluse, developing friendships in college will be central to your happiness.

Becoming a Leader

A leader is one who, among other things, motivates, teaches, trains, and organizes others. Those skills will help you in almost any career—whether you want to flip Whoppers at Burger King or become President of the United States. If you develop leadership skills in college, these will keep the door of management open for you. You may never want to manage anybody, but it's nice to be prepared enough to have the option.

Being a leader doesn't mean you have to run the country. But wherever you wind up, you will spend most of your time dealing with a small circle of people. Be a leader for them.

Bob Rogers tended to stay away from leadership positions until his black belt in tae kwon do thrust him into a leadership position. Because he had achieved so much in this discipline, he was automatically seen as a

leader. He didn't feel comfortable immediately, but his skill allowed him to offer strong leadership to the group. He felt that the experience gave him a chance to "see different leadership and teaching approaches and to hone leadership skills."

How do you become a leader? Well, if you haven't done it before, start small. Volunteer to head a committee. Then put as much energy into it as your studies allow. The most important part of your activity is gaining the goodwill of those you work with. As your confidence increases, accept more responsibility. Run for office. If you win, great—accept that as a sign that your peers respect you. If you lose, don't be discouraged. As Winston Churchill said, "Success is the ability to go from one failure to another with no loss of enthusiasm."

WHAT MAKES A GOOD PARTICIPANT?

- Contributes ideas
- Organizes events
- Volunteers to help
- Follows through on commitments

WHAT MAKES A GOOD LEADER?

- Has a vision of where the organization can go
- Makes decisions
- Motivates others
- Sets goals
- Plans and organizes
- Listens carefully
- Inspires people
- Delegates responsibility
- Shares credit
- Isn't arrogant
- Acts diplomatically
- Recognizes others' achievements and contributions

Don't worry if you've never led before. Give it a try and see how it feels. You may hate it, but you might love it. Either way, it pays to know. Student activities often have resources to help you develop leadership skills such as workshops and seminars.

Doing Volunteer Work

There are many good reasons to volunteer. Volunteering offers the chance to develop both leadership and team-building skills. Also, you'll typically interreact with a diverse group of volunteers, which will enrich your life perspective and enhance creativity.

Gretchen Van Fossan, national program manager for the Points of Light Foundation, says, "Service is an incredibly valuable experience both in and out of college, particularly if you're willing to step out of your own familiar and comfortable environment in order to participate with others in community work. Helping people in situations that are different from the ones

you've grown up in and working in a group with diverse perspectives are invaluable in building a real and balanced view of the world around you."

Increasingly, schools are making community service part of the core curriculum. For example, at the University of Maryland School of Law, the entire clinical program is centered on volunteer work. In order to graduate, students must integrate two hundred hours of community service into their regular coursework. To meet that requirement, some law students have helped local high school students reclaim abandoned properties in the depressed Baltimore neighborhood of Park Heights. "One group is white and one is African-American," says Daniel P. Henson III, commissioner of housing and community development, "but there's a great camaraderie between them." Next, UM is opening a law office in one of the formerly abandoned buildings to take on everything from landlord-tenant disputes to misdemeanors.

Several companies encourage community service as part of their company philosophies. For example, take IBM, which has implemented numerous community service programs to help their employees balance the demands of their jobs and their personal and family lives. One such program, Community Service Assignments, allows IBM employees to continue earning their salaries while working for nonprofit organizations.

CSA helps selected nonprofit tax-exempt community service organizations in their time of need, and at the same time supports IBM employees with special talents in the efforts to help such organizations.

Volunteer work can also be great for relieving stress because it takes you out of yourself. Your history final will seem less catastrophic after you've worked an afternoon in a children's hospital ward, or played basketball with a fatherless child, or analyzed a famous painting with a group of high school students.

Your participation in service projects also says something very positive about you: your future employer will know that you care about people. Therefore, on the job, the chances are greater that you'll treat others with sensitivity and respect. When you face unexpected snags, for instance, you'll be less likely to take out your frustrations on those around you.

If you've been a volunteer or feel that volunteering is an important part of your "life philosophy," your future employer will have reason to believe that you are a good hire—conscientious, ethical, and concerned about the well-being of others, not just your own advancement. Employers want to hire people who will be role models for others; they want people who care about others above and beyond the rudiments of the professional relationship. Good citizenship is good business.

Organizations

So where do you begin? There are literally hundreds of clubs on and off campus. Here are several ways to find out more about campus activities:

- Student activities office
- School newspaper
- Campus fliers
- Orientation week activities
- Friends and siblings

Start brainstorming about what you might like to join. Then gather information and join up. Start small if you're not used to groups. Try one and then another a few months later. Here are a few suggestions:

CAMPUS ORGANIZATIONS

Alumni Association
Amnesty International campus
    representative
Association for African-Americans
Chess club
Crisis intervention center
Residence hall association
Greeks (fraternities and
    sororities)
Honorary service societies
International student club
Intramural sports and
    recreation
Karate club
Marketing club

Political groups
Pre-law Society
Red Cross campus
    representative
Religious groups
Sailing club
Ski club
Student bar association
Student government
Student media
Student newspaper
Student Union
Women's Groups
Yearbook

VOLUNTEER ORGANIZATIONS

Campus hospital
Childhood abuse center
Drug addiction clinics
Home for the mentally retarded

Hospice program
Hospital care
Humane Society
League of Women Voters

March of Dimes
Mental health services
Nursing homes
Planned Parenthood
Political campaigns

Public library
Red Cross
Ronald McDonald House
Sierra Club
World Wildlife Federation

ACADEMIC AND PROFESSIONAL HONORARY SOCIETIES

Phi Beta Kappa
Tau Beta Pi
Phi Kappa Phi
Blue Key National Honor Society
Mortar Board

Golden Key National Honor
Society
Who's Who Among American
College Students

Setting Limits

To what extent should you participate? This varies according to who you are. For example, if you're a skilled opera singer or lead the nation in a competitive sport, you may have to focus entirely on that to be the best. Take Steve Kendall, for instance. Steve's college grades were average, but Steve was captain of his college tennis team. Although his rigorous training schedule and travel left him little spare time, his athletic and academic record prompted the college recruiter for Procter & Gamble to seek Steve out for an interview during his senior year.

"Because I was successful in a competitive sport, Procter & Gamble believed I would apply the same principles of diligence, effort, teamwork, and competition to my future career," says Steve. P&G's faith was well placed: Steve worked for them for several years before accepting another position as sales and marketing director of Nabisco.

So what if your forehand is unimpressive? Does that mean that extracurricular activities are off limits? Of course not.

Leigh Talmage, for example, didn't focus on any one activity, as Steve did. She spread herself out and joined several organizations. Leigh, now a trader for a foreign bank, was president of her sorority, qualified to be a member of scholastic honorary societies each year, and spent two semesters in London. "Get activities under your belt," advises Leigh. "That's what counts the most at interview time." Leigh is one of five women out of 250 people in the world who trade in international debt. Leigh is considering another career, working for a nonprofit organization. "All of the activities and leadership positions I held in college have given me solid, transferable management skills," she says. "Because of these skills, I feel comfortable moving from one industry to another."

"It's problems with people, not problems in engineering, which constitute the real power struggles," says Steven Fisher, a senior engineer for Westinghouse in San Francisco. "If you swallow your ego and learn from others in your small group, you'll pick up the commonsense aspects of the job which the technical training you receive in college doesn't provide."

Steven, who graduated from Stanford with a degree in mechanical engineering, cites extracurricular activities as the best way to learn about people and how to get things done: "That's how you prepare yourself to be successful in the long term with a company. You must realize how people work, what motivates them, and what the company can do to help them be most happy and most productive."

If you're shy and you're not used to being around people, it may be enough to join one organization and participate in it so that you become comfortable with the other members and perhaps run for office. Stretch yourself, but take things in steps, not quantum leaps.

What If You Don't Get Accepted into Organization X?

Does that mean you've failed? Of course not. You only fail if you don't try. It sounds trite, but it's true.

I didn't get a lot of the things I applied for in college, but I didn't let it stop me. In my freshman year, I didn't make it into the freshman honorary society. I was disappointed. But before I said "To hell with it," I stopped to think about *why* I didn't make it in. Had I blown the interview? Was I not well-rounded enough? Were my grades not good enough? Most of the answers to these questions were "yes," and the other people who made it were better-qualified than I was. Throughout the next year, I worked on the areas that needed improvement, and at the end of the year, I applied for the sophomore honorary society. I got in.

I was seriously disappointed when I applied for the Rotary scholarship and didn't even make the first cut. I had invested a lot of time and energy into filling out the lengthy application, getting all my professors to write me letters of recommendation, and fully researching the three countries in which I wanted to study. They wanted an "ambassador of goodwill," which

I thought I could be! But there were others who were more qualified: I had to accept that.

And there were pluses that came from that disappointment. I learned how much I truly loved studying other cultures. I swore to make travel a major life priority. I also met fascinating people who were also applying for the scholarship: one of them, a unique person who spoke fluent Chinese, Spanish, and French, became my true love for the next two years. (He didn't make the first cut either.)

When you get a job after college, you may initially be passed over for a promotion you want. Chances are you were not as well qualified as the person who got the job. Find out specifically what you can do to ensure that you get the next opening, and *take action*.

How you deal with defeat says a lot about your overall character. If you learn in college how to handle defeat graciously, you'll be well prepared for the working world, where you'll need to transform tough situations into new challenges and opportunities.

So don't let defeats defeat you. Look at the situation in a broader context. Extract the positive things you have learned and go on to the next thing. Don't let temporary setbacks take any wind out of your sails.

Dealing with Your Supporters (and Detractors)

Any time you join a group of people and you assert your opinions about what you think the organization should or shouldn't do, you will have some people who will agree with you and others who won't. Sometimes, especially if you are leading an organization, you will have to stick your neck out for what you believe in while communicating to others your vision of what the group can do.

Be cool. If people always agreed with you, you would be among a dull group. The best ideas and the best teamwork come from stimulating discussions that allow all points of view to be considered. When people disagree with you—and sometimes during college and in the real world they will disagree violently with you—keep a positive attitude and remain confident. Acknowledge their opposing viewpoints and thank them for their suggestions. Remaining mature and controlled will help you put the situation into perspective and allow you to reaffirm your position. Remember, leaders are sometimes unpopular in some camps. That's okay. It's helpful to get used to this feeling in college—to let your skin get thicker—so that you will be more resilient in dealing with people of varying maturity levels once you start working.

Part of being both a leader and a participant is learning how to draw out the best suggestions and ideas from others. Often, discussing your thoughts with your colleagues helps you to crystallize an already good idea of your own. Recognize that sometimes it's good to change your mind, to concede someone else's points or plans. This is all part of developing your judgment.

7

The Real World

Working Part-Time

> I don't like work—no one does—but I like what is in work—the chance to find yourself. Your own reality—not for others—what no other person can ever know.
> *Joseph Conrad,* Heart of Darkness

The summer after his freshman year at the University of Wisconsin, Jeff Colquhoun worked at the Kellogg factory near his parents' home in Michigan. Occupation? Well, what does one do at a cereal factory? Eat and run?

Guess again. Jeff frosted flakes. And when finished with his frosting duties, he stuffed coupons by hand into boxes the machines had missed. His was a manual counteroffensive to mechanical incompetence. It was an incredibly boring job. But for Jeff it was by no means a waste of time.

Besides earning money to help pay tuition, Jeff learned several things that helped clarify his career direction.

1. The Kellogg experience opened Jeff's eyes to people whose back-

ground differed from his. There were many people there who hadn't had Jeff's advantages whom he might never have encountered in his "ordinary" college experience or in a more typical summer internship for the up-and-coming college student. The job helped Jeff appreciate his education. He developed real respect for people from all walks of life who worked hard for a living, regardless of job title.

2. He did not let the boring aspects of the job interfere with his work or his attitude. For the purpose of sanity, he stretched his mind and imagination. He went through the letters of the Greek alphabet forward and backward. He marveled at the mind of the engineer who designed the machine. (He thanked God for him, in fact.)

3. Jeff learned that when you're not in an ideal situation (we seldom are), you've got to expand your mind and envision a broader context. Idle is bust.

Thirteen years later, Jeff is a doctor of ophthalmology in New York City. He went through years of studying and rigorous on-the-job training in emergency settings and operating rooms. What he learned at the Kellogg factory that summer in college—to see even the most difficult or mundane tasks in a broader context—helped him in his pursuit of medicine.

Joy Wake, a marketing planner at Hallmark in Kansas City, Missouri, had several part-time jobs during college. As the youngest of nine children, Joy supported herself 100 percent through college. She had several work-study jobs and one summer internship in Washington, D.C. And she saved enough money to travel one semester through Europe.

"Hallmark hired me because I had worked hard to put myself through college," Joy says. "They believed in me because I had a successful track record. They knew I could overcome obstacles. They also recognized that I had done different things to make myself stand out."

Instead of attending school during the day and working at night, Chris Barnett did the opposite. He got an entry-level job paying $185 a week selling space in the yellow pages. He took three classes at night per semester. Although it took Chris two additional years to graduate from college after transferring from the University of Southern California to Columbia, he feels the trade-off—financial and experiential—was worth it.

Chris is graduating this spring. He has been promoted three times within the last two years and is now supervising eleven people. It's true that Chris hasn't had time to join extracurricular activities or participate in intramural sports, but he has, at age twenty-four, earned a living, put himself through school, and maintained a 3.2 grade point average at an Ivy League college. He's learned firsthand about leadership through direct professional experience.

Gaining work experience in college is one of the best ways to prepare for your future. First, you learn to support yourself, partially or entirely, which tells your future employer that you have a sense of commitment, responsibility, and financial savvy. Second—and more important—you acquire skills and techniques that will prepare you to work with others.

What Work Is Best for You?

Almost any job you have during college will benefit you in ways far greater than the financial. Obviously, some jobs are better than others. Before you take the first job you apply for, spend some time learning about yourself and the kinds of jobs available on and off campus.

Phoebe Finn applied to several expensive acting schools in New York and London while studying drama at the University of Maryland. To support herself and save money, she drove the campus shuttle bus at night. Not glamorous for someone aspiring to be Meryl Streep, but the job served its purpose. It allowed her to save money and attend the London School of Dramatics. Phoebe's London experience helped her land her first big job in the Folger Shakespeare Library's production of *Macbeth*.

Of course, if you've got your sights set on a highly competitive field, it may be worth it to take the extra steps necessary to get a job providing experience that will help you later on.

"Broadcasting is fiercely competitive," says Nancy Kilroy. To prepare herself during college at Yale, Nancy worked at National Public Radio, where she learned how to interview people, how to be persistent, and how to pull together information for a five-minute broadcast. "Experience is everything in broadcasting," says Nancy. "You'd better learn early on that most people have already worked at least two jobs in the profession by the time they graduate."

What to Consider

As discussed in Chapter 3, there are three basic areas of work: working with people, information, or objects. You might enjoy each of these areas, but if you're like most people, one appeals to you more than the other two.

Richard Bolles, the author of *What Color Is Your Parachute?*, identifies several characteristics that can help you analyze what area best suits you. How do you answer the following questions?

PEOPLE-RELATED SKILLS

Taking Instruction
- Do you like to take instruction and then carry out a plan?
- Do you enjoy executing and providing support services?

Serving
- Do you like helping, teaching, waiting on, or serving others?

Sensing, Feeling
- Are you intuitive with respect to the needs of others?
- Are you generally responsive, empathic, warm, and able to understand the position of others?

Communicating
- Are you a good listener? Do you question others?
- Do you enjoy writing, giving speeches, giving instructions to others?

Persuading
- Do you like to influence, inspire, and recruit others?
- Do you like publicizing and promoting causes, people, or things?

Performing, Amusing
- Do you like to entertain others?
- Do you like to dramatize your point of view or your own experiences as a means of teaching others?

Managing, Supervising

- Do you like to plan, oversee, and develop programs with people?
- Do you like to encourage and critically evaluate others, using your expertise to help them to improve?

Negotiating, Decision-Making

- Do you like to discuss, confer, and resolve difficult issues?
- Are you skilled in conflict management?
- Do you appreciate and consider opposing points of view?

Founding, Leading

- Are you able to work with little or no supervision?
- Do you have maverick qualities? That is, do you like to forge your own, possibly better path?
- Can you enlist the enthusiasm and the support of others?
- Do you delegate authority? Do you trust others to execute a job?

Advising, Consulting

- Do you enjoy helping others resolve a physical, emotional, or spiritual problem?
- Do you enjoy being an expert, reading, and keeping up with what is happening in one field?
- Do you make effective use of contacts? Do you give others insight and perspective on their problems?

Holistic Counseling

- Do you like to facilitate the growth of others by helping them to identify solutions to their problems?

Training

- Do you like to teach others through lecture, demonstration, or practice?

INFORMATION-RELATED SKILLS

Observing

- Do you like to study the behavior of people, information, or things?

Comparing

- Do you enjoy analyzing two or more different things?

Copying, Storing, and Retrieving
- Do you like keeping records, storing data, memorizing, filing, or reviewing information?

Computing
- Do you enjoy working with numbers, taking inventory, solving statistical problems, using a computer, budgeting, projecting or processing data?

Researching
- Do you like uncovering hard-to-find facts and information?

Analyzing
- Do you like to break things down, taking information apart and examining it?

Organizing
- Does giving structure and order to things turn you on? Do you always have a place for everything? Do you typically classify material?

Evaluating
- Are you a diagnoser or inspector? Do you like to assess, decide, appraise, and summarize information or situations?

Visualizing
- Are you able to perceive patterns and images? Do you picture things you want to do before you do them? Do you enjoy painting, drawing, or designing?

Improving, Adapting
- Do you like to take what others have developed and expand upon it? Are you good at improvising, improving, and arranging?

Creating, Synthesizing
- Do you like to pull together seemingly unrelated things? Do you like to develop new concepts, approaches, and interpretations?

Designing
- Do you like to create models, sculpture, or other things?

Planning, Developing
• Do you like to oversee and carry out a plan? Do you prioritize and develop strategies?

Expediting
• Do you naturally tend to speed up a task by organizing your objectives ahead of time? Do you have a sense of urgency or immediacy?

Achieving
• Do you enjoy accomplishing tasks or specific goals? Do you like to increase productivity and create results?

OBJECT-RELATED SKILLS

Manipulating
• Do you enjoy working with your hands? Do you like using your body to move objects?

Working with the Earth and Nature
• Do you like nurturing, weeding, harvesting?

Feeding, Emptying (Machines)
• Do you like placing, stacking, dumping, and removing things from machines?

Monitoring (Machines)
• Do you like monitoring and adjusting machines, pushing buttons, flipping switches, adjusting controls?

Using Tools
• Do you enjoy using hand tools?

Operating Equipment or Machines
• Do you like to have specialized knowledge about equipment or machines?

Operating Vehicles
• Do you like to drive, pilot, or steer vehicles?

Precision Working
- Do you like jobs such as keypunching, drilling, sandblasting, making miniatures, or performing other specialized tasks with your hands?

Setting Up
- Do you like to construct or set up displays, machinery, or equipment?

Repairing
- Do you like to restore, repair, or do preventive maintenance?

As a freshman, you may not be able to complete this questionnaire. But as a junior or senior, you'll have many more experiences under your belt. For now, just get a general idea of your strongest suit.

Below is a list of job possibilities.

COMMON JOBS FOR COLLEGE STUDENTS

Campus

People	Information	Objects
Resident assistant	Word processor	Library aide
Campus guide	Administrative assistant	Lab technician
Health aide	Secretarial aide	Mechanic
Study tutor	Writer (yearbook or campus newspaper)	Maintenance assistant
Lecturer	Researcher	Groundskeeper

Community

People	Information	Objects
Waiter/waitress	Legal assistant	Short-order cook
Salesclerk	Secretary	Gas-station attendant
Host/hostess	Word processor	Technician
Bartender		Gardener/yard worker

Where to Find Work

Many colleges have job placement centers right on campus. Often campus jobs are listed there, and professors may also list job vacancies there (babysitting, housework, construction, house-sitting). You'll find a wide range of jobs and hours. Getting a job through a placement center can also put you in contact with professors who may introduce you to fields you might not be exposed to through your major.

The Co-op Experience

Another way to get "real-world" experience is to enroll in a cooperative program. These programs are sponsored by a wide range of corporations and are designed to give students work experience while they are taking classes. You can find out more about these programs through the college placement center.

Mick McCormick, a director of sales for Nike, worked in a co-op program during college. He studied electrical engineering and finance and worked for IBM as a hardware and software programmer. In addition to providing him with a stable income during college, co-op experience helped him to realize that he did not want to work with computers all day. At the same time, it gave him invaluable computer experience.

"I have the technical knowledge to do word processing, PowerPoint presentations, and other computer applications I use in my present work. I also learned a lot about my working style. I needed a career where there were no barriers to getting a job done. I don't thrive when there is strong managerial control over my work."

If Waiting on Tables Is Not for You . . .

If you decide to forgo a traditional part-time job, such as waiting on tables, for a more educational, experience-earning job, such as working as a legal clerk, you'll have to demonstrate to your potential employer that you are worth hiring despite your limited experience. If you can convince the person interviewing you that you are a quick learner, extremely reliable, motivated above and beyond what is expected, and truly interested in pursuing a career in that area, chances are you'll get the job despite your youth and inexperience.

Remember that the

people interviewing you were once in your place. A determined and inquisitive mind and the capacity to work hard and achieve enabled them to be where they are today. If your potential employer believes you have the same qualities that contributed to his success, it is in his best interest to hire you. After all, you will be graduating in a few years, and you could be an attractive employee. Ask for the chance to prove what you can do. Both you and the employer could have a lot to gain.

If you don't get the experience-earning job you sought, don't despair. Follow up your interviews with a thank-you letter and reconfirm your interest in the company. If you try again six months or a year later, the company may be in a better position to take you on as an apprentice. If you know that the experience gained on the job would be more valuable than the wages you would earn and you can afford it, volunteer for the first six months. It might pay off in the long run.

The experience that a "real-life" job will provide could make the difference when you are competing for the job you most want during your last semester of college. If you have solid job experience, you will probably get hired even if the other candidate has superior grades and a more impressive background. You learned firsthand about the job, and consequently you have much more to offer than someone without such experience.

Whatever the part-time job you hold—be it gas-station attendant, hotel clerk, or real estate apprentice—you'll learn to juggle work, school, and other activities while sustaining your motivation and sense of self-reliance. You'll have the best-rounded education upon graduation; you'll gain satisfaction from knowing that you are self-reliant, independent, and responsible for your own accomplishments; and you'll gather important data to help you make career decisions in your junior and senior years.

A Final Note

Jenny Harris has been out of college for three years, and she is a producer for business news at CNN. She believes the key to her success (in addition to good grades) was her commitment to part-time work and internships. "I tried to get exposed to as many different industries as possible to get a first-hand look at how that industry worked. After working as a paralegal in a law firm for several summers, I realized that maybe I didn't want to be a lawyer. I had to sit back and rethink my plans."

Jenny worked on a committee at Cornell University that brought speakers to campus. While on the committee she did a variety of jobs—advertising and promotion, budgeting, setting up for the speaker. She enjoyed the work, but she didn't feel that she would enjoy doing it as a career. After reflecting and talking with other professionals, she decided that broadcasting might be a career she would enjoy.

In order to see what broadcasting was like, she worked for the student-run radio station at Cornell. That work allowed her to experience reporting, broadcasting, writing, and news meetings—all of the facets that go into putting together a broadcast. She liked it, so she applied for an internship with the prestigious MacNeil/Lehrer news program in Washington, D.C. During her internship there, the Gulf War broke out.

"I got to be in the newsroom and experience the excitement. After this internship, I was convinced that this was the field I wanted to pursue. When I graduated, I worked for CNN as an intern for four months without pay before I was hired as a production assistant.

"All of my jobs and internships provided me with a perspective. I knew something was missing when I was working for the law firm; I wasn't happy or comfortable in that work environment. I never would have discovered what I really liked without getting the firsthand work experience that I did."

8

Intern We Trust

Getting the Internship

I think the most valuable thing a college student can do while in college is to intern in his or her field of interest," says Stephanie Ward, who was the director of casework for Big Brothers/Big Sisters in Dallas. Internships help you learn if the profession you're considering is what you really want for a career. If you do, the internship gives you credibility in the job market and a leg up on those with no experience.

"I was responsible for hiring caseworkers," explains Stephanie. "What type of internship, how they performed while at their internship, and references from their internship carried more weight in my hiring decision than grades. If a decision came down to two applicants, and one had more experience in the field than the other and could verbalize what he or she had learned and discovered about him- or herself, then this would be the applicant I would hire."

Even if the only thing you discover from your internship is that you don't like the work, you're still ahead. You will have invested only your summer, not your life. Sometimes students really enjoy the coursework in a particular field, but when they actually have the opportunity to do the job, they find they don't like it. That happened to Jill Ruvidich, who had wanted to be an accountant since high school. "I really enjoyed studying accounting; however, an internship between my junior and senior years proved I found the real stuff extremely boring."

Rod Garcia, admissions recruiter for the MBA program at the University of Chicago, says that internships are very useful for people who don't yet know what they want to do. "Internships give students an idea of what's out there. The experience that even an unpaid internship provides is just as valuable as, if not more valuable than, some of your key college courses."

Rama Moorthy, an engineering sales specialist, loved her engineering courses in college. She did well in her classes and received several job offers. "When it came down to it, none of the actual jobs interested me. I decided to get an MBA and apply my engineering degree in a way I would enjoy.

During graduate school, I made sure to intern in several different areas so I could see what it was like doing the work I was studying. This time, when I graduated I had a much better idea of what I wanted to do."

Brigitt Berry, a quality development consultant, had several different internships in college. One of the most valuable came about through a representative she met at the college's career fair. "Different professionals had come to the college to talk about their fields of expertise. I sat down with a human resources representative and spoke with him at length about the profession—what it included and what it would take to enter the field. I was really impressed with him and what he had to say. When I look back on that conversation, I have to smile, because I asked him all sorts of questions that were of interest to me but never really bothered to ask him what he did with his company or if he liked his profession. I spent no time making it a two-way conversation.

"Two days later, I went to the college career center to get his address and found out he was the vice president of personnel for a Fortune 500 company. I wrote and asked if I could spend a month with his company in New York. He was impressed with my quick request and flew me to New York six months later. During my experience with his organization, I learned that I was not at all interested in the communications department, but that I *was* interested in the training and development department."

In addition to giving you a ground-level view of the profession, internships can also open the door for full-time employment when you graduate. So keep in mind that the organization you intern for will be checking you out, too. Rita Rather is a management information systems senior at the University of Illinois. An honor student with a strong personality, she so impressed management at the Cellular Telephone Company in Chicago during her internship last summer that they offered her a full-time job upon her graduation this spring.

Internships During School

Jim Cochran, an economics major from Los Alamos, New Mexico, had three internships during college. From each one he learned something different.

During his sophomore year, Jim had an unpaid internship working twelve hours a week with a commercial real estate company, Kimmel Property Management. This was Jim's first exposure to business, and it enabled him to build confidence and to establish valuable contacts. Four years later, when Jim began his first job out of college, he talked with the president of Kimmel to ask advice on his future career. Today, Jim is still in contact with several people from his first internship.

The second internship was in a law firm where Jim worked ten hours a week during the school year. Jim learned here that he did not want to become a lawyer. He still did not know what he really wanted to do, but at least he was learning what he did *not* want to do.

During his senior year, Jim worked ten hours a week for Merrill Lynch. He wanted to explore finance and investing and to continue making contacts. He enjoyed the job at Merrill Lynch, but didn't feel passionate enough about it to make it a career. He opted not to pursue a career in investing and got his first job with a real estate consulting firm.

When you know what you want to do, it can be valuable to let one internship lead to another in the same field of interest. This shows future employers that you are not only interested in them, you are *very* interested in them. Gordon Bock, a former reporter with both *U.S. News & World Report* and *Time*, was the youngest news director ever at Columbia University's radio station during his sophomore year. One day, the nationally syndicated Campus Radio Voice called for an intern. Gordon said, "I'm interested." He was hired, and over the next two years he was heard over the air at 460 colleges nationwide, interviewing celebrities and newsmakers. That internship led to the most prestigious one of all: becoming the first undergraduate in the history of the school to teach communications at Columbia's Graduate School of Journalism.

The result: when Gordon graduated, he moved immediately to a reporting job with AP Dow Jones in New York, writing radio copy. Three months later, he was hired by UPI New York at a third-year pay scale (based largely on his college jobs), and four years after that, he was hired by *U.S. News & World Report*. At the age of twenty-six, when many reporters are moving from one-town to three-town beats, Gordon was given a job covering eight states and half of Pennsylvania at a major national magazine.

Landing good internships, Gordon says, can be very important. And once you have them, he says, make the most of them. "Be gung-ho about whatever you do."

Summer Internships

"Summer activity is a great indicator of future job success," says Dee Milligan, first vice president and director of insurance marketing for Kemper Financial Company in Chicago, who interviews and hires many graduates straight from college. "I want to see that the applicant has taken initiative. I'm not interested in someone who has just messed around and not thought about using his or her summers wisely."

Dee says that working during the summer in a standard corporate environment gives students the opportunity to learn about the workplace—by diving in and experiencing it for themselves. It's the kind of education you can't get in the classroom.

Brenda White is from Ainsworth, Iowa, a town of five hundred people. She attended Augustana, a small Lutheran college in Illinois. During her junior year, Brenda applied for a nonpaying summer internship with the United Nations. She was selected as one of twenty college students in the country to come to New York.

Although the internship was nonpaying, Brenda talked to several people at the financial aid office at Augustana to see if she could get funding. And she did.

The most valuable part of Brenda's experience? She became "street smart." She learned to survive—and thrive—in a big city. After that summer in New York, Brenda felt herself a match for any environment.

Jeff Cantany is an economics major who hopes to work for a nonprofit agency in international development. To qualify, he needs to go into the Peace Corps, and they require construction skills. So what did he do the summer after his freshman year? He worked for a builder in New Mexico. He earned a good salary, learned a trade, and was introduced to a culture very different from that of his native New York.

Winter Internships

Many companies and firms have programs for students during the winter semester break. During his senior year at Columbia, Tim Dalton had a full-time four-week internship in January with the Lawyers Committee for Human Rights in New York City. Tim worked with other volunteers on LCHR reports about human rights violations and refugee issues.

"I learned about issues not covered in the newspapers," says Tim. "Although I wasn't paid, the internship was invaluable because I gained insight into the nonprofit organizations which rely heavily on volunteers. I provided them with much-needed labor, but most of all, I enjoyed the work."

Internships After Graduation

Think about internships after college, too. Kim Caldwell already had a B.A. in art history when she began her six-month internship at the Metropolitan

Museum of Art in New York City. Kim was able to work in several administrative areas of the museum and to visit other museums in the city. She got the job through Aniso, a monthly job posting put out by the American Association of Museums.

"Becoming involved in a professional organization kept me abreast of openings in the museum field as well as informing me of the latest trends in museum policies," Kim said.

No Pay? Okay!

Internship work seldom provides a paycheck. Particularly in some industries, unpaid internships are the norm. Your reward is the experience. This means, quite obviously, that you may have to work a part-time job to help pay for your living expenses.

I was a summer intern in Washington, D.C., between my sophomore and junior years. I worked without pay for Common Cause, a grass-roots lobbying organization. I attended Senate and House hearings and reported on the Clean Air Act and the daily debate on the constitutional amendment to balance the budget.

On the less glamorous side, this internship didn't pay the bills. Therefore, I worked as a waitress at an Italian restaurant atop an apartment building overlooking the Washington monuments. Because the restaurant was expensive, I made good money in tips, so I only had to work three nights a week.

I remember working on the Fourth of July and feeling glum because all my friends were down on the Mall watching the fireworks and listening to the Beach Boys concert. However, I was lucky to be in Washington. I was also lucky to have a part-time job that enabled me to have my nonpaying, though thoroughly rewarding, summer internship.

Meeting Mentors

Lisa Heinlein, a special-education teacher, learned a great deal about how to be an excellent teacher from watching other great teachers. "Allow yourself to be taught," Lisa says. "Don't be afraid to try things and make mistakes—that's how you learn."

Lenny Feder, now a senior at Columbia, had his first internship during his sophomore year. He worked for three weeks at American Marketing. Though he had held a lot of different jobs, this was his first experience in the corporate world. His boss, who happened to belong to the same fraternity as Lenny when he had attended college, served as a mentor. He let Lenny sit in on meetings, allowed him to help plan projects from Day One, and even gave him advice on what type of suit to wear. "My mentor gave me a sense of what skills I'd need in the business world. But I couldn't just copy him. I learned those skills by myself—with my mentor serving as a guide."

Through your internships, you'll meet people who can be your teachers. Choose two or three people whom you respect to be your mentors. Pick their brains to find answers to the following questions:

- How could I do my job better?
- What could I do at school to better prepare myself for this industry?
- How did you become interested in this industry?
- What are your toughest challenges?
- What part of the job do you like most?
- What will be the toughest challenge facing the industry over the next five years?
- Where is the growth potential?
- If you were interviewing me today, would I get the job? If not, why?
- What qualities do you look for in a qualified applicant?

Getting answers to these questions will help you learn about the profession and about yourself. You'll gain insight and your employers will gain respect for your initiative.

Developing a Professional Self-Image

One of the transitions you will have to make when you start your first job after college is the change from seeing yourself as a student to seeing yourself as a legitimate professional. Internships can give you the opportunity to develop your professional self-image.

Carla Schnurr spent a summer on a fellowship in science and mass communications. The fellowship, which was sponsored by the American Association for the Advancement of Science, placed fifteen students in reporting positions in radio, television, newspapers, and magazines around the country.

Carla joined the science desk at *The Atlanta Journal-Constitution*, where she was assigned stories along with other science reporters. She learned by doing. The editor would give her a story, and it was her job to research it, conduct the pertinent interviews, and write it. The editor and the other re-porters coached her as she worked through each phase of the job.

"I gained confidence by being thrown into new situations where I was expected to perform as a professional rather than as a student. The intern-ship helped me to develop my 'reporter's persona,' to be comfortable talk-ing with all kinds of people as an adult. I remember being very nervous on my first interview, with the new director of the American Cancer Society. As we began talking, however, I became interested in the person and the work he did. From then on, I lost my feelings of shyness around people in the prominent positions; my interviewing skills really grew with that newfound confidence."

The people Carla worked with became mentors and role models. "They have become real friends in the workplace. Through their experience, I got to see alternative routes to my goals, which I might not have thought of on my own."

How to Get the Internship

Let's hope that I've convinced you that an internship is worth pursuing. Now what? First, know that you *will* get a job as an intern. Banish all doubts—they aren't going to help you. Believe you are going to succeed.

Second, realize that securing an internship is very much like interview-ing for a "real" job at the end of your senior year. In fact, the whole process of writing your résumé, interviewing, and landing the internship is *exactly the preparation you'll need* for your full-fledged job search upon graduation. Now, for the practical steps.

What to Do

1. Get a copy of one of the current summer internship directories for col-lege students, or make an appointment in your school's career office. I also recommend Betsy Bauer's *Getting Work Experience*. (See Appendix 2 also.)
2. From the college directory and/or other resources, make a list of the in-ternship positions that interest you. Select at least twenty.
3. Review your list carefully, thinking about which skills a potential em-ployer might look for in an applicant.
4. Take stock of your qualifications. Look at the skills listed below and ask yourself two questions: (1) Which of these skills can I offer my potential employer? and (2) What other skills not listed here can I contribute to

the internship positions? In the column on the right, add your own words to describe your strengths and to give examples of something you've done that illustrates your know-how. For instance, if you've served as the head of a school club, describe how this experience helped you develop leadership abilities. The more specific you are, the better prepared you'll be for your job search.

SKILL LIST   MY STRENGTHS IN THIS AREA, AND AN EXAMPLE OF WHAT I'VE DONE THAT DEMONSTRATES THIS ABILITY

Organizing

_____

_____

_____

Working with others

_____

_____

_____

Developing ideas

_____

_____

_____

Writing/researching

_____

_____

_____

Prioritizing time

_____

_____

_____

Observing _____

_____

_____

Repairing things _____

_____

_____

Founding/leading _____

_____

_____

Paying attention to detail _____

_____

_____

Following instructions _____

_____

_____

Speaking in public _____

_____

_____

Other _____

_____

Where to Go

Geography may also play a part in which internship you choose. For instance, if you're interested in banking, New York, Chicago, Los Angeles, or San Francisco would be great cities to work in for a summer. If you're interested in computers, you could work in almost any large metropolitan area, though California's Silicon Valley might be the best. Maybe you don't know which career interests you yet. No problem. Half your classmates don't know either, but they're not taking steps to find out. Pat yourself on the back. Okay, that's enough. Now, back to work . . .

If you can afford it, seek contrast. If you're from a small town, apply to a big city. The more diversity you experience, the more versatile you'll be. Working in new cities conveys maturity, confidence, and determination to your future employers. I waited tables on the weekends so I could afford to intern a summer in New York. I'm from Arizona, so living in Manhattan for three months was an educational experience in itself!

When to Apply

Begin early. If you want to get an internship between your sophomore and junior years, ideally you should have your résumé, cover letter, and list of target companies ready the summer after your freshman year. Also, since you may not get a response from any of your top five picks, plan to send letters to at least fifteen other companies. From the twenty letters you send, expect to receive at least two offers.

Whom to Contact

Since you have considered internship possibilities based on your skills and your career interests, it's time to narrow your scope by choosing the five internships you'd like to contact first.

1. Desired career: _____

   Name/address/phone number of organization:

   _____

   _____

   Contact person: _____

2. Desired career: _____

   Name/address/phone number of organization:

   _____

   _____

   _____

   Contact person: _____

3. Desired career: _____

   Name/address/phone number of organization:

   _____

   _____

   _____

   Contact person: _____

4. Desired career: _____

   Name/address/phone number of organization:

   _____

   _____

   _____

   Contact person: _____

5. Desired career: _____

   Name/address/phone number of organization:

_____

_____

_____

Contact person: _____

How to Apply

Now that you know which organizations you want to contact, here's what to send:

- A *résumé* briefly stating your objectives as an intern, your education, your work experience, and your extracurricular activities. Be prepared to provide three references, and notify these people that they may be contacted by your prospective employer. (See the sample résumé on page 138.)
- A *one-page cover letter* explaining your interests, abilities, and reasons for choosing this organization. This letter, like your résumé, should be flaw-lessly written and typed; see the example on page 139. Have a couple of your friends or your composition professor read it for clarity and accuracy. Make sure you're sending the letter to the right person. Don't rely on the information in your internship directory. It's a changing world, so call the company to verify their address and the contact person.
- A *letter of recommendation* from a professor or employer (not one of your three references). The right recommendation can make a big difference because it can help separate you from the pack. When you approach someone to write a letter, let him or her know why you are asking for a letter. It is helpful for a teacher to know that you have chosen her because you are proud of the research project you did in her class, and not simply because she gave you a good grade. (See the sample letter of rec-ommendation on page 140.) Be sure to thank the professor or employer for the letter.

About two weeks after you've mailed your cover letter, résumé, and let-ter of recommendation, call the person to whom you wrote. Make sure he or she received your letter, and ask when a decision will be made. Reiterate your interest in the company, but also let the person know that you have other summer job options.

Is an interview required? If so, read Chapter 12.

S A M P L E   R É S U M É

Mary Ann Van Camp
6680 North Anywhere Avenue
Duluth, MN 55806

Education: College sophomore
English major, Business minor
University of Georgia
Athens, Georgia

Objective: Summer internship in Marketing or Sales.

Employment:
April 1999 to
present

Administrative assistant, Adler & Adler
Public Relations Agency. Responsibilities
include working with clients and partners,
answering mail, and routine paperwork.

March 1998 to
April 1999

Hostess, Spaghetti Company
Restaurant.

Activities: Resident Assistant, Coronado Dormitory,
University of Georgia. Responsibilities include organizing dorm functions, helping
students adjust to college, and providing
support during difficult times.

Member, International Students Club;
Spurs; Sophomore Student Honorary
Society. Participant in philanthropy program.

High School Highlights: President, Thespian Society. Organized
actors' league, performed for charities,
worked with professional actors in the
community.

Graduated with a 3.2 GPA. Mainstream
High junior-year representative to Girls'
State.

References available upon request.

S A M P L E   C O V E R   L E T T E R

6680 North Anywhere Avenue
Duluth, MN 55806

September 30, 1999

Mr. Ryan Rinaldi
Pillsbury Company
Pillsbury Center
Minneapolis, MN 55402

Dear Mr. Rinaldi:

I am a sophomore majoring in English and minoring in business at the University of Georgia. My goal is to work for Pillsbury this summer as an intern in either sales or marketing.

Attached is a copy of my résumé and a letter of reference from one of my professors. As you can see from my résumé, I am committed to achievement, both in and out of the classroom. An internship with Pillsbury would provide me with an unparalleled "real-world" experience. Because I am a dedicated, energetic, and inquisitive worker, I would be a benefit to Pillsbury as an intern.

I will be calling before October 15 to inquire further about internship opportunities. In the meantime, if you have any questions, don't hesitate to call me at 313-555-1017.

I look forward to speaking with you soon. Thank you for your consideration.

Sincerely,
Mary Ann Van Camp

SAMPLE LETTER OF RECOMMENDATION

September 25, 1999

To Whom It May Concern:

I met Mary Ann Van Camp the first semester of her freshman year. Mary Ann was enrolled in my Western Civilization course, and she immediately impressed me as a top-notch student. She came to see me during office hours, asked questions about class lectures and writing assignments, and followed up after tests to ensure that she had learned all the pertinent information. Seldom do college students today take the extra time—especially in a survey course—to get to know their professors and to seek their help outside of class.

Although Mary Ann received a B for the course, her efforts deserved an A for the amount of time she devoted to a class normally taken by sophomores. The first semester of college is a tough adjustment period for any student, and those who persevere to learn the material, not just to get a good grade but for the sake of learning, are truly distinguished. I know Mary Ann will get more than most out of college because she tries harder.

I highly recommend Mary Ann for a summer internship at your company. Her delightful personality, coupled with her intellect and desire to learn, would be an asset to any company or organization.

Please feel free to contact me.

Sincerely,

Dr. Robert Timmons
Department of History
University of Georgia
Athens, GA 00010

Don't Give Up

If no organization in your field of interest is listed, find one on your own! In Appendix 1 at the back of this book, you'll find a directory of many businesses in the United States currently offering summer internships for college students. Although this is an excellent reference list, don't depend on it completely. Some of the most rewarding internships are those you research and find yourself. Use this list to land your first summer internship, but for the following summer, go for the challenge of landing the job no one else could find. Sell yourself to the organization, which may not have an established internship program.

Rama Moorthy suggests that one way to learn about a company and to get your foot in the door for an internship position is to try to meet some of the recruiters who come to campus to interview graduating seniors. "Ask them if you can meet with them briefly in between their interviews and then use the opportunity to find out what kinds of internships they offer or if they would be open to creating an internship position."

If you can convince an employer to "make a position" for you, you'll be successful at selling your ideas and getting support after you graduate. The more you develop these "maverick" qualities, the more fearless you'll become. To be effective, you must believe in yourself. If you learn early to convince others to believe in you, you'll be several steps ahead of the game.

Once You Begin Your Internship

Some internships are better organized than others. Jonathan Bober, a curator and art professor at the University of Texas, says that internships are valuable only if they are extremely well organized. Otherwise you may spend your time running errands rather than learning about the field. Keep in mind that you will often need to be the initiator to make your internship as valuable as possible. It's up to you to formulate some goals—what you want to learn about this career.

Pam Zemper knew she was good at understanding how an organization ticks—seeing the broad patterns. When she began her internship at an ad agency in Austin, Texas, her goal was to learn every department of advertising. She chose this particular agency because she would gain experience in television, radio, print, and public relations. "The agency I interned for had agreed to give me a chance to work in each division. But when I got there, I realized it was up to me to seek out extra projects in those areas."

Pam formed a mentoring relationship with an account executive who gave her background reading in many areas of the business. "This material was written by an advertising agency and gave me a working knowledge of the process and the vocabulary. I was able to apply this information during my internship and talk comfortably with the other executives." After graduation, the agency offered her a job.

When Things Go Wrong

What happens when you make your first mistakes on the job? Well, if you're not making any mistakes, you're probably not trying hard enough. Mistakes are the process by which we learn. One of the main purposes of an internship is to learn some lessons that will make you better prepared once you start your "real" job after college.

Jim Burke, the CEO at Johnson & Johnson, has a favorite story about his former boss. General Robert Wood Johnson discovered that Burke had failed miserably at one of his really innovative ideas—a children's chest rub. Johnson asked him, "Are you the person who cost us all that money?" Burke nodded. "I'd like to congratulate you," the general said. "If you are making mistakes, that means you are making decisions and taking risks. And we won't grow unless you take risks."

If you mess up on the job, admit it, correct the mistake, discuss it, and, above all, learn from it. The greatest fool is one who will not admit his or her own mistakes and get help from others when necessary.

When things aren't going as you expected, it's time to figure out why. Were your expectations realistic? Internships will involve some drudgery; it's not going to be exciting every minute you're there. However, if you're not learning and experiencing what you hoped for at least part of the time, there are steps you can take to help remedy the situation.

- *First*, set up a time to meet with your supervisor. Tell him or her what you see as the problem and what you think the possible solutions are.
- *Second*, discuss what you believe the goals and objectives should be. Then ask your supervisor for feedback.
- *Third*, clarify with your supervisor what he or she wants you to accomplish, and together establish some specific goals for the remainder of your internship there.

Evaluating Your Performance

Some organizations have formal evaluations. If yours doesn't, be forthright in asking for an honest appraisal of your work at the conclusion of your internship. Remember, you'll be able to improve only if you can take constructive criticism from those with more experience.

The following is a list of categories on which an employee is typically evaluated. Use the list to grade yourself in each of these categories. If you believe you're doing an *excellent* job, put an E next to that item; if a *satisfactory* job, put an S; if a *poor* job, put a P. Then go over the list with your manager. Ask for specific tips on how you can improve on your weak areas.

PERFORMANCE REVIEW

Quality of work	Planning and organizing	Communication
Quantity of work	Delegating	Working with others
Problem solving	Self-control	Business savvy
Decision-making		

OTHER CHARACTERISTICS

Creativity	Adaptability	Attitude
Initiative	Persuasiveness	Maturity
Teamwork	Leadership	Foresight
Judgment	Self-confidence	

OVERALL EVALUATION

- Your strengths: _____

- Areas that need improvement: _____

  _____

- Supervisor's comments: _____

  _____

Where Do You Go from Here?

If you love your internship and decide that another summer at the same company would be valuable for your professional development, set things up for the following year. Many companies have an interest in cultivating students two summers in a row so that they can make them a job offer upon graduation. Just make sure to secure greater responsibilities for the next summer. This way, you'll continue to develop your skills as well as make new contacts.

Then again, you may wish to keep your options open and work for another organization the following summer—in the same industry or a completely different one.

Adam Edwards, a senior at the University of Michigan, is completing his third internship at Microsoft. He feels his experience as an intern has benefited him in many ways. "The most tangible benefit of the internships is that by doing well at them, I give Microsoft the incentive to hire me when I graduate—these days it's comforting to have a job lined up after graduation." Adam has also gained valuable knowledge about his field. "I learned a computer language at Microsoft that is taught at my school—I learned it before I took the class, so I had an advantage over people who were learning it for the first time. I've gained enough knowledge about how software is developed so that I could potentially develop commercial software using methodologies and technical skills I learned on the job at Microsoft."

9

Windows on the World

Traveling at Home or Abroad

The world is a book and those who stay at home read only one page.
St. Augustine

The use of traveling is to regulate the imagination by reality and, instead of thinking how things may be, to see them as they are.
Samuel Johnson

Peeople travel for a variety of reasons: study, work, leisure, and to volunteer. Regardless of the motivation, encountering the world offers immense personal and professional rewards. For one thing, travel can be a deeply enriching experience. By venturing out of your safe, familiar environment, you gain insights about humanity and also about yourself.

Your understanding of other cultures expands, and so does self-awareness—important elements in developing a healthy view of the world.

Globalization has become the buzzword of the twenty-first-century job market. Travel is now a practical asset for today's career seeker. Janice Bellace, deputy dean at the University of Pennsylvania's Wharton School of Business, said in an interview for the Kaplan Staff/Newsweek "Tipsheet," 1999 edition: "Twenty years ago you could still go to work for a large Amercian company and have limited exposure to business outside of the United States. That's not true today. You can't be in a major form or investment bank without being part of the international market."

Even if you're not planning a career in business, job recruiters in other fields also look favorably on students who have traveled outside the United States. A summer or a semester abroad tells a potential employer that you possess attractive character traits such as the desire to learn and the courage to explore, key attributes for the kind of innovative thinking today's industries long for. Immersing yourself in another culture also develops in you the universally prized skill of *adaptability*. Your ability to adjust quickly to any situation, group of people, or environment bodes well for every occupation, particularly in today's multinational work environment.

Marty D'Luzansky taught English in France while on a Fulbright teaching assistantship after he graduated from college with a major in French. He ended up working as a trade consultant with the New Zealand Trade Development Board. "I can't stress enough how important it is to take a year between undergraduate school and whatever it is you think you want to do," he said. "My overseas experience has provided me with the cross-cultural skills essential to help me effectively advise New Zealanders on the best way to succeed with their products or services in the U.S. market. The ability to see the United States from a foreign perspective is critical to my work."

The World as Your Classroom

Hong Kong. Buenos Aires. Cairo. London. Paris. Milan. Faraway cities like these can be your first exposure to other people, cultures, and languages. World travel can even jump-start a career that you'll love. Diane Roberts is a case in point. As she traveled through Europe, Diane became enamored with historic churches and, more specifically, with the restoration work necessary to keep them intact. Diane's curiosity led her on a search for studios where stained-glass restoration was done; the artists there told her that the churches and buildings in the United States were just then becoming old enough to need restoration, and they recommended that she pursue a career in restoration at home. Today

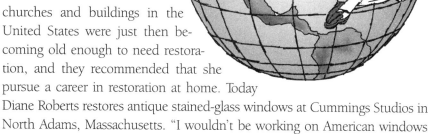

Diane Roberts restores antique stained-glass windows at Cummings Studios in North Adams, Massachusetts. "I wouldn't be working on American windows today if I hadn't spent that time in Europe," she says.

Spending time in another country can also help you clarify career goals. Susan Finnemore studied one semester at York College in England. On weekends she traveled with friends around Great Britain. In the youth hostels where she stayed, she noticed advertisements for "work camps." (Important tip: There are many jobs abroad. Some can be found on the bulletin boards of youth hostels, train stations, and schools.) One "camp" in which Susan worked was on a Welsh estate, where she received wages and lodging. The camp paid for food, and Susan cooked the meals.

Susan's parents are both professors, and Susan had always planned to go straight from undergraduate school to a master's program in history. Travel gave her the perspective to reconsider her options. "If I can travel through Europe," Susan thought to herself, "I can do anything." Instead of going to graduate school, Susan decided to pursue a career in publishing. She is now the psychology editor for college textbooks at Prentice Hall, where she's found her niche.

Your travel experience, however, doesn't have to be as structured as the examples cited above to be worthwhile. Bill and Jonathan Aikens spent three months cycling through Europe with little else on their minds except taking in the scenery. Yet they learned valuable lessons along the way. Be-

tween the two of them, they spoke five languages. Besides English, Bill spoke Spanish and French; Jonathan spoke German; *both learned Italian en route!* Travel can, therefore, provide another very specific, very tangible skill: speaking a foreign language.

In some fields, the more exotic the language, the more marketable that skill. UPI Beijing correspondent Mark Delvecchio skipped several rungs on the journalism ladder this way. Reporters can work ten years to win coveted overseas positions—and some can wait entire lifetimes for such jobs, to no avail. Mark, however, rose out of a reporting job for a small-town Connecticut weekly to his job in China in just a little over four years.

An energetic reporter, Mark made rapid progress on the basis of hard work, becoming city editor of a daily after only three years in the business. However, when a job opened up on UPI's foreign desk in Washington, D.C., Mark says that it was his college year abroad in China, plus his University of Connecticut master's degree in Chinese history, that made the difference. "Few American reporters speak Chinese," he says. A few months after arriving in Washington, Mark was sent to Beijing. He was twenty-eight years old.

Learning About Yourself

Travel teaches you about other places and other people, but most important, it teaches you about yourself. For example, I spent the fall semester of my junior year in Segovia, Spain, a town of some forty thousand people about sixty-five miles northwest of Madrid. I lived with a delightful Spanish family and attended a local Spanish college, for which I received university credit. I partied—in Spanish—with friends from the town while the other Americans partied (in English) with each other.

On weekends I took the train into Madrid and explored other nearby towns. Once, my Spanish friend Ma Paz took me outside Segovia to visit her family's village: population, twenty-five. It was out of a storybook. The only public building was a small church where a friar came to perform mass each Sunday.

Ma Paz's father, a farmer, lived with her mother in a small house next to a barn overflowing with cows. Her grandparents' house was only a ten-minute walk away, alongside a path bordered by gorgeous, rolling Spanish hills. Her grandparents showed us where they made wine from grapes they pressed themselves. They were intensely curious about my life back in the United States, asking many questions about my family, my hometown, and my university. We talked long into the night.

I felt lucky to meet these generous people. When I reminisce about my semester abroad, it's not the Prado, the Alhambra, or the eight-hundred-year-old castles that leap to mind first, but my experiences with people such as Ma and her family, who taught me much more than just how to be fluent in Spanish.

The lives of other travelers have also been enriched in ways similar to mine. Sue Flynn, for instance, traveled and worked extensively throughout Europe and South America prior to earning a law degree in public service. Sue's reflections on her experiences abroad prompted her to say the following: "If you can understand and relate to the conditions in different countries, whose people have backgrounds so different from your own, you can come back to the United States and relate to almost any situation."

Linda Montag grew up in Pittsburgh and attended Grove City College in Pennsylvania. Although her school offered study-abroad programs, Linda knew she could distinguish herself by getting work experience in a foreign country. So, with the encouragement of one of her German professors, she secured a work-study program in Germany for one summer and one semester in the field of insurance.

"My time abroad helped me develop self-confidence more than anything else I did in college," says Linda, who is now an assistant vice president of a German commercial bank headquartered in Frankfurt. "It was the first opportunity I had to truly assert myself and depend on myself completely to do everything—from finding my way around, to learning my job, to becoming proficient in a foreign language."

Where Do You Want to Go?

Maybe you'd like to visit France because you studied French in school. Maybe you'd like to visit Ireland because your ancestors were Irish. You've also thought about Canada or Mexico because they're closer, and therefore more convenient to visit. Below, make a list of five countries that interest you and, more important, tell *why* they interest you.

1. _____ , because _____ .

2. _____ , because _____ .

3. _____ , because _____ .

4. _____ , because _____ .

5. _____ , because _____ .

If no particular country stands out in your mind as the place you really want to go, take your travel wish list and do some information-gathering:

* Talk to professors.
* Talk to friends who've traveled.
* Read whatever you can about the countries that interest you.

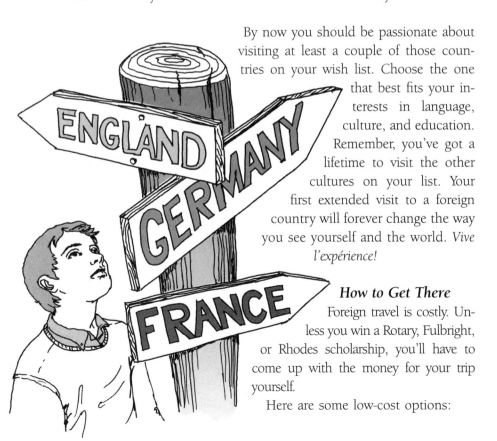

By now you should be passionate about visiting at least a couple of those countries on your wish list. Choose the one that best fits your interests in language, culture, and education. Remember, you've got a lifetime to visit the other cultures on your list. Your first extended visit to a foreign country will forever change the way you see yourself and the world. *Vive l'expérience!*

How to Get There

Foreign travel is costly. Unless you win a Rotary, Fulbright, or Rhodes scholarship, you'll have to come up with the money for your trip yourself.

Here are some low-cost options:

1. *You can take a year off from college to work, then travel.* Work hard to save money for the entire first semester, and then travel for six months—or as long as your money lasts. You can travel by train with a backpack and stay in inexpensive youth hostels. It's safer, but not essential, to travel with a companion.

    Advantage: You can plan for and take your trip without any outside interruptions. You can fully immerse yourself in travel: six months is a good chunk of time in which to see several different countries or concentrate on only one.

    Disadvantage: You'll be one year behind your classmates in school. However, this is actually an advantage, because you'll graduate with one more full year of experience over other applicants. Don't let peer pressure stop you.

2. *You can work in London or Paris as an au pair or nanny, taking care of children in the homes of affluent families.* In exchange for your services, which also may involve light housework, you receive free room and board and sometimes a small salary.

    Advantage: This is a cheap way to learn about other cultures. It affords far more experience than, say, living in a college dorm. Usually you have weekends free to explore the city and the surrounding countryside.

    Disadvantage: Frequently you will not have the time to venture beyond your central city unless you are traveling with the family. The job itself can be quite demanding.

3. *After you graduate from college, you can become a Peace Corps volunteer.* This requires a two-year commitment in one of sixty developing nations, working in such areas as nutrition, agriculture, education, or hygiene. Contact your local Peace Corps office for more information, or call 1-800-424-8580. If two years abroad is too long for you, shorter assignments are also available. The Young Men's Christian Association (YMCA) and Amigos de las Americas both offer summer volunteer programs that might better meet your objectives.

    Advantage: If you don't know a foreign language, the Peace Corps will teach you. You would work with a team of other volunteers in a small town or village. You would learn a great deal about the developing country and the people who live there. This is probably one of the most eye-opening experiences you can have abroad. Its rewards are not in dollars, but in experience. Also, being a Peace Corps volunteer tells potential employers that you are both tenacious and hard-working.

    Disadvantage: Peace Corps assignments are typically rigorous, and a two-year commitment is a significant amount of time. So consider the cost before you make a commitment.

4. *You can contact the Council on International Educational Exchange.* The Council on International Educational Exchange is a nonprofit member organization of nearly two hundred universities, colleges, and youth service agencies. It runs service projects in Denmark, Poland, Portugal, Canada, Turkey, Spain, and other countries. These two-to-four-week programs involve voluntary community service—such as renovation of historical sites, forestry, or social work—in exchange for room and board. There are also long-term service projects, including semester-long programs on Israeli kibbutzim.

 Advantage: There's no better way to learn about yourself than through helping others—the personal satisfaction and confidence gained through volunteer work is more than worth your time and effort.

 Disadvantage: Again, unless you choose to volunteer during the summer, you'll lose out on time in school. Your time will probably be very structured on these trips, too. Also, conditions can often be quite rustic.

5. *You can study abroad—for a summer, a semester, or a full year.* Nearly all colleges sponsor programs abroad for credit, and most of these programs are open to students from other schools. In addition to joining a program sponsored by an American university, you can enroll directly with a foreign university, in a program designed for foreign students. There are programs in virtually every country—if you really want to study in Finland or Bora Bora, or both, you probably can.

 Almost every college campus features summer- and semester-abroad programs for credit. Check with your foreign language, art history, or humanities departments for details, or perhaps your school has a separate office for study abroad.

 Advantage: This is a great way to learn the language and the culture while earning college credit. Living with a family abroad can be one of the most delightful ways to experience the country in depth. Also, you can usually apply for financial aid.

 Disadvantage: Cost. Often these programs are very expensive, including airfare and spending money as well as tuition and room and board. Fortunately, most colleges encourage students to apply their financial aid packages toward study abroad. Another disadvantage is that the host family the placement service thought was just right for you may turn out to be less than all you'd hoped for. This is rare, however; most programs thoroughly screen the families to make sure that they will provide a nice home, good food, and a pleasant atmosphere for their guests.

6. *You can contact Semester at Sea.* This program offers students college credit while they travel by ship to several designated countries. Check with your study-abroad office for details.

    Advantage: Students are able to see many different countries by ship, a thrilling means of travel by anybody's standard. You can also earn up to sixteen units of college credit.

    Disadvantage: This is an extremely costly program. Since you are on a ship most of the time, you won't put down roots in a particular country. Also, because most of the students are American, you are essentially transporting America by cruise ship to wild and exotic places. "The best way to waste a summer or a semester abroad is to hang out with other Americans," says Susan Finnemore. Some of the adventure is definitely undercut. Finally, instead of traveling by yourself, you are in a group—all the time.

7. *You can enlist in the armed services.* You're trained in a marketable skill, and you get to travel around the world. Other armed services besides the Army have ROTC programs; consult your local recruiter or your on-campus ROTC office.

    Advantage: When you get out, you'll be able to continue your education with a healthy subsidy from Uncle Sam or enter the job market, whichever you prefer. You might also want to consider ROTC. With this program, your undergraduate tuition at a host institution is partially paid for (usually the program pays 80 percent) and you have the advantage of not worrying about what you're going to be doing once you graduate.

    Disadvantage: You have little choice in where you will to be stationed, and the time commitment is relatively lengthy—usually three to four years.

8. *You can apply for a travel scholarship.* You just might qualify for a grant or scholarship to study abroad. It is relatively easy to get scholarship money for study in non-Western countries. For example, Max Ward, a senior in Asian studies, spent a semester studying in China. His trip to China was funded by the University of Texas and the Institute of Asian Studies in Chicago.

    Advantage: According to Max Ward, his experience "provided a chance for me to see a completely different way of life from my own." It moved him so much that he planned to go back to China after graduation to work. (He is now working part-time for a legal aid service, where he has had the opportunity to work with Chinese businesspeople.)

Disadvantage: Depending on your school, competition for travel scholarships can be fierce. Your knowledge of a foreign language, however, narrows the competition for scholarships. In the spring of her first year at Columbia's School of International Affairs, Elizabeth Thompson decided that she wanted to go to Egypt to brush up on her Arabic. (She had learned some Arabic while abroad in the past.) Elizabeth, a native of Detroit who had attended both Harvard as an undergraduate and Columbia's graduate school on full scholarship, could not afford to go on her own. When she asked an academic adviser if there were any scholarships that would send her to Egypt, he pulled an application for a grant out of the drawer. "In Middle Eastern affairs departments," he explained, "there are sometimes more grants than students." Elizabeth spent that summer in Egypt. Since then, she has taught in Syria for a year and has been admitted to Ph.D. programs in Middle Eastern studies, both at Columbia and Berkeley.

Additional Search Strategies

Here are some other sources of information about traveling abroad:

1. *The Internet and the World Wide Web.* Get on-line and click on a search engine; then type in the words *study abroad* or *foreign travel* and see what you can find. If you know which country you want to visit, type in that country's name; many countries have Web sites. Also check out "chat rooms" and "bulletin boards" where you can get tips from other travellers.

2. *Travel agencies.* Look in the yellow pages under "Travel Agencies," then call and ask about student programs. Travel agencies also have information on which U.S. cities sponsor international events. They often offer package deals that can make travel a bargain. Your on-campus travel agency is a great place to shop for such bargains. Students are often eligible for travel discounts from airlines and hotels. Agencies may also offer reduced rates on airfares, tours, and other travel items. You can also get an International Student Card, which allows you to visit museums and other attractions worldwide at reduced rates.

3. *International education offices.* Many campuses also have an international education office set up to help you. They have information on programs in places as diverse as the Orient, South America, and Russia. Vince Perez, for instance, had always been interested in international relations as a sophomore, so he applied for a job with the Association for International Students in Business and Economics (AIESEC) through the international

education office on his campus. Although Vince was from the Philippines, he got a paid job—$1,000 a month—in New Jersey with an American firm. Through an exchange program with Rider College, AIESEC arranged for Vince to live with an American family. Vince enjoyed the program so much that he became President of the AIESEC for the Philippines. He attended seminars in Australia, Singapore, Belgium, and Washington, D.C. Vince's sister joined the same organization and landed a job in Denmark, where she now lives and works. "AIESEC was my big breakthrough," says Vince, who is now director of an international trading firm, Lazard Frères, in London.

Travel Essentials

Check with your health clinic to determine whether you will need to be immunized before leaving the United States. Some immunizations must be completed *weeks* before you leave, so plan ahead.

For any type of foreign travel, you'll need a passport. These are available from courts and post offices throughout the country, as well as from designated passport agencies in most major cities. You may also need a visa for travel to some countries. For visa information, you can contact the country's embassy or write to the Office of Passport Services in Washington, D.C., for visa requirements.

It's Never Too Late

If you can't afford the time or cost of travel during college, don't worry. Cathy Stanley and Kim Corley waited until after graduation before they went abroad. For two months they traveled, carrying backpacks and using Eurailpasses. They explored England, Spain, Germany, Switzerland, Italy, and Greece. When they returned, Cathy began her job as a sales representative for Procter & Gamble and Kim began her career with IBM.

Howard Sklar graduated from UCLA with a degree in French history, but he didn't think his education was complete. "I'd spent four years cramming my head full of names, dates, literature and facts—but to tell you the truth, I hadn't the slightest idea of what French culture is in real life. I'd never seen it. I'd never lived it."

Howard decided to experience French culture firsthand from the seat of his bicycle. For three weeks, he took in the French countryside as he pedaled his way from Paris to Pouilly. Near the end of his trip, he finally realized what fascinated him about France. It wasn't the language or the history or the great works of art and literature. Rather, to his surprise, Howard found the heart and soul of France in its wine. Today Howard works as a wine importer in California.

Rich Matteson didn't travel during college either. Instead, he worked for one year as a restaurant manager after graduation before joining Up With People, the performance organization dedicated to promoting international understanding. After traveling to Belgium, Denmark, and Finland, Rich decided to become a full-time staff member with Up With People. He travels all over the world and stays with host families while organizing tours and performing with the cast. So don't be discouraged if you can't see the world right now. An opportunity to travel may open sometime in the near future. If it does, be sure to go for it.

Travel Opportunities in the United States

Although our focus up to this point has been on foreign travel, travel doesn't have to be international to be valuable. After her sophomore year at

Brown University, Melissa Halverstadt spent twelve months hiking, kayaking, and mountain-climbing in the wilderness education program at Prescott College in Arizona. She learned to lead, cooperate, conserve, and plan—survival skills in the truest sense.

So if you cannot venture outside of the United States yet want to experience the world, never fear. There are plenty of activities and programs you can join right on your own campus and in your community that will "bring the world to you."

Where to Get the Facts

ON CAMPUS

1. *Contact the International Students' Organization.* Almost every campus has an ISO group where students from around the world join Americans in an exchange of culture, ideas, and good times (often centered around delectable cuisine). If there is no such organization on your campus, begin one yourself. Each week, someone from a different country gives a speech or slide presentation, followed by refreshments and the opportunity to meet everyone. Also, dinners or banquets are held where a group of people will provide the regional cuisine, and perhaps demonstrate a traditional art or form of dress.

2. *Visit the campus residence for international students.* You could apply for a job as a desk clerk or as a food server. Or drop by sometime when you can introduce yourself to several students. Give them your phone number and tell them you would like to get together for lunch or dinner. Remember, they want to learn just as much about America as you want to learn about their culture.

3. *Volunteer to be an English tutor.* This is a great way to intimately learn about the culture of a foreign country through fellow students who will become your friends. Also, you can derive a lot of personal satisfaction from knowing that you are helping to open your culture and country up to someone else.

IN THE COMMUNITY

1. *Work in an ethnic restaurant or in a business run entirely by people from another country.* Expose yourself to a different set of customs and values.

Ask questions about their home country. How is it different from the United States? How do they perceive Americans? What have they learned from Americans? What has been the biggest cultural barrier?

2. *Read the newspapers to find out about cultural events.* Frequently there are cultural festivals that feature music, dance, and foods from foreign lands. If you have time, get involved in a steering committee to plan such an event. Chances are you'll meet fascinating people from the community who will keep you posted on similar events.

3. *Contact Americorps.* Americorps is like the Peace Corps, except that the assignments are here in the United States. You can work for little or no pay in places like American Indian reservations, inner cities, or remote rural communities. Like the Peace Corps, Americorps involves hard work and commitment.

Other Horizons

There are many ways to enrich your travel experience before, during, and after your trip. Brushing up on the language, reading about the history of the country, and learning about the people before you go can make you feel more at home right from the start.

Let's say you've chosen to visit France. Before your trip, you may want to listen to some French-language tapes and practice the most commonly used phrases. (It helps if you've studied the language in school, but it's not essential.) What are other considerations?

- **Art.** Every region of the world has its own unique art forms. You may want to research the region you intend to visit.
- **Literature.** Read works by native authors as an entertaining way to learn about the country you are visiting.
- **History.** Invest in a paperback on the country's history so that the sights you see will have greater significance for you.
- **Music.** Listen to local radio stations during your trip. This will help you understand the language and expose you to the country's music.
- **Philosophy.** Who were the philosophers that influenced cultural development? How has their thinking affected everyday life?
- **Politics and Economics.** Think about the way the country is governed. How does it differ from the United States? What are the pluses and minuses? What is the economic system?
- **Business.** What is the local commerce? What are the major industries? Is the country rich in natural resources, human resources, agriculture,

or technological advances? Which American companies thrive in the country?

No matter where you plan to go, from Peru to Japan, getting a sense of the country beforehand will help you feel better upon arrival. You can learn and adapt on the road by carrying a guidebook as a useful reference and road map.

This is only a partial list. Don't stop here! Make foreign or domestic travel a goal. Your travel adventure may just be the most valuable experience of your college years.

10

Networking

Mapping Out Your Career Strategy

The need to be opportunistic, to think on your feet, again underscores the importance of tuning in to people—of hearing not only what they say, but the larger and underlying meaning as well.
Mark McCormack, in What They Don't Teach You at Harvard Business School

Don't wait for the business connections to come to you," says Chris Salgado, an operations manager at Morgan Guaranty. "You have to talk to as many people as possible, and don't be afraid of asking questions. The more aggressive you are at asking questions, the more information you'll have on which to make a decision." By visiting his school's career services office when he was a sophomore, Chris had a competitive advantage over his classmates who waited until the last minute to investigate career contacts.

Networking involves all the activities that result in contacts. Therefore, at the core of networking is a commitment to develop good relationships. Meeting people; making your career needs known to friends and relatives; keeping in touch and on good terms with past and present classmates, professors, employers, co-workers, relatives, friends, and virtually everyone else you know—all are important elements of mapping out an effective career strategy. Learning to network effectively can mean the difference between landing a job or receiving a form letter that reads, "Thank you for your time, but . . ."

Your career network represents the connections you already have with the people you know, as well as those you want to establish. Therefore, Nancy Forsyth, a business graduate from the University of New Hampshire, advises, "Be gutsy. You can't expect people to help you out if you don't do something for yourself." Nancy built strong relationships with her professors and the counselors at the career services office. "Your mentors in college have the best connections, and they care about helping you assess what you should do," says Nancy, who became an editor for Boston publisher Allyn & Bacon. "But students must make the initial effort to seek these people out."

Although he had been a highly qualified student, the editor of his college magazine, and voted "Most Likely to Succeed in Journalism," David Herndon found that getting his first good job was not just a matter of talent and hard work; it also involved "circumstance and opportunity."

"You've got to be around to get around," says David, a *Newsday* features editor. After graduating from Columbia's Graduate School of Journalism, David had to spend three years doing odd jobs (including compiling sections for an encyclopedia, which was "like writing high school book reports") before he finally got his break. Ironically, it came from a former fellow student who had landed a job with *Sport* magazine and asked David to write a few articles. David did, and was then recommended for a job as sports editor at *The Village Voice*. He got the job, and over the next five years he made up for lost time, moving from sports editor to managing editor (at age twenty-nine) to features editor for *Newsday*.

In his book *Achievement Factors: Candid Interviews with Some of the Most Successful People of Our Time*, B. Eugene Griessman writes: "Opportunities are usually for the moment, and as they pass by, there is often only a brief moment to grab them." Therefore, keep in mind that contacts are everywhere, in the classroom and out, in the office and out.

The Career Search

Why not use your career search as a launching pad for networking skills? Basically, for career-search purposes, networking means making contact with people who can

- Tell you about a specific job
- Put you in touch with someone important at a company that interests you
- Keep you in mind for a job that will open up in the future
- Coach you in your career pursuit
- Provide you with inside information
- Introduce you to someone who can give you valuable information
- Hire you

Why is networking—or making career or business contacts—so important? For one thing, you always need people contacts, whether you're looking for a job or not. (Your GPA will not be your best friend.) Second, you need people to tell you firsthand how to make the transition from super college student to super job applicant. Meeting people who can help you in this transition will be more helpful than reading ten books on how to get the job of your dreams.

In fields like finance, connections can be everything. John Carrigan, thirty years old, has his own seat on the Chicago Board of Trade. He says his first contact in the field was made through a friend from high school. His three summer internships, and the contacts he made, were a foot in the door for his first post-college job trading futures for Paine Webber.

Where to Begin

First, take inventory of your summer internships and part-time jobs. Did the work interest you? What do you most value from your college classes and activities? What was most enjoyable?

Use the answers to those questions as clues to finding the jobs that interest you most. Then talk to people who have those jobs now. This advice should sound familiar, since you've already been "networking" with your professors, friends, and employers since your freshman year.

If possible, ask your networking contacts if you can observe them on the job. You want to get an accurate picture of a typical workday. Would you like to be alone or with people? Would you rather be closely supervised or independent? What environment would you like to work in? Would you like to travel?

George Fraser, author of the networking book *Success Runs in Our Race*, remembers one of his first jobs working in a department store stockroom. "I worked hard and looked constantly for opportunities to be promoted, and in doing so, I learned a basic principle of networking: start wherever the door of opportunity opens, be it in the mailroom or the back room. I see so many young people who want to start in the front office, if not higher. It doesn't work that way. Everything good that happened to me during this period was a result of people telling other people good things about my attitude. I learned the importance of developing good relationships with my co-workers. If you work hard and well with other people, you don't always need to job-hunt. Often, the jobs come hunting for you."

Cultivating Contacts Now and in the Future

Much of your success in work will depend on the relationships you have with other people. If you learn early to pick people's brains, to perceive what makes them successful, and to incorporate their qualities of success, you will be far ahead of your contemporaries. Know that you have much to learn from your mentors and your "role models" in business, but you have equally as much to learn from all of your other work associates.

Networking doesn't mean just making yourself visible to those in a position to give you a promotion, though that is important. It also means cultivating relationships with all the people behind the scenes, the people who actually get things done—the receptionist, mail clerk, messenger, office manager, janitor—people whose jobs go mostly unrecognized by the corporate hierarchy. It involves a willingness to learn anything from anyone who works with you, in *any* capacity.

"You never know where you will run into someone again," says Nancy Wingate. "You may not think much of the receptionist or the intern or the classmate next to you, but they may be sitting across a desk interviewing you down the line. It pays to treat everyone you work with with respect and consideration."

Robert Girardot, a chemical engineer at CSX Corporation, agrees. "You never know who's going to be your boss one day." He remembers when an unpopular guy became the boss. "I'm not saying you should be phony . . . but do not participate in office gossip. Be a booster. If you don't have something good to say about a co-worker, boss, or company, don't say anything." Do you remember the Golden Rule you learned way back in kindergarten? Well, it still applies, even in your professional life. Not only is following the Golden Rule the right thing to do, your career will also function better in the long run. Therefore, maintain high ethical standards.

Business Week columnist Paul Nadler says he always sends postcards to the office's photocopying personnel. He depends heavily on quick and efficient photocopies, especially at deadline time.

Building relationships with all different kinds of people will help you if you ever want to be in management. As a manager, you are a leader, organizing and inspiring and working with others to achieve professional and personal goals. How do you learn the principles of good management?

"Not by reading about great leaders whose experience is so foreign it makes it impossible to identify with them," observes Andrew S. Grove, former CEO of Intel Corporation, in a *Fortune* magazine article. Grove does not endorse wilderness excursions, climbing down poles, or whitewater rafting as the secret to management success. Good leadership and good management is learned, according to Grove, "the same way each of us has learned the important, unteachable roles in our lives, be they that of husband or wife, father or mother: by studying the behavior of people who have made a success of it and modeling ourselves after them."

Networking means learning from others. It also means being a teacher to others when you have the knowledge, experience, and expertise to give someone else guidance.

John and Elizabeth were hired right out of journalism school by a major financial news weekly. Each held entry-level editorial positions. John was eager to learn, inquisitive, and helpful to co-workers in his training seminar. When Ann, a new co-worker, was having a hard time figuring out the computer system, John took the time to sit down and help her figure it out. He wasn't much more experienced with it than she was, but he figured he'd learn by helping. When they couldn't resolve a glitch, John was the one who went to the seminar instructor and asked for help. Not only was the instructor happy to help John and Ann solve the problem, he also became interested in the sample article they were working on. And he was impressed with John's editorial eye. This gave John the opportunity to get to know a senior editor in an informal situation, sincerely and without any grandstanding.

Elizabeth had a different approach. During the instructor's seminar, she continually interrupted the other trainees, interjecting her opinion based on her vast experience working at her father's newspaper in a midsized midwestern city. Once, when Ann asked Elizabeth to share her experience about working for her father's newspaper, Elizabeth refused. Instead, she looked briefly at Ann with a bored expression and said that she'd love to if she had the time, but that right now she was "consumed" with a special feature proposal for the magazine.

At promotion time, Elizabeth was still laboring on her uncommissioned special feature while John was promoted to assistant managing editor, with responsibility for developing a financial news column for college graduates. The senior editors believed John would be a better long-term choice because he was a superior teacher, listener, communicator, and motivator. In short, John was a role model. Elizabeth, on the other hand, didn't receive the promotion because her poor attitude closed the doors of opportunity.

How Have You Networked?

Have you networked during your summer internship or in a part-time job? Even if you have only waited on tables, think of how your success depended on your co-workers. Seriously.

An excellent waiter who is liked and respected by his co-workers is far more effective—and therefore more profitable—than the average waiter. Why? Because if the host or hostess likes him, he'll get his tables turned (cleared off and set) faster than the others. If the cook likes him, he'll get occasional special orders for his "preferred" customers. If the manager realizes how valuable his work and his good disposition are, he or she will make special arrangements—like letting him work as much or as little as he wants to accommodate his school schedule—just to keep him. Finally, the customer—the ultimate recipient of this entire team process—stands a greater chance of being pleased with the service. Therefore, this waiter will probably get a better tip—one of his goals in the first place.

Good human relations will help you in any job. Although some people have a natural knack for dealing with people, others have a hard time. If you are in the latter category, take heart. There are resources that can help you understand how you can better relate to people and how you can help other people feel comfortable relating to you. The classic self-help book on this subject is *How to Win Friends and Influence People* by Dale Carnegie. In it, he outlines six basic principles for successful interaction. (There's so much common sense here, it's easy to take this formula for granted. Don't.)

1. Become genuinely interested in other people.
2. Smile.

3. Remember that a person's name is to that person the sweetest and most important sound in any language.
4. Be a good listener. Encourage others to talk about themselves.
5. Talk in terms of other people's interests, not your own.
6. Make the other person feel important, and do it sincerely.

Networking is a relatively new word for, among other things, effective human relations. Wholesome, old-fashioned characteristics like good manners, sincerity, a positive attitude, and a generous spirit never go out of style. Together they formulate the essence of a winning career strategy.

Finding a Mentor

If you haven't already, find yourself a mentor. A mentor is a teacher, a coach, a guide, a guru—somebody you have a rapport with and a respect for in your chosen career field. A mentor is less a model than a teacher. (Whitney Herzog, for example, was a mediocre baseball player but has become one of the game's most successful managers.)

So how will you meet your mentor? Will he or she appear to you magically? Probably not; you must take the initiative. Seeking out a mentor will help you define yourself and your chosen career path, so choose carefully. Asking yourself two smart questions will help you get started on your quest:

1. *Which professors most inspire you?* Talk to them after class. Ask them for special assignments.
2. *Whom do you know that works in your field of interest?* Perhaps your mentor will be a manager at an office where you have a part-time job or a summer internship. Set up an appointment to talk with that person about your career goals, and ask him or her for input or suggestions.

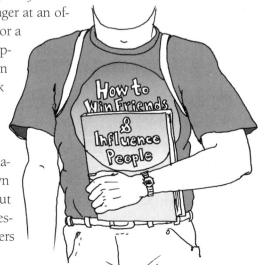

To be effective at networking, that is, cultivating good professional relations, you must first examine your own character and personality. Think about those people you most admire (professors, movie stars, politicians, characters from literature, etc.). Think about the people who've had the greatest and most positive influence on you. What distinguishes them from the rest of the herd? Why do they appeal to you? Why do they stand out? Learn how to ask questions of the people you work with who have more experience and more knowledge than you do. Take notes. Watch them in action. Analyze what they do. Study the people who are excelling in their fields; obviously they are doing something right.

One other thing: it's important that your mentor be someone you can get to know. If you want to be a playwright, Shakespeare might be an ideal, but he's dead; Arthur Miller might be a model, but he lives in New York City. Why not cultivate a relationship with the drama professor at your local college?

Thomas Easton, New York bureau chief of *The Baltimore Sun*, found his career shaped dramatically by a mentor. In college he was reluctant to specialize in any one area. He was interested in everything, from film to history to political science. When he graduated, he had a vague idea that his broad range of interests might make him suitable for journalism, but he wasn't sure.

Then, during a job interview for a chain of Connecticut weekly newspapers, he met editor John Peterson, who had won awards as an investigative reporter. The two hit it off right away. Peterson's great curiosity and energy matched Easton's. "I asked him once if he wanted me to go out for coffee," Easton says, laughing. "And he said, 'No, I didn't hire you to get coffee. I hired you to get stories. Get out there.' "

Because of his mentor, Easton made an extraordinary career jump. After two years on the weekly, he worked for a daily for six months, went to business school, and ended up on one of the best papers in the country. Easton says that the *Sun* weighed two things heavily: his business degree and a stellar recommendation from Peterson.

The Mentor Dynamic

Within your career-strategy network, there will be people whom you admire more than others because of the quality of their work. Mentoring relationships naturally tend to form around a shared interest or passion within a particular field. Therefore, your boss might be a potential mentor, but it could just as easily be someone in a different department with whom you've worked on a specific project. Many fields and industries even require new employees to form a mentoring relationship. In these situations, senior members are matched with newcomers for the purpose of advancing the work.

If someone takes a special interest in you because you have been an apprentice—taking on extra assignments, staying late to help on a special project, etc.—this person is likely to give you advice that is not commonly available to others at your level. For instance, you may learn how to best prepare yourself for a promotion. Or you may receive detailed advice on how to do your present job more efficiently. Therefore, seek out ways to work with or for the people on whom you want to model your professional life. Then learn as much as you can from them.

I also recommend that you look to a number of different people for guidance, not just one person. The world has become so specialized that a single individual cannot possibly keep up with all there is to know in a chosen domain. For example, at last count, there were at least three different types of eye surgeons, who operate on three different areas of the human eye. Therefore, plan to draw information and support from several people, according to their areas of expertise.

In order to learn from other people, you must demonstrate an inquiring mind. Ask questions, and be willing to disclose what you do not know. Be open to feedback. Ditch any attitude of arrogance; it won't get you anywhere. I'm not saying that you shouldn't be confident—you have to believe in yourself—but have the wisdom to know what you can learn from others.

What does a successful mentor-protégé relationship look like in the working world? The answer: a two-way street. Harvard Business School graduate Linda Hill, the author of *Becoming a Manager: Mastery of a New Identity*, writes that good mentoring relationships are always mutually beneficial. "The mentor offers advice and opportunity; the protégé delivers results," explains Hill. In other words, the mentor's input yields fruit. You are improving, or you are growing in your understanding of a concept, as a direct result of the mentor's influence in your professional life. This tangible evidence of personal growth and development is gratifying not only to you, but to your mentor as well.

Who Are My Contact People?

Throughout college, you've pushed yourself to branch out, experience things, meet people, and ask questions. Beginning with your junior year, narrow your focus to the career you think you want to pursue.

Here are some good people to contact:

• Company representatives who have registered with your career services office

- Company recruiters listed in the publication *Job Choices* (this is revised and updated yearly)
- Members of your school's alumni association who are in fields you want to pursue
- Professionals in your hometown
- Professors at your university
- Your parents' friends; your siblings or their friends
- Authors of books you've read in your field of interest
- People who have given speeches in your career area

Of course, this is only a partial listing, but it should at least get you started. Keep a checklist of important people you want to meet in order to gather information. Try to meet and speak with one key person a week during your junior and senior years. Keep notes on your conversations so that you can make comparisons and analyze the advice you're given.

Getting Connected

Networking, for the purpose of mapping out a career strategy, entails six simple yet critical steps. First, you will need to make contact with people who already work in your field of interest. Therefore, make a list of anyone and everyone who is even remotely related to your selected career or job. If you can't think of at least five people to contact, you're not thinking hard enough.

Second, create a list of questions to ask the contact person. The goal of the questioning process is to determine whether the career path you are on is truly the right one for you. Here are a few questions to get you started:

- What are the pros and cons of working in the industry?
- Of working in that company?
- Of the company's philosophy?
- What does and doesn't appeal to the company?
- What has he or she enjoyed the most? disliked the most?

Remember, finding the answers to these questions will help you assess whether the field and the job are right for you.

Third, with each contact you make, take notes on the responses you get to your questions. Some contacts may even offer to call potential employers on your behalf. Be sure to ask each contact person with whom else you can speak in order to gather more information.

Fourth, while you have the contact on the phone, make the most of the opportunity. For instance, if the conversation went well, plan to ask permission to use the contact's name as a future reference. Be prepared, however, for a "no" response, and try not to take it personally. The individual may not feel familiar enough with you to give an honest reference.

The previous step leads naturally to the fifth one: Prepare yourself for unexpected outcomes. For example, your contact person may invite you for an interview, so have a calendar nearby so that you can set a date. Likewise, poise yourself for rejection. You may have caught the contact person at a bad time. If you sense that, ask if there is a better time for you to call.

Finally, regardless of what happens, always thank the contact person for his or her time. Then follow up with a brief note of appreciation.

Accessing Key People

Within every company or industry, there are key people. These key people are given job titles such as "chief executive officer," "executive director," "president," or "dean." Although the titles may vary, the power usually doesn't. These are the decision-makers of that institution; therefore, they are the people you need to gain access to.

Making contact with them, however, can be tricky. To contact the key person, you must first make a good impression on the person in the other power seat: the *administrative assistant*. Treat the administrative assistant with as much respect—or more—as the other people you intend to contact. Tell him or her why you would like to see the key person. Explain why you are interested in the company, and talk about your experiences and abilities. Also, ask for information on the company so that you can study it before your meeting with the key person.

The administrative assistant is the eyes and ears for the person you need to speak with. He or she is skilled at knowing exactly what his or her boss values and looks for, so this individual is the first in the chain of people to win over.

If the administrative assistant does not grant you an appointment with the key person, be gracious. Thank him or her for his or her time. Later, send follow-up letters to the administrative assistant as well as to the key person, restating your interest. Often the initial "no" is a smokescreen. Your diplomatic, consistent follow-up may secure the appointment, so don't give up.

Face-to-Face with Key People

Mapping out a career strategy eventually translates into meeting the administrative assistant and other key people for the first time. Although one of your objectives for this initial encounter is to research the company or industry, your primary goal is to make a favorable impression on the people you meet. Doing so may lead to future employment at that establishment, or at the very least *open the door* to some great contacts. That's why some people refer to this stage of career strategy as "getting your foot in the door."

When meeting someone for the first time, you will want to present a professional, courteous, and direct demeanor. Therefore, right at the start, clearly state your interests and your reasons for wanting to interview this person. (This is especially crucial with a professional whom you have not met previously.) Be poised and well dressed, and don't smoke right before the meeting. You'll probably have only two or three minutes to set up the lunch appointment or half-hour meeting, so make the most of it by being prepared. Consider the following sample dialogues.

FIRST INTERVIEW

YOU:	Hello, Ms. Marshall. Thank you for taking time to see me today.
KEY PERSON:	My pleasure. What can I do for you?
YOU:	As your assistant probably told you, I am one year away from graduating from State A&M with a degree in architectural design. Since your firm has designed some of the most outstanding buildings in this state, I wanted to express early interest in working with you someday. I wondered, specifically, if I might be able to set up a luncheon appointment with you or one of your junior associates so that I could learn firsthand about the qualities you seek in graduates you hire as first-year associates.
KP:	I admire your foresight. Unfortunately, I am swamped right now and would not be able to take two hours to meet with you. However, there is one exemplary employee who has worked with us for two years and who graduated from your school. His name is Jordan Simon, and he may be available to give you some advice.
YOU:	I would appreciate speaking with him. Thank you very much for your time. I hope we are able to see each other in the next year.
KP:	You're welcome. My assistant will be happy to give you

Jordan's phone number. He manages our other office. Tell him I sent you. Good luck.

PHONE CONTACT WITH JORDAN SIMON

YOU: Mr. Simon, I am a junior at State A&M and will graduate next year with a degree in architectural design. Cynthia Marshall recommended that I speak with you about how I might best prepare to work for your firm someday. May I take you to lunch sometime next week so we can talk further?

JS: I exercise at lunch every day, but I'd be happy to meet you for breakfast if you tell me why it would be worth my time.

YOU: Gladly. I have a 3.6 GPA and two summers of experience working for your competitors, and I have put myself through school. I am a hard worker and a team player, and I have a very creative mind. I'd like to speak with you in person to pick your brains and find out how you think, plan, and organize your time.

JS: That's a good start. Where and when would you like to get together?

Before the actual appointment, make a list of good questions to ask. You shouldn't be doing all the talking. Instead, you should be listening and asking what else you can do to prepare for success. Be confident, but don't be cocky. You may end up with an apprenticeship, which can get you in the door at graduation time.

Narrowing Your Choices

Once you have completed several phone contacts and meetings, you enter the narrowing phase of your career pursuit. On the basis of all of the information you've gathered over the last three years, narrow your choices down to two or three career domains. For example, if you have strong people skills and you want to be in management someday, sales may be the place to start. If you're strong in information skills, you may want to begin in an entry-level position in market research.

If you're strong in the area of objects, you may want to begin as an apprentice with a craftsperson or a professional in your technical area of interest.

N E T W O R K   M A P :
C H A R T   I T   O U T !

SYLVIA ROBINSON
Alumna; VP, Interstate Bank

CHARLES DEAN
President, Hometown Bank

MARY ROLATTA
Ex-employee

AL RUBEN
VP, Finance

JOHN SLOAN
Now has own business

MARK CORTEZ
Financial Planner, Merrill Lynch

ANNE GIBB
Teller

Career Network Map

Field: _____

Job: _____

Contact people:

1. Entry-level
    a. _____
    b. _____
    c. _____

3. Former employees
    a. _____
    b. _____
    c. _____

2. Upper-level
    a. _____
    b. _____
    c. _____

4. Alumni who are now in the field
    a. _____
    b. _____
    c. _____

Impressions of the industry:

Pros

Cons

_____   _____
_____   _____
_____   _____

Once you've narrowed down your career search to a few companies within a particular industry, make a list of the employees you'd like to set up appointments with. (Again, one way to gain access to these people is through their administrative assistants.) You may not be able to talk to all of them, but writing down their names will help you figure out whose advice may have the greatest impact. They are the ones you will want to make every effort to contact first.

Therefore, to maximize the efficiency of your employee list, consider these questions: Who do you think is the most happy in his or her job? Why? Is it the company, or is it that person's approach to the job—or maybe a combination of both? Questioning as many people as possible, in a very diplomatic way, will give you volumes of information with which to make a good decision.

There you have it. As you can see, networking involves far more than just meeting people and gathering information for your own purposes. Keep in mind that it's a two-way street. Sure, you will gain a lot from others, but not unless you're prepared to contribute to them as well. If you can't help someone directly, at least be prepared to thank them in earnest for their support. In turn, when you can, determine to help others who are less experienced than you. Take pleasure in knowing that you're being a mentor or role model to them, just as others have been to you.

11

Paperwork

Résumés, Cover Letters, and the Job Application

Thought is the soul of act.
Robert Browning

Brevity is the soul of wit.
William Shakespeare

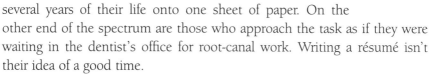

People vary in their reactions to writing résumés. Some students, for example, are excited about it. They look forward to the challenge of condensing several years of their life onto one sheet of paper. On the other end of the spectrum are those who approach the task as if they were waiting in the dentist's office for root-canal work. Writing a résumé isn't their idea of a good time.

How about you? Are you ready to promote yourself on paper? Whatever your degree of anticipation, writing a résumé is an absolutely essential component of a successful job search. In this chapter, we will help you craft an effective one as painlessly as possible. We will also assist you with two other aspects of paperwork, namely, the cover letter and the job application.

The Job Search

According to William Potter, vice president of A Better Résumé Service in Chicago, the key to a successful job search is

- To know yourself
- To know your market
- To know how to market yourself effectively

By now you are well on your way to developing knowledge in two of these areas. From Chapter 2, "Discover Who You Are," you learned more about Potter's first recommendation, *to know yourself*. In Chapter 3, you tackled Potter's second recommendation, *to know your market*, by investigating the majors and jobs that interested you. Congratulations—you have covered a lot of ground!

Now you are ready to pick up Potter's third job-search recommendation: *marketing yourself*, which is the focus of this chapter. Marketing yourself is where résumé writing comes into the picture. Effective résumés will open doors to interviews. Therefore, to market yourself effectively, you will need to craft a résumé that identifies your unique skills and qualities.

Planning Your Dream Résumé

Your career direction will find its shape, and its name, in increments. In other words, everything you study and explore now will contribute to the résumé you send out during your senior year. Your résumé will summarize the whole shebang—academic achievements, extracurricular activities, and work experience.

What do you want your résumé to look like? Thinking about the answer to this question now will help you achieve the résumé of your dreams. Consequently, the résumé of your dreams will help you land the job of your dreams. So begin planning now!

Many students resist writing their résumés for as long as they possibly can, usually until the second semester of their senior year. While this procrastination is understandable, in most cases, it is not helpful in finding a job. Wait until the second semester of your senior year and you may find yourself distributing political tracts at the local mall—for the opposition party—at minimum wage. So why tempt fate when it is so easily outfoxed? Start thinking now about how you'd like your résumé to look. Can't picture it? I have a suggestion: write it out.

MY DREAM RÉSUMÉ

(By the second semester of my senior year)

My grade point average is _____.

My major and minor are _____.

My career goal is _____.

My academic honors include _____

_____

_____.

My extracurricular activities include _____

_____

_____..

I had a summer internship doing _____

at _____.

I traveled to _____.

I worked part-time as _____

_____.

My references are:

1. _____

2. _____

3. _____

Okay, now you know what you want to accomplish for your future. The first step toward getting there is to focus on the here and now. What does your current résumé look like? Do you have a current résumé? If not, now is definitely the time to begin thinking about it. Why? Because you want to land that internship, don't you? What about that part-time job? Regardless of the type of position you seek, a résumé will always reflect favorably on you. It allows your prospective employer to see what you have accomplished thus far—your experience, skills and abilities, and any special training are there at a glance.

So, how do compile your current résumé? You can begin by taking a look at what you possess that might be attractive to a prospective employer. Don't be afraid to toot your own horn—as long as it's all true and not exaggerated, of course! Completing the sentences below will help you begin to craft the résumé of your dreams.

My objective is _____.

I am currently studying _____.

I graduated from high school in _____.

Academic recognition that I received in high school included _____

_____.

My past work experience includes _____

_____

_____

_____.

I have special training in _____

_____

_____.

I am especially good at _____

_____

_____ .

My other abilities include _____

_____

_____ .

Classes that I have had that are relevant to the position that I seek are

_____

_____

_____ .

My references are

1. _____

2. _____

3. _____

First Impressions

Experts emphasize that your résumé gives potential employers their first impression of you. A good résumé can help you get your foot inside an interviewer's office door. For that reason, your résumé may be the most important element of your job search. In addition to making a good first impression, your résumé also serves as a springboard for a prospective employer's questions. And later, it's a reminder on file of who you are.

A survey involving the top one hundred U.S. companies by Robert Half, author of *How to Get a Better Job in This Crazy World*, revealed the four leading reasons that résumés are disregarded: 36 percent of all résumés

contain distortions or lies; 19 percent have spelling errors; 12 percent fail to provide sufficient detail; and 10 percent give irrelevant information. Your career planning and placement center probably offers assistance in eliminating mistakes like these, so be sure to make an appointment with them. For now, here are the basic ingredients of an effective résumé, in the order that they should appear:

1. *The heading.* A résumé should begin with your name, address, telephone number, and E-mail address (if you have one) so that an employer will know how to reach you, should he or she be interested.
2. *The job objective.* Next on your résumé comes the job objective, which should be stated in one sentence. Including a job objective on your résumé, however, isn't always necessary, nor is it always the best approach. "By stating a job objective," writes Robert Half, "you potentially rule yourself out of being considered for other jobs in that same company, jobs that do not match precisely with the objective you've stated."

    One solution to the job objective dilemma is to drop the job objective altogether. Another option, however, is to write separate, "specialized" résumés, each prepared with basic honesty, but beefing up the qualities you want to accentuate. For example, let's say that your education and background have made you suitable for positions in marketing, selling, and advertising. Obviously, any of those areas might provide permanent employment for you, but one résumé that attempts to cover all those bases might lack the necessary focus. Therefore, three specialized résumés should be created. One will emphasize the marketing aspect of your experience. The second will focus on your sales background and your accomplishments in selling. The third will have your advertising experience at the forefront. When you're invited for a marketing job interview, you will give the interviewer the version of the résumé that highlights that aspect of your education and experience.

Since you can't, however, be all things to all people all of the time, Half recommends that you also prepare a "general" resume so that "the disparate major focuses of your experience are given equal weight."

3. *The body.* The body, which is the largest portion of your résumé, consists of four parts: (1) education; (2) job history; (3) activities; and (4) achievements. List these items in reverse chronological order, beginning with the most recent. Include any skills relevant to the type of employment sought, such as ability to speak a foreign language, or secretarial or computer skills.

The Cover Letter

To get your résumé noticed, you'll need an ace cover letter. A what? A personalized letter that accompanies your résumé. You might think the best cover letter would contain a curling arrow and a boldface message reading "Résumé Below," followed by a full line of exclamation points:

!!!!!!!!!!!!!!!!!!!!!!!!!!!!!!!!!!!!!!!

That might not be such a bad idea, but unfortunately this is not the kind of cover letter most employers have come to expect. The cover letter is not the domain of the abstract-expressionist avant-garde existentialist career hunter. Not as of this writing, anyway.

Basically, a cover letter lets you do two things: herald your résumé and secure the interview. By taking your highlighted qualities and personalizing them, a good cover letter convinces the reader to pay attention to your résumé. Therefore, take just as much care in preparing the cover letter as you do in preparing your résumé. To make your cover letter visually appealing, print it on personalized stationery, or at least on good-quality paper. Then briefly state your most compelling qualifications and request an interview. Also, be sure to mention the reason why you'd like to work for the company.

In short, the goals of your cover letter are

1. To express interest in the company and a specific position
2. To engage the reader's interest so he or she is compelled to read your résumé
3. To mention a specific date when you will contact the person if he or she does not contact you

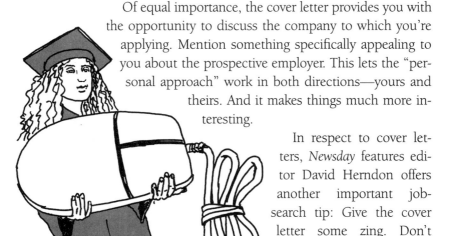

Of equal importance, the cover letter provides you with the opportunity to discuss the company to which you're applying. Mention something specifically appealing to you about the prospective employer. This lets the "personal approach" work in both directions—yours and theirs. And it makes things much more interesting.

In respect to cover letters, *Newsday* features editor David Herndon offers another important job-search tip: Give the cover letter some zing. Don't dwell on the reasons it would be a good experience for you to work for the prospective employer; rather, always stay focused on how you can help the company. "Tell [the prospective employer] why it would be a good experience for him to work with you." Then follow up with a phone call two weeks later.

Thank-you notes following interviews are neither necessary nor expected. All the more reason why it's so important to send them. They need not be elaborate. Just say thanks.

The Job Application

Like your other work papers, the job application should be neat and well-thought-out. If you can, fill in the application at home. But before writing on the actual application, write your responses first on scratch paper. That way, you can refine your thoughts before committing them to paper.

On the pages that follow is a fairly comprehensive sample job application. Fill it out for practice. Then look at your responses later and see what you think. Are you crisp and to the point? Are your examples convincing? Would *you* be interested in interviewing *you* after reading your application?

Some sample cover letters, résumés, and thank-you letters follow. Remember, résumé writing and other paperwork are simply marketing tools. On average, job recruiters will spend only about thirty seconds looking at your résumé; therefore, you want to give the very best impression.

The way you dress, speak, and follow up are also tools of self-promotion. Again, you may see a key person only briefly, but you want to make a lasting, winning impression. If you follow the advice in this chapter, you will.

Please print in ink. Attach separate sheets if necessary.

Name: First, Middle, Last	Social Security No.

Home Address: Street City State Zip	Home Phone

How long at present address?	Are you in the U.S. on a temporary visa?

In emergency, notify (Name/Address/Phone)

List any friends or relatives working with the company, by name and relationship.

Have you ever worked for us or one of our subsidiaries?

Have you ever applied for work here before? if so, when?

Do you own or have access to a car?

Has your license ever been
suspended or revoked? If so, why?

EDUCATION

Circle the Highest Grade Completed:	High school 1 2 3 4 College 1 2 3 4	Graduate school: 1 2 3 4 Degrees:

	High school	**College**
Names of school, date entered, location		
Graduation date and grade-point average		
List major and minor fields		
Scholastic honors		
Any academic or disciplinary probation? If yes, explain.		
List extracurricular or athletic activities.		
List part-time jobs.		
How did you spend your summer vacations?		
Are your proud of your college record? Explain.		

WORK EXPERIENCE

From / Through / Most recent employer / May we contact?

Address   Phone

Current or final supervisor

Starting position and salary

How did you get the job?   Why did you leave?

What did you like the best about the job?

What did you like least about the job?

From / Through / employer before No. 1 / May we contact?

Address   Phone

Current or final supervisor

Starting position and salary

How did you get the job?   Why did you leave?

What did you like the best about the job?

What did you like least about the job?

From / Through / employer before No. 2 / May we contact?

Address   Phone

Current or final supervisor

Starting position and salary

How did you get the job?   Why did you leave?

What did you like the best about the job?

What did you like least about the job?

Please summarize any relevant experience which uniquely qualifies you for this job.

REFERENCES

List three persons, not relatives or former employers, who have known you for the last five years whom we may contact.

NAME	ADDRESS	YEARS KNOWN
1.		
2.		
3.		

State your own personal definition of this position:

Please tell us why you want this job and why you think you would be successful.

ACTIVITIES

Excluding religious or political groups, with what organizations do you now work?

What are your hobbies?

What magazines or newspapers do you regularly read?

How many hours do you watch TV per week?

What types of books do you read most often?

Below are some of the reasons why some people want to join our company. Check the four that are most important to you and the four that are least important to you.

	MOST	LEAST
The chance to be with a growing company.	_____	_____
The company's liberal pension policies.	_____	_____
The chance to learn through experience.	_____	_____
The opportunity to be promoted.	_____	_____
The opportunity to sell.	_____	_____
The company's reputation.	_____	_____
The profit-sharing program.	_____	_____
Freedom from routine.	_____	_____
Job security.	_____	_____
The opportunity to travel.	_____	_____

What do you consider your most important accomplishment?

What has been your most serious disappointment?

Describe your most competitive situation and the steps you took to achieve success.

What do you consider to be your three most important assets?

In what three areas would you most like to improve?

Are you willing to travel? To relocate?

When can you start work?

S A M P L E   C O V E R   L E T T E R   N O.   1

Melanie McFadden
9 Circle Street
Columbus, Ohio 43216
(614) 555-1234

April 10, 1999

Mr. James Ward
Director of Operations
Database International
5510 Mainway Drive
Los Angeles, CA 90086

Dear Mr. Ward:

I am a senior majoring in computer science and information processing at the University of Florida

I have followed the success of Database International. You are recognized nationally as a leader in the industry and have a reputation for providing exceptional ongoing training programs for your junior programmers.

Enclosed is my résumé outlining my academic, extracurricular, and work experience of the past four years.

If you would like to call me to set up a personal interview, I can be reached at (614) 555-1234. If I don't hear from you by April 29, I'll call you.

Thank you for your consideration. I look forward to hearing from you soon.

Sincerely,

Melanie McFadden

SAMPLE COVER LETTER NO. 2

Sandra Magioco
9 College Road
Baltimore, Maryland 21203
(410) 555-1776

February 5, 1999

Ms. Margaret Jimenez
XYZ Department Store
9 Fashion Street
New York, NY 11351

Dear Ms. Jimenez:

I was recently speaking with Joanne Stewart, a manager with your store. Because she is familiar with my work, she strongly advised me to send a copy of my résumé to your office regarding the opening as an assistant buyer in your sportswear department.

I feel confident that after reviewing my résumé, you will see that I am a worthy candidate. Besides having a strong background in sales, I have worked closely with buyers for many years. Not only do I have skill in fashion display, customer service, and managing employees, I understand the demands of the retail fashion industry as a whole.

The opportunity to work with you is appealing. I look forward to your response and hope we can meet soon to discuss my résumé and work history further. Thank you for your time and consideration.

Sincerely,

Sandra Magioco

S A M P L E   R É S U M É   N O.   1

Jennifer Andersen
4332 Rookwood Street
Cleveland, Ohio 44101
(216) 555-3452

JOB OBJECTIVE:
Position as programmer with supervisory responsibilities.

EDUCATION:
- B.A., University of Florida, 1999. Computer science/information processing major; liberal arts minor. GPA: 3.4.
- Junior semester abroad in Florence, Italy. Studied history, art, music, Renaissance literature, and Italian.
- Rotary scholarship finalist, May 1998. Alternate for one year of study in Fyfe, Scotland.

WORK EXPERIENCE:
- Anderson, Inc., 1999 to present.
  Created computer programs using Java for privately owned company in Cleveland.
- Tutor Computer Science Center, University of Florida, 1998–1999.
  Tutored freshman and sophomore students in math and computer science.
- Borrans Corporation, Columbus, Ohio; summer intern, 1996–1998.
  Programmer and operations trainee, responsible for training new employees and experienced employees in need of additional instruction.

ACTIVITIES/HONORS:
- Vice President, College Democrats, 1997–1998. Recruited students to participate in city, state, and local political campaigns.
- Treasurer, Campus Achievers: 1996–1998. Honorary student service society.
- President, Student Union Activities Board, 1996–1997. Coordinated activities from Parents' Day to spring break vacations.

References available upon request.

S A M P L E   R É S U M É   N O.   2

GEORGE RAPPAPORT
154 West 78th Street
New York, New York 100019
(212) 555-0030

JOB OBJECTIVE:
Entry-level accounting position with medium-to large-sized public accounting firm.

EDUCATION:
Bachelor of Science in Accounting with English minor, University of Maryland, 1999. GPA: 3.6.
- Dean's List, six semesters.
- Junior semester in Mexico City, Mexico. Studied Spanish and Mexican heritage while living with a Mexican family.

WORK EXPERIENCE:
- Internal Auditor, 1997 to 1999, HealthCare Insurance Agency, Baltimore, Maryland.
  Managed nine corporate accounts. Responsible for training and supervising staff of twelve.
- Summer Intern, 1998, Kenase Accountants.
  Experienced work in a small accounting firm firsthand. Managed four of the company's ten largest accounts as well as eighteen long-term clients.
- Summer Intern, 1997, Business Management Legal Associates.
  Performed legal accounting and tax preparation for partners and associates.

ACTIVITIES:
- Volunteer, Big Brother program, 1997–1999. Coached and served as "big brother" to two underprivileged teenagers.
- President, Blue Key (national senior honorary society), 1999.
- Scholarship Chairperson, Phi Kappa Psi Fraternity.

References available upon request.

S A M P L E   R É S U M É   N O.   3

GRETL PAHNNE
11 North Oracle Circle
Santa Barbara, CA. 93103
(805) 555-9000

EDUCATION:
• University of California, Santa Barbara—Bachelor of Arts in Oral History, May 1999.

MAJOR COURSEWORK:
• Rhetoric, Religious Theory, PASCAL Programming, Political Science in the Modern Age, Squash.

EXPERIENCE:
Tutor
• Dual Discovery Center, 800 Sproul Plaza, UCSB, Santa Barbara. Tutored socially disadvantaged high school students in various academic disciplines, with an emphasis on algebra and geometry.

Sales Associate
• The May Company, 1000 Maypole Lane, Primavera, CA. Marketed state-of-the-art organic disinfectants. Involved in all aspects of business, including cash and credit transactions, daily book- and record-keeping, and inventory.

Political Assistant
• Assistant to Representative Boris Bear, 8 Beach Front Bonanza Boulevard, Bora Bora, CA. Performed administrative tasks, including word processing, maintaining headquarter files, and telephoning constituents. Assisted with door-to-door survey in reelection campaign; coordinated neighborhood voter registration drive.

Volunteer Work
• Advisor, Big Sister program, Santa Barbara. Planned recreational activities for three inner-city teens.
• Pollster, Campaign to Re-elect Jerry Brown. Worked at midtown Los Angeles headquarters on voter survey phone bank. Solicited voter preferences through assertive phone skills.

PERSONAL:
• Captain, UCSB Varsity Squash Team; UCSB Humanitarian Award (1998).

References available upon request.

SAMPLE THANK-YOU NOTE NO. 1

John Rhies
2001 Northshore Drive
Detroit, MI 48231

February 25, 1999

Mr. Mark Nordbrach
Manager, Personnel Department
Wesley Manufacturing, Inc.
500 Sylvan Avenue
Redwood City, CA 94063

Dear Mr. Nordbrach:

I appreciate your taking the time to talk with me about entry-level management positions at Wesley.

I am especially interested in spending a day in the field with one of your division managers. I am anxious to see the workings of the job you discussed—in progress.

If I don't hear from you by the end of the week, I'll call you on Monday morning, March 8.

Again, thanks for your time and consideration.

Sincerely,

John Rhies

S A M P L E   T H A N K - Y O U   N O T E
N O.   2

3000 Sutro Boulevard
San Francisco, CA 94143

April 8, 1999

Ms. Alison McCormack
National Recruiter
ABC Paper Products
9 Ellwood Avenue
San Francisco, CA 94142

Dear Ms. McCormack:

Thank you for taking the time to discuss with me the position of product manager with ABC Paper Products.

Though we didn't have a chance to discuss my part-time job, I believe it qualifies me for the position even more than my summer internships. Working ten hours a week over three years for the Reynolds Advertising Agency as a clerk gave me firsthand experience with designers and production people. I was able to learn over an extended period the long-term ramifications of the wrong—and the right—paper decisions. This long-term view provided me with more insight than my three-month summer internship.

If I don't hear from you within the next week, I'll call you on Monday, April 19. I'm keenly interested in the position and the company.

Again, thanks for your time.

Sincerely,

Kevin Sullivan

12

Your Third Degree

Interviews

The worst thing you can possibly do in a deal is seem desperate to make
it. That makes the other guy smell blood and then you're dead. The best
thing you can do is deal from strength, and leverage is the best strength
you have. Leverage is having what the other guy wants. Or better yet,
needs. Or best of all, simply can't do without.
  Donald Trump, The Art of the Deal

L ike making a deal, there is a special art to interviewing," says Anne Marie
Myers, who coaches people on how to prepare for interviews.
"You have to convince the prospective employer that they need you
to work for their company. But to do that, you have to first convince your-

self." Ninety percent of the interview, Meyers says, is based on the confidence and image you project.

So what's the worst that can happen during an interview?

When asked to describe how you function under pressure, you let out a high-pealed shriek, double over in your chair, and laugh uncontrollably—so hard, in fact, that tears are rolling down your face, soiling your new suit. Unable to breathe, you gasp periodically. The recruiter, visibly frightened, buzzes the secretary at her outer alcove and asks for a box of Kleenex, which the secretary does not have and which she is asked, in an imperative panic, to *find* . . .

Or, in place of hysteria, you are stricken with amnesia.

RECRUITER:	Tell me about yourself.
YOU:	Who?
RECRUITER:	You . . . yourself. Tell me about yourself.
YOU:	I don't remember.
RECRUITER:	Well, Jim, thank you for your time. We'll be in touch.
YOU:	Jim???

If the above scenarios seem unlikely, you can relax about interviewing for your first big job. The more typical ways of fouling up during interviews—which *everybody* has, at some point, done—are far less embarrassing and much easier to correct.

Be Prepared

Sarah Greenspan's first interview is a good example of what can happen to an ace candidate who starts off unprepared. And Sarah is a crackerjack. Hardworking, outgoing, smart as a whip, athletic—generally and specifically on the ball. The kind you'd love to hate if she weren't so nice.

Sarah's first choice was Xerox. Their corporate headquarters was located on the East Coast, near her hometown. The company philosophy was one she admired, and the starting salary for sales reps was very attractive indeed. Sarah was, in a word, psyched.

But, as you may have guessed, psyched was not enough. The problem was that Sarah was *too* psyched and *too little* prepared. Because she was uninformed, unrehearsed, and unprepared, the recruiter spent only fifteen minutes with her despite her impressive credentials—top of her class, student body vice president, and employee of the Campus Copy Center.

What do I mean by "unprepared"? Back to Sarah.

XEROX INTERVIEWER: Sarah, I'd be interested to know a little about how you've overcome defeat.

SARAH: Well, um, let me think. I tend to be pretty successful when I put my mind to something. Um, I guess there was the time I was running for homecoming queen. I lost. And I mean, I was really busy, it was my junior year, I was student body vice president, I was working part-time at the Campus Copy Center (we had *Xerox* machines, by the way), and I guess I didn't really have the time I would have liked to devote to promoting myself. I mean, I still think I could have won. But I got over it.

This was minute 7 of the interviewing process, and the clock was still ticking. By minute 14, Sarah was being thanked for her time and ushered to the door. What was wrong with Sarah's response?

First, Sarah was out of sync. She was still trying to sell her invincible being when the recruiter was specifically asking for a candid discussion of failure. She wasn't listening, a common problem of interviewees. Because she wasn't listening, the rest of her response sounded scattered and insincere. That wasn't the moment to plug Xerox—the recruiter had her résumé; he could read; he knew she'd worked with their photocopiers and was familiar

with the product. What he was looking for was Sarah's response to defeat—*real* defeat. He wanted to see her capacity to evaluate herself, under adverse circumstances, and do something constructive.

There are two obvious lessons to learn from Sarah's mistake. The first one is this: When you are being interviewed, focus on what the interviewer is saying, then respond accordingly. The second lesson is even more to the point: Prepare answers in advance to common interview questions, like the one Sarah was asked.

Back to Sarah, this time under better circumstances, in her interview with Gallo, where she was offered a job.

GALLO INTERVIEWER: How have you overcome defeat?

SARAH: Well, I very much wanted a university fellowship for a year's study abroad. I had been thinking about a career in international relations. I wanted to see Europe, and I knew I probably wouldn't have another chance to immerse myself in a foreign culture. I put all my eggs in one basket. I didn't apply for other study-abroad programs, and in April, after the second interview, I was nixed. Despite being seriously disappointed, I regrouped. I contacted the International Council on Economic Development and found out about volunteer programs in Latin America. I worked at the Campus Copy Center that summer, saving money, getting work experience, and taking my mind off what I didn't get. That fall, I immersed myself in Latin American studies and applied to the Council's volunteer program in Bolivia. I was accepted, and the following May I was off. I think now that this was the best I could have hoped for. I was able to help other people and at the same time learned self-reliance. I found out about the world, and about myself.

Notice the difference in Sarah's response. She didn't try to dodge the question or reframe it to suit her agenda. She was clear, while showing a capacity for reflection and honest self-appraisal. She also showed that she had the ability to create value from failure, which is an asset in any job situation.

Further, Sarah was able to reveal a lot about herself without blowing her own horn. From her answer, the recruiter could deduce motivation, tenacity, concern for others, and self-reliance. He could see, in short, complexity and capability from a response that used up a total of 90 seconds. He liked what he saw and made her an offer. (Sarah also received offers from Lever Brothers and Carnation.)

Let's look at another example. Alan King was extremely well qualified and well prepared for his interview with Shearson Lehman. He had researched the company and the position; he had spoken with several employees and did an excellent job of communicating his background and his career aspirations. But when the interviewer wrapped up the conversation, he said: "Alan, you have excellent credentials and I'm sure you'll be very successful when you begin your career. However, I don't think you're what we're looking for." Alan, thinking quickly on his feet, said: "If Shearson seeks employees who are quick starters, inquisitive, hardworking, dedicated, and committed to making things happen, then you should hire me. If you want an employee who won't be dissuaded by obstacles or excuses, and if you want someone who will continually lead others in finding new and creative ways to solve problems, I'm your candidate. If Shearson doesn't seek these qualities in their employees, then perhaps you're right. Perhaps I'm not what you're looking for."

The interviewer, who closes every interview with the phrase "I don't think you're what we're looking for," liked Alan because he overcame an objection with self-confidence and poise. He didn't take no for an answer. Shearson sought leaders—not complacent followers.

I routinely interview college graduates for positions as sales representatives. The more specific the applicants are about what they've done and how those experiences have affected them, the more I'm convinced they'd be valuable employees. It's not enough just to say what you've done; you also have to demonstrate that you've thought about how that experience has contributed to your personal and professional development.

To illustrate my point, I will briefly describe real interviews that I conducted with two applicants. The first applicant had all the right "canned" responses. He had obviously prepared for the interview by reading a book about interviewing, but he hadn't prepared by thinking through his responses in order to distinguish himself from all of the other applicants. He just didn't stand out from the crowd. He came across as rather ordinary and predictable. He also did not exude interest, enthusiasm, or confidence.

Toward the end of the interview, I gave him another chance to show some initiative: I gave him my business card and told him to call me if he had any questions about the position or about career opportunities within the company. Perhaps he could have redeemed himself if he had called later with specific questions. He could have written a follow-up note. I never heard from him again. Despite his high grades and work experience, we didn't call him back, either.

At the start of the second interview, I was skeptical because the applicant was a graduate of Yale. (I'm not a Yale grad.) This was an outrageous prejudice, I realize. But it's a good example of a mind-set, which you will undoubtedly encounter with some interviewers in one form or another and will have to bulldoze your way past with confidence, preparedness, and authenticity.

I asked the second applicant, whose name was Ted, some of the usual questions. He responded with enthusiasm, imagination, and humor. He didn't strike me as someone who would be bored by the possibility of work. He'd played intramural sports, was involved as a class officer, had had a summer internship with clinical psychologists in the Bronx, and for two years had volunteered with the Big Brother program. He also had high aspirations. He asked about career-track opportunities and my own career path within the company, and he talked about the future he envisioned for himself. Within the first five minutes, Ted managed to throw my prejudices right out the window. I asked him what some of his lifelong career goals were. He said: "I want to go into politics in the second half of my career. I want to be President."

We hired him. His determination, his track record, and his belief in his own ability made him a winner in my book. He'll succeed because he believes he can. By the way, if he does run for President at some point, he's got a campaign manager in me.

Back to the prejudice for a moment. Perhaps you'll have to overcome a stereotype someone may have of people who did or did not attend your school, or a prejudice about the activity you did or did not join. You *will*, one of these days, have to overcome some kind of bias to get a job. Relax. Everybody else faces the same kind of situation. There were interviewers who were undoubtedly unimpressed by the fact that I had *not* gone to Oxford on a Fulbright, followed up by two years in Ethiopia with the Peace Corps, capped by a year in Paris at the Cordon Bleu, before my return stateside to pursue a career in marketing.

The trick is to be yourself. Doing so may win them over. However, if they know the real you and still aren't impressed, realize that you probably wouldn't have liked working there anyway. How could you be happy working for an organization that didn't value your personality and abilities? Instead, determine to give the interview your best shot; be direct and professional. Identifying and overcoming objections, as well as bad attitudes, is part of being a pro at the interviewing process. It's also part of being a successful team player once you're hired.

Your Interview

You've marketed yourself with your résumé and cover letter. Now comes the big sell. You'll need to describe your experience so that your interviewer knows you're prepared for the job. Rehearse for confidence. And by all means, follow up after the interview. Here are some tips:

1. Before the interview, *do some research*. Check out the organization and the position. The better prepared you are for the interview, the more confidence you will project. Talk to people who work at the company or who hold similar positions for rival firms. Go to the library and research the company. Look in the Standard and Poor's Register of Corporations or the Moody's Manual. Check *Forbes*, *Fortune, Hoovers,* or other business magazines. Look for the organization's web page on the Internet. Learn the organization's history and the current business climate. This is the type of knowledge that helps people at both ends of the interviewing see-saw. Not only will your readiness impress your interviewer, it will also help you decide whether the organization interests you. So develop questions about the company and the job ahead of time, then find the answers from your research.

2. *Rehearse.* Before your interview, rehearse answers to questions likely to be asked. Ask friends to play interviewer and give them a list of questions to ask you. When you communicate effectively, your interviewer will be convinced of your abilities beyond your "paper" credentials. If you do not have someone to help you role-play, set up mock interviews at your career services center. You may even want to record a practice interview of yourself on a video camera and then play the video to see how you did. Without sounding arrogant, become comfortable with and confident about your accomplishments. You want the interviewer to know that you are ambitious and self-assured.

Even after you've asked a friend to help you simulate an interview, continue to think and brainstorm about the really tough questions you're likely to be asked. For practice, go on all the interviews you're offered, even at companies you're not seriously considering. All the while, keep an open mind. The company you may be least interested in initially could be the very one that impresses you most.

3. *Dress for success.* Your appearance says a lot about you, so invest in one good interviewing shirt, suit, and shoes. Have your hair cut and styled. Look neat, alert, and enthusiastic. Again, you're promoting yourself, so you want to present the best "you" possible. Don't take any shortcuts.

4. *Relax.* If you've followed the first three steps, you have every reason to be confident as you walk into the interviewer's office. So relax, be yourself, and enjoy the experience.

Some Interview Tips

Now for a few tips from a combat veteran. Steve Kendall, a recruiter for Nabisco, appreciates interviewees who are animated, sincere, and forthright. "I want to see the applicant use examples to convince me of his or her qualifications and potential for success," says Steve.

"Let the interviewer set the pace," he continues. "The biggest turn-offs in job interviews are pat answers riddled with anxiety and interviewees who control the interview too abrasively in the first part of the conversation. Use the time in the last quarter of the interview to ask questions and gather information about the company."

Common Interview Questions

When Steve Kendall conducts an interview, two of his favorite questions are "Why are you interested in working for my company?" and "What are some examples of how you persuaded others to your way of thinking?" (How would you respond right now to those two questions?)

In addition, here are some of the most common questions interviewers ask college graduates. Use the sample answers as a starting point for figuring out answers of your own.

- *"Why should we hire you?"* (Worst possible response: "Because.")

    This is a springboard from which to list the qualities that will make you a great employee. Be brief in giving your reasons, and use specific examples to illustrate your points:

    > I'm conscientious, tireless, and committed to going above and beyond what is expected of me. Last summer, as an intern with the New York Stock Exchange, I was always the first one in to work and the last one to leave at night. I made several excellent acquaintances, including the president of Merrill Lynch, who offered me a part-time job during the school year.

- *"Tell me about your education."* (Worst possible response: "It's over.")

    This question is meant to find out how much emphasis you've put on your academic education. If you've made good or great grades, terrific. If you haven't, explain why: you worked twenty-five hours a week; supported yourself and your foster family of five completely; took eighteen units each semester; got your pilot's license; and so on. If you've learned a lot by taking rigorous courses from demanding teachers, say so, but only if it's true. Never fudge in an interview. In addition to being unethical, padding your own story in an interview is painfully obvious to people who recruit for a living.

Although my GPA is 3.2, I've made 4.0 for the last two academic years. I took serious classes, looked to my professors as mentors, and truly challenged myself. I'm proud of what I've learned during college.

- *"Tell me something about yourself."* (Worst possible answer: "Taurus, Cancer rising, Moon in Sagittarius.")

  Like the first question, this is an open-ended query. Your interviewer is interested in seeing what you choose to include in your answers. Open-ended questions reveal a lot about who you are: Are you an achiever? Are you detail-oriented? Are you reliable? Are you a fast learner? Are you good at balancing several things at once? Would you have a cool head in a hot situation? What about the personal side of you? How are you perceived by others? Are you frequently available to help? Are you patient?

  Your response to one open-ended query helps answer many questions all at once. Notice how the applicant below manages to skillfully answer the question while letting her personality shine through.

  > I'm an enthusiastic, determined, and highly self-motivated person. I take a great deal of pride in being successful in work and play. I've tried hard to develop my outside interests—some of which my friends and family consider crazy. I like to skydive, spelunk [crawl around in caves], and read science fiction. I also love organizing big groups of people—for outdoor park concerts, the annual summer Renaissance Festival, canoeing trips, etc. My greatest weakness is that I have so many interests, I tend to take too much on at times.

By analyzing the responses to some of these questions, you can see how much you must "think on your feet" to answer questions in positive, concrete, and self-affirming ways. But the more responses to questions you've thought through and rehearsed, the better you'll be able to "close" your interview.

Here is an additional list of frequently asked questions for you to think about and rehearse. (You'll notice that some of these questions are similar to those in Chapter 2, on defining who you are. Compare the answers from your freshman year to the answers to your interview questions. How have you changed?)

- Tell me about a specific goal you have set and achieved, at school or at work.

- How much energy do you have? Describe a typical day and week.
- Describe any experience you have had that is relevant to this job.
- Where do you see yourself five years from now?
- Where do you see yourself ten years from now?
- What was your greatest defeat, and how did you overcome it?
- What is your greatest accomplishment?
- What do you do in your spare time?
- What is the last book you read?
- What book has had the greatest impact on you?
- What interests you most about this job?
- How would a previous employer or professor describe you?
- How would your friends describe you?
- What interests you most about this job and this organization?

How You Will Be Evaluated

There are a number of different categories in which your interviewer will evaluate you. On a scale of 1 to 5, with 1 being the lowest and 5 being the highest, rate yourself in the following areas. Then think of one or more specific examples to support your rating and write the examples down in the spaces provided below:

- *Solving Problems and Setting Priorities:* Able to understand and take action to solve even the most complex problems.

  Number rating: _____

  Example: _____

  _____

- *Achieving Goals:* Consistently sets and achieves goals; results-oriented.

  Number rating: _____

  Example: _____

  _____

- *Motivating Others:* Effective at communicating a personal point of view to others.

  Number rating: _____

  Example: _____

  _____

- *Working Well with Others:* Works well with and gains the respect of co-workers.

  Number rating: _____

  Example: _____

  _____

- *Responsibility:* Follows through on commitments made to co-workers and clients.

  Number rating: _____

  Example: _____

  _____

- *Tenacity:* Determined to work well through even the most mundane parts of the job.

  Number rating: _____

  Example: _____

  _____

- *Detail-oriented:* Pays attention to even the smallest details while keeping the larger goals in focus.

Number rating: _____

Example: _____

_____

- *Vision:* Envisions a mission beyond the immediate game plan; can see all the way to the championship.

Number rating: _____

Example: _____

_____

- *Resilience:* Bounces back from defeat. Treats setbacks as stepping stones. Explores other avenues despite the difficult nature of the situation. Consistently tests new ideas.

Number rating: _____

Example: _____

_____

Other Criteria

Basically, most companies will evaluate you as Excellent, Good, Fair, or Weak on four points. They are:

1. *Personal qualities:* How do you come across? Are you strongly motivated or sluggish? Are you energetic or lazy? Do you have long-term goals or are you aimless? Are you articulate or shy? Friendly or boorish?
2. *Professional qualities:* Are you reliable? Are you honest? Can you inspire others? Are you able to juggle a number of projects at once? Are you decisive? Do you follow through?
3. *Accomplishments:* Can you describe your proudest achievements? What have they taught you? How have you grown from the challenges you've faced?
4. *Potential:* Do you consider the long term? Do you place high value on

continuing your education and building new skills? Will you be a good investment for the company? Do you show signs of long-term interest in the industry, or will you be off to business school in one year?

These are the kinds of questions interviewers have in mind when they sit down with you. You will find favor in their eyes if you can answer their questions with clarity.

A Match Made in Heaven

The interview process is designed to make sure that the applicant and the organization are a good match. Therefore, as you diligently rehearse answers to an interviewer's questions, don't forget to prepare questions of your own. The answers you receive will help you confirm whether or not the organization you're considering is the right one for you. To help you determine this, here is a list of questions you'll probably want to ask:

- *Job training:* What will be the job training procedure for my position?
- *Learning opportunities:* Does your organization provide an employee development program or other kinds of learning opportunities?
- *Advancement:* What is the opportunity for advancement for someone who not only does his or her job, but goes beyond that?
- *Reporting structure:* What is the reporting structure for this position?
- *Facilities:* May I have a tour of your facilities, especially the area that this position occupies?

If you have other concerns or questions you want answered, by all means voice them during the interview. One word of caution, however. Inquiries about the number of vacation days, the medical benefits, the pension plan, and other nitty-gritty items should be saved until later. These issues are typically discussed when you are close to being offered the job, which rarely happens in a first interview. Although you have every right to know these things before you make a final decision to accept or reject the job, there's no reason to bring them up prematurely. Doing so will make it seem as if your primary concern is money and benefits, rather than making sure that your qualifications fit their needs. (The chapter that follows will discuss how to initiate a conversation about your employee package and how to negotiate a salary.)

Your career services office is likely to have a number of books and videos on how to research companies and how to interview effectively. The career services office will also have information on companies that come to interview on campus. For example, most companies will give the career services office large notebooks describing the history of the company and the various positions available. Again, make sure that the company will be a good match for you, and vice versa. Many career offices also link company home pages to their Web sites. You can make sure that a company will be a good match for you only if you have sufficient information. Get it. It will allow you to be savvy and well-informed in your interviews.

Handling Rejection

At some point during the interviewing process, you'll have to deal with rejection. One way to handle it constructively is to call the employer and dis-

cuss the reasons you didn't get the job. What you learn from this discussion may help you in future interviews.

Another constructive means for handling rejection is to keep a positive attitude. Keep reminding yourself: "I will find a job." Commit yourself to that end. Believe in your capabilities and overcome all objections.

It was hard for Chris Nelson, who majored in economics. After graduate school, he searched for three years for a good banking job. He kept his head up, realizing that the perfect job was "just around the corner." Finally, he landed a job with First Boston. If you are talented and work hard, he says, the only other quality you'll need is perseverance.

Some Final Points

No matter how the interview goes, be sure to send a thank-you note. You never know what's going on behind the scenes. The company's first choice may turn down the offer, or the person who was hired may not work out a month down the road. In that case, your last piece of correspondence may tip the scales your way. Always be ready for the unexpected. Eventually you'll succeed.

13

You're Hired!

How to Land the Job

> The true objective is to take chaos as given and learn to thrive on it.
> *Tom Peters,* Thriving on Chaos

You did not laugh uncontrollably during any of your interviews. You did not misplace your identity. You were confident and authentic. We're talking home run.

Now come a few very important details. After each interview, write a thank-you note and then wait two weeks. If you still haven't heard from the company, call the interviewer to see if you're still under consideration. If so, request an appointment to see them again. If they don't grant you a second interview, ask nicely for the time frame on the decision process.

Do They Want You?

At this point, you'll have some indication of whether you're in or out. If you're still in, one or more of the following things could happen:

1. *You spend a day in the office or in the field* to get a feeling for the job first-hand. If the interviewer doesn't propose this, request it. Seeing where you will spend a significant portion of your waking hours will help you further discern whether this job is really for you. Be observant and try to get a "feel" for the work atmosphere. Do the employees seem enthusiastic and friendly? Is the work environment safe, healthy, and pleasant? Checking this out before you accept the position could mean the difference between a job you like and a job you hate.

2. *You're invited to dinner or lunch* so the prospective employer can observe you in a social setting. Two quick tips: don't order alcohol, and avoid smoking if they don't. Also, plan ahead how you want to come across. Are you friendly or abrasive? Are you well-mannered or boorish? Do you spill your drink on your future boss's white divan? Do you listen to others, or do you dominate conversations? Be sure to exhibit your star qualities of enthusiasm and graciousness.

3. *You could meet again with the interviewer,* in which case you will probably be introduced to others in the company. Meeting employees is a golden opportunity to learn more about the organization, even if all you have the chance to do is observe. Don't count on the recruiter alone to provide you with a composite picture of the company.

4. *You're flown to the home office.* This is optimal, since it's in your best interest to know the philosophy and daily workings of the company. You will be introduced to lots of different people. Hold fast to your energy! You need to be as sharp and enthusiastic in your final introduction as you were with your first one. (After it's over, you will be able to wilt and take a much-needed break.)

5. *You take a series of tests*—analytical, verbal, logical, etc.—during your continued interview process. You may also be requested to complete a personality inventory.

These extra steps vary from company to company. The bottom line, however, is to remain poised, inquisitive, and attentive. Act as though you want the job—even if you haven't decided. After each interview, send an additional follow-up letter or note.

Do You Want Them?

Once you've finished the second interview and talked with your "contacts," you will probably know if the job is right for you. If it's your only job offer, you may have to take it. That's okay. Give the job your very best shot. In the process, you may grow to like it more than you thought you would. If not, there's nothing to stop you from seeking out other positions.

Once you've decided that you want the job, you will need to find out about the *employee package*, such as salary range and benefits. As stated in the previous chapter, you need to use discretion about when to discuss these matters. Usually, the interviewer will bring up the employee package during the second interview. If not, you can open the conversation yourself in this way: "I am wondering about the salary range and benefits. Is it all right if we talk about this now, or will this be covered another time?"

Here is a list of what you'll need to know:

- What is the starting salary?
- Is there a bonus?
- Will you have the use of a company car?
- Is travel involved? If so, how much?
- What are the projected timetables for promotion?
- Is the job a "career track" position?
- Does the benefit program include medical and dental benefits?
- Is there a profit-sharing program?

- Is there a retirement plan?
- Is there a tuition-reimbursement program?
- Does the company cover travel and moving expenses?
- What kind of formal training will you receive?
- When can you start?

If you have several job offers, list the pros and cons of the company in which you're most interested. Here's an example:

ACME COMPANY EVALUATION SHEET

Pros	*Cons*
Company car	Relocation necessary
Bonus and salary	Too much travel
Interesting job	Will need to work overtime
Growth potential	Solitary job
Fortune 500 company	No formal training
Great co-workers	Six-month probation period

As I mentioned earlier, you'll meet more and more people as you progress through the interview process. Keeping up with so many names and faces can get confusing. To help you remember the important details, I suggest that you take notes. As soon as the introductions are over, and while the names are still fresh in your mind, write down what you want to remember about the people you've met. Below is a sample for you to follow.

People I've Met at the Company So Far

NAME	DATE MET	WHAT I NEED TO REMEMBER ABOUT HIM/HER

Here's what your notes might include:

Henry Jones	*2/16/99*	*Vice President of Operations; plays golf; 4-year-old daughter takes karate lessons.*

Here's space for you to jot down the real thing.

1. _____ _____ _____

_____

You're Hired!

2. _____ _____ _____

_____

3. _____ _____ _____

_____

4. _____ _____ _____

_____

5. _____ _____ _____

_____

6. _____ _____ _____

_____

7. _____ _____ _____

_____

8. _____ _____ _____

_____

9. _____ _____ _____

_____

10. _____ _____ _____

_____

Poising Yourself for an Offer

After you have all of the answers to your questions, ask your interviewers if they have any more questions for you. If they do, answer them. If not, state that from what you have heard and all the information you've gathered, you would very much like to work for them. Personalize your closing conversation. Tell them what has impressed you about their company, and be specific. Recount examples from the past few weeks or months that have led you to your conclusions. When you are finished, pause for a moment so that the interviewer has an opportunity to provide input. If the interviewer's comments seem vague and no job offer is forthcoming, then ask plainly, "What happens next?"

As the final stage of the interview process draws to a close, the interviewer may ask if you've interviewed with any other firms. Be honest, but be on your guard. Even if you're not interested in the other companies, don't let them know that. You want to hold on to your bargaining power. If they think that they're the only company you are interested in or that is interested in you, they may make you a low offer.

If you're offered the position on the spot, *don't* accept. Tell the company you need some time to think it over, but make a commitment to call back with your answer. Then review the list of pros and cons with your mentors, supervisors from your college jobs, professors, friends, parents, or other family members, such as your spouse or partner.

Negotiating Salary

"When I accepted my first job out of college with the accounting firm of Touche Ross, I had two other offers from well-respected firms," says Donald Mason, who now works in Dallas for a private firm. "Because Touche Ross knew I was attractive to several employers, they offered me more money to start than the typical college grad."

In your first job out of college, you don't have tremendous bargaining power, but you do have some. So use it.

Employers never offer their highest or even their middle-range salary. They start low because they expect to negotiate with you. Push for a higher salary. Point out that you're more experienced than most people who have been out of college for two or three years because you gained four years of real-world work experience during college. You're much more qualified and promising than the average college grad.

Don't push so hard that you alienate your new boss. But if you get $2,000 over the initial offer, terrific. If you haven't done anything in college to prove that you are better qualified than the rest of the pack of applicants, take what you're offered. On the job you can prove that you're worth the best raises.

Accepting the Offer

When you accept an offer, do it gracefully. After you've ironed out the salary issue, accept with a positive, reaffirming statement, such as "I'm very pleased to be a part of your company."

This is your first official chance to bond with your new manager. You may want to take the initiative at the outset and ask about goals for your first year on the job. What defines minimum requirements? What sort of performance exceeds requirements? What do you have to do to be outstanding in your first year? Together, you and your manager may want to put some specific goals on paper so that you have something to refer to throughout the year. At salary-review time, you will have something concrete with which to gauge your work, a contract of sorts between you and your manager.

Tying Up Loose Ends

Write thank-you letters to the companies you turned down. Thank them for their time. You may want to call those who gave you special attention. Expressing these kinds of courtesies leaves all doors open for the future.

You might also write thank-you notes to those who turned you down. You'll probably be qualified to work for them in the future. Maintain a favorable impression in their minds.

When to Start

When should you start? That depends on how you're planning to celebrate finishing off college. If you've been waiting to backpack through Indonesia with your suitemates and have slept with a map of the South Seas above your pillow for three years running, don't forsake that for a briefcase and suit. The briefcase will be there when you get back, and student loans don't come due until nine months after graduation. Take the time while you've got it. If, on the other hand, you can't wait to close in on that corner office, go for it. The job is yours. You can still see the world in two-week intervals during your paid vacations.

Other Incidentals

You'll have to fill out insurance and benefit forms. You may also have some training, either "soft" or formal. Even if you are hurried right into your job with the minimum of instruction, don't worry. Ask questions. Solicit advice. Work hard. Learn all you can.

Starting your new job may scare you as much as starting college. Be patient with yourself. This period of adjustment will be easier and shorter than those of your peers who are less prepared for the real world. In the meantime, keep using all the techniques you learned in your internships and other jobs. Within about six months, you should feel like an ace who's been with the organization for years!

14

Outlooks and Insights

Succeeding on the Job and in Life

It is as though I had lost my way and asked someone the way home. He says he will show me and walks with me along a smoother path which suddenly stops. And now my friend tells me: "All you have to do now is find your way home from here."
Ludwig Wittgenstein, Culture and Value

I went to the woods because I wished . . . to front only the essential facts of life, and see if I could not learn what it had to teach, and not, when I came to die, discover that I had not lived.
Henry David Thoreau, Walden

No matter what your first job after college happens to be, it marks a new beginning. It also marks a point of departure. If you started with the company and the job of your dreams, great. Your job right out of college might also be less than terrific. But you have to start somewhere, building your skills, meeting people, and developing good work habits. That's a positive, exciting challenge.

You may go through any number of changes at the outset of your career: from your new job to a string of promotions, to a better job with another company, to a smaller company, back to school, or even to begin your own company. Your first job, however, is like a blank page. You fill it in as you go. And your possibilities are limitless as long as you pursue them.

Games People Play

In the working world, people measure personal success by all kinds of things—how much money they make, what their job is, how many people they know, how many dates they have, what kind of clothes they wear, what kind of car they drive, and how they balance career and family responsibilities.

Many of these things have to do with *appearances*, not *reality*. They reflect what people want others to think, not necessarily who they really are. Know the difference between the two and be true to yourself and your values. The best job in the world isn't worth much if you are not happy. Similarly, no amount of money or possessions will make you any more satisfied with yourself if you aren't already content with who you are.

This book is about defining those things that are important to *you*, and you alone. So resist comparing yourself to those around you. That's a game you'll never win. There will always be people who are better off and people who are worse off than you. In college and in life, it's important to do what you believe is important and what you feel is right.

People may not always agree with you, especially if they are threatened by your abilities. The going will often seem hard. That's okay. Preserve your integrity and don't let anyone get the better of you. Your satisfaction will come from knowing that you took the high road.

President John F. Kennedy said it best in his 1961 inaugural address:

> For of those to whom much is given, much is required. And when at some future date the high court of history sits in judgment on each of us, recording whether in our brief span of service we fulfilled our responsibilities to the state, our success or failure, in whatever office we hold, will be measured by four questions: First, were we truly people of courage? . . . Second were we truly people of integrity? . . . Third, were we truly people of judgment? . . . Finally, were we truly people of dedication?

Character and Ethics

You are working very hard to prepare yourself for a rewarding career. You are diligently studying, you are accomplishing goals, and you are honing your people skills. Without a doubt, the time and energy you're spending to develop these qualities will not be in vain. However, of all the qualities you will need to succeed, one of the most easily overlooked is *character*.

By character, I don't mean your personality type. You could have an open, endearing, and charming personality, or a closed and not very fluid personality, but still have a lot of character. Some of the best leaders in their fields are introverts.

What I do mean by character is the ability to be *ethical*. Although ethics is somewhat hard to define, it's a human quality that's easy to spot. Usually ethics is marked by a concern for other individuals. Ethical people consistently exhibit a willingness to live up to the commitments they make, and they don't shrink from considering how their decisions affect those around them.

In your job, you'll face decisions that are difficult to make. When the answers aren't obvious, you can always seek wisdom by asking yourself the following questions: Would others approve of my behavior if they knew about it? Would I want someone else to behave similarly? Is what I'm doing right for the organization? Is what the company doing right? If not, how will I handle it? What are my own personal standards, and how do I define them?

Here's a prime example of ethics at work. In journalism, the unwritten but accepted rule for quoting someone is that if the person says something to you but then adds, "Don't print that" *after* the statement was already made, then you are allowed to print it. But several journalists I've talked to said they would not print the quote if it was made by a "civilian," meaning a nonpolitician or anyone unfamiliar with the rules of the press. The reason? Plain fairness. That's the cornerstone of ethics. Begin thinking now about your moral views, especially as they relate to work. Particularly if you aspire to be a leader, character is crucial.

Taking Risks

After graduate school, Bob Kinstle took a job with a consulting firm in Virginia. The company's main business was with defense contracts, but the group's charter was to develop computer information systems for the commercial market.

One of his first assignments was to manage a project for a large bank in New York City. Over the next several months, the project team grew in size as he designed and implemented the system. At the end of the first year, the project began to wrap up, and the number of people assigned to it dwindled until there was just Bob. The company began to doubt its desire to penetrate the commercial market and prepared to abandon all future work with the bank. Bob, however, was certain that there was much more work to be done.

"I began to consider leaving the company and pursuing the bank as an independent contractor. The choice was difficult. I had a 'promising career' with the company—I was the youngest associate manager, having been promoted to that level faster than anyone else in the company's history. Yet I longed for the freedom to set my own work schedule—to be my own boss," explained Bob.

"There really was no way to know the consequences of leaving the company. Would they accuse me of stealing their client? Would the bank be willing to work with an independent consultant located in Virginia? What if the project really was over and no further work emerged? Could I find other contracts?

"After weighing the risks, I decided to make the change. I resigned from my position and notified the bank that I would be interested in continuing business with them. Largely because of the relationships I had developed over the previous year, the bank agreed to give me a small enhancement project related to our original work.

"This small project has grown over the ten years I have been a consultant for the bank. My office is located in my home. I connect to the bank's computers via modem. Trips to New York continue, although the frequency has decreased. The bank is satisfied, knowing that they can contact me twenty-four hours a day, seven days a week. And I am happy feeling free to pursue contracts that interest me, setting my own schedule for work and designing systems that reflect my personality and preferences."

Pam Zemper has also experienced the advantages of risk-taking. She believes her professional growth came when she began taking risks that brought about positive results for her company. If you know yourself, your strengths and weaknesses, and you have learned to think critically, you will be able to make decisions that fulfill your dreams. Taking calculated risks can mean the difference between an outstanding career and an average one, between a zestful life and an ordinary one.

Throughout this book, I have encouraged you to

- Apply yourself academically
- Gain work experience, both through part-time jobs and through internships
- Keep active in extracurricular activities

By following my suggestions, you should develop the inner resources to make these same kinds of critical career decisions when opportunities arise. Like Bob and Pam, you will be equipped to take risks that will lead you down a career path you'll love.

"All of us reach points in our lives when we can 'play it safe' or walk into the unknown," says Bob Kinstle. "I'm not advising recklessness; however, after you've weighed the risks and rewards, you may still need to take a leap of faith to begin a new path."

Calling It Quits When It's Time for a Change

At some point in your career, you will leave your job for another one. When the time comes for you to hand in your resignation letter, you'll want to make sure that you leave on good terms. Career coach Joyce Lain Kennedy advises: "At any job level, act like a manager and resign gracefully. Don't burn bridges when you quit your job."

The reasons for leaving on good terms are evident. Making enemies could come back to haunt you in the form of poor references or a tainted industry reputation years later. To avoid these pitfalls, Kennedy offers some tips to help you bow out in style:

- *Avoid quitters' remorse.* Be sure that you really want to leave your present job.
- *Get the new offer in writing.* Make certain of your ground with the new organization before announcing your departure.
- *Write a cordial resignation letter.* Always give at least two weeks' notice, or whatever length of time your company requires. Never risk negative language in your letter. Simply note your new position and employer and the date you'll be leaving.
- *Meet with your boss.* Workplace courtesy requires that you let your boss know you are leaving before you tell your co-workers, so set up a time to meet with him or her in private. Also, offer to help train your successor or otherwise ease the transition.
- *Don't boast.* Bragging about your higher new pay could create discontent in the workplace.
- *Don't bad-mouth the company or its employees.* Although you may have reason to complain, negative comments will get you nowhere. When pressed for the reason for your departure, simply point out that your new job is too good to pass up, which should be true.

Being Happy

It takes a strong commitment and hard work to maintain a healthy balance on the job and off. Being happy won't just happen. Like anything else, you have to work at it.

Once you've landed your job, take pride in what you do. Have concrete objectives that will guide and direct you. Concentrate not just on job success but on overall happiness. If there is any one point I want to make in this chapter, it's the importance of striking a balance between your personal life and your professional one. Remember, your job is only one aspect of your life.

Kenneth Olsen, former CEO of Digital Equipment Corporation, knows all about making things happen on the job and off. In a graduation speech to students at his alma mater, MIT, Olsen reflected on his thirty years of work since graduating from college: "Running a business is not the important thing. Making a commitment to do a good job, to improve things, to influence the world is where it's at. I would also suggest that one of the most satisfying things is to help others to be creative and take responsibility. These are the important things."

"Your most precious commodity is not material," says Charles S. Sanford, Jr., CEO of Bankers Trust New York Corporation. "It is and always will be your time." If you keep work in balance with other things in your life, Sanford advises, you can accomplish even more on the job. "Read a little poetry, enjoy friends, and most of all, don't take yourself too seriously. In the final analysis, whatever you have accomplished won't be worth much unless you've had fun."

Okay, so the cynic in you cries: How much time did these CEO's spend working in their twenties and thirties? Good point. They probably spent a lot of time, but were they happy? How did all that time at the office affect their families? Also, you have to ask yourself, "Do I want to be a CEO?" Some people would say "No thanks." I traded in the corporate life to run a small business that is part of a large corporation. That was right for me and my life goals. You have to carefully weigh the trade-offs of your long-term goals with what you are doing—and enjoying—in the short term. Most of the working population thrives quite happily in intermediate positions between entry level and the top of the heap. They find a balance between work they enjoy and spending time with their friends and family.

Maybe you won't have all the money in the world, but you will have time to enjoy those things that count the most when you're ninety—a job you liked, a lifestyle you enjoyed, and the opportunity to contribute to your own growth as well as to that of others.

Thoughts for the Journey

I began this book with a personal anecdote, so I'd like to end with one. It has to do with becoming discouraged. And it is a story without which this book truly would have no closure.

About three months before I finished the manuscript for this book, I was exhausted. My job was quite tedious—not because the work itself had changed, but because my approach to it had shifted. I had little time to see my friends, and at night I just wanted to go to sleep early. Boring. In short, I was doing all those things I have said throughout my book never to do. Realizing that I wasn't being myself, and knowing for a fact that I wasn't having a good time, I decided to take a break to get back the perspective I knew was missing.

Egypt was the place for perspective. Why Egypt? It was exotic, distant, and vastly different from life as I knew it. Also, one of my interests is travel, and after spending part of my junior year in Spain, I made a personal promise to visit as many countries as I could. So off I went for the first time on a vacation by myself, leaving my "normal" life and my work behind me.

When I saw the age-old pyramids at dusk, renewed energy and inspiration filled me. The pyramids symbolize balance, perfection, human achievement, and teamwork. Seeing the achievements of an ancient culture that have survived for thousands of years left me with a feeling of great awe and real humility. I wondered how many monuments from America's civilization would survive four hundred years, let alone four thousand.

Clearly, the Egyptians saw no limits to what they could accomplish. They saw things not in terms of what they were in the moment, but of what they could become in time. They looked to the possibility instead of the limitation. They made dreams into realities.

"Well, bully for Tut," you say, "but what has this got to do with college and careers and human potential?" The answer is that the pyramids helped me recover my "edge"—my own potential. The tensions loosened up inside of me, and confidence took over.

My perspective restored, I was free to concentrate on challenges—including work, the book, and my personal life—with confidence and energy.

Throughout your life, the inspirations that motivate you will ebb and flow. You won't always feel inspired, and you won't always perform at peak. The important thing to remember when you reach an impasse is not to panic. Remove yourself from the ordinary—through reading *Don Quixote* or going to a concert or an exhibit or taking a day trip by yourself. Maybe your most relaxing time is spent watching a football game or a weekly sitcom. That's fine. Just allow yourself time to unwind and replenish your own central energy source.

David Glenn, a division manager for Chevron for thirty years, reflects: "Live in the now—in the moment. It is easy to get so focused on a goal or destination that you forget to enjoy the journey. Every day in our jobs and families we are challenged to be, for the moment, with someone rather than too busy. Perhaps one of the benefits of becoming established is that we can enjoy the journey more."

The Blue Sky Ahead

You have a lot to be proud of. If you are reading this book for the first time as a freshman, you get credit for getting this far and for committing yourself to making college and your career pursuit everything it can be. Good for you.

If you are reviewing this chapter for the last time and you have a job lined up and are wondering how four years could have come and gone so fast, take time to pat yourself on the back. Look down from where you are now, realize how far you've come, and be proud of your accomplishments. The next peak you scale—your first job—is very similar to the challenges you've had the last few years. Accept the new challenges that are before you. And in addition to doing a good or great job, give to the world something of what it has given to you—through your family, your friends, your activities, and your actions. Don't be typical. You are unique. Show the world the special gifts and contributions that only you have to offer.

And so, here's to your unique success story. Here's to the ability you have to dream the dream and make it real. Go change the world! Good-bye and good luck.

Afterword

A few things have changed since I wrote the first edition of this book. After its publication, I spent over six years as a director of marketing. During that time, I managed a staff of over twenty and learned firsthand about people, their motivations and character—what they are really made of and how they act when the going gets rough.

Over a year ago, I left New York and moved to Denver, Colorado. I run a small business within the larger company for which I have worked for fifteen years. I am an anomaly in today's business environment, since I have been with the same company since I graduated from college. I am fortunate that my company has allowed me to custom-create my job, which is based on my abilities, interests, and performance. It is equally fortunate that I am able to live in my location of choice. I still take hiring people very seriously, because it is the most important decision any manager can make. It is the manager's perspective I now have that I would like to share with you as you continue to refine and improve your knowledge base and life-long skills.

What Do Employers Look For in People They Hire?

In addition to the obvious qualities of teamwork, leadership, communication skills, problem-solving abilities, and technological aptitude, there are some not-so-obvious qualities that, if cultivated, will allow you to have tremendous advantages in the world of work, and possibly in your personal life as well.

- *Knowledge.* More than any other ability, your capacity to learn, to grow, to ride the rapids of change and actually enjoy the chaos, will be one of the greatest indicators of your long-term employability and promotability.
- *Commitment.* While people may have a number of jobs throughout their careers, the rule of thumb for accepting any job is giving it a two-year commitment. If you leave before that, you will have a red flag on your résumé about your stability and your ability to keep your word.
- *Ability to adapt to change.* Realize that change is constant. There is a balance between being able to keep your word and job commitments and being prepared for two to three other jobs should your current job end unexpectedly. If your company is bought or downsized and has a series of layoffs, you will have a backup plan. While I have been with the same company for years, I have always kept backup game plans. This has made me more confident in my current job, while providing me with a type of mental insurance against the unknown.
- *Ability to differentiate yourself.* People who stand out the most have a passion for their work. They don't take any job for granted. They apply themselves to their current job while keeping in mind the next step they are striving to reach. They have a positive attitude, and they ask themselves what they could bring to the job that is special and different from what anyone else could offer. Being able to answer this question for yourself is essential to any job you will ever hold.
- *Courage.* Employees who are courageous don't run from responsibility, nor do they lose their cool when the going gets rocky. They know that the ride will often be rocky as well as smooth and that this in-between state is where the fullness of life really is. To be truly alive is to deal with any challenges you face in an honorable, courageous way. It also means owning up to self-imposed personal setbacks so that you can learn from them and avoid continuing the same self-defeating behaviors.

Finally, another kernel of advice for you to consider: There are plenty of things that may happen in life that are painful, discouraging, and unfair. But if you can detach yourself from difficult emotions and see the whole of yourself, the whole of someone who is causing you pain, and the whole of a hard situation, then you can give thanks for your lessons and truly be in a state of grace instead of a state of resentment. Try to take stock daily of what you appreciate in yourself, in others, and in the world as a whole. It is easy to find things to complain about, but people who triumph are able to make peace with hardship and accept the whole of what life has to offer—what is real in both the positive and negative aspects of human experience.

So identify what is special that you have to offer yourself, your community, and the world. Develop those gifts and commit to them, especially in the difficult times. Your indomitable spirit will triumph and you will have the fullness of life you deserve.

Appendix 1

Companies with Summer and Winter Internships

Below is an abbreviated directory of internships updated from *Peterson's Internships 1995* and *Princeton Review's America's Top 100 Internships*. This list will give you an idea of some of the companies that offer internships. Remember, this is only a very small sampling of the companies offering internship programs. In addition to requesting more detailed information about the programs listed below, don't forget to contact businesses you are interested in that don't advertise formal internship programs. Some of them will allow you to create internships to suit your individual needs. An asterisk (*) indicates internships on the *Top 100* list.

Advertising and Public Relations

Abramson Erlich Manes
1275 K Street NW, Suite 300
Washington, DC 20005

*Backer Spielvogel Bates
The Chrysler Building
405 Lexington Avenue
New York, NY 10174
(212) 297-7000

Bozell Public Relations
75 Rockefeller Plaza, 6th Floor
New York, NY 10019

*Hill and Knowlton
420 Lexington Avenue
New York, NY 10017

*Hill, Holliday, Connors, &
   Cosmopulos Advertising, Inc.
200 Clarendon Street
Boston, MA 02116
(617) 437-1600
www.hhcc.com

*Ruder Finn, Inc.
301 East 57th Street
New York, NY 10022
(212) 593-6332
www.ruderfinn.com

*TBWA
292 Madison Avenue
New York, NY 10017

*Widmeyer Group
1875 Connecticut Avenue NW, Suite 640
Washington, DC 20009
(202) 667-0901

Business and Technology

Aetna Life and Casualty
151 Farmington Avenue, RSAA
Hartford, CT 06156

American Management Association
135 West 50th Street
New York, NY 10020
(212) 903-8021
www.amanete.org

*Arthur Anderson
33 West Monroe Street
Chicago, IL 60603
(312) 580-0069
www.arthuranderson.com/careers

*Apple Computer, Inc.
1 Infinite Loop, MS 38-3CE
Cupertino, CA 95014
(408) 996-1010 or 1-800-473-7411
www.apple.com

BMW of North America
300 Chestnut Ridge Road
Woodcliff Lake, NJ 07657-7731
(201) 307-3974
www.bmw.com

*The Boeing Company
P.O. Box 3703 MS 6H-PR
Seattle, WA 98124
(425) 965-4004

*Citibank
Summer Associate Programs
575 Lexington Avenue,
    12th Floor,
    Zone 3
New York, NY 10043
(212) 559-3580

*Coors Brewing Company
311 Tenth Street
Mail No. NH210
c/o College Recruiting Representative
Golden, CO 80401
(303) 279-6565

Federal Reserve Bank of Chicago
230 South La Salle Street
Chicago, IL 60604
(312) 322-4748

*Frito-Lay, Inc.
7701 Legacy Drive
Plano, TX 75024-4099

*Genentech, Inc.
460 Point San Bruno Boulevard
South San Francisco, CA 94080

*Hallmark Cards, Inc.
2501 McGee Trafficway
Kansas City, MO 64141-6580
(816) 274-5111

*Hewlett-Packard
SEED Program
3000 Hanover Street,
    Mail Stop 20-AC
Palo Alto, CA 94304-1181

*Intel Corporation
1900 Prairie City Road
Folsom, CA 95630
(916) 356-8080

Kimberly-Clark Corporation
2100 Winchester Road
Neenah, WI 54956

*Kraft General Foods
University Relations
Three Lakes Drive
Northfield, IL 60093

*The LEK/Alcar Consulting Group
12100 Wilshire Boulevard, Suite 1700
Los Angeles, CA 90025
(310) 442-6500

*Levi Strauss & Co.
P.O. Box 7215
San Francisco, CA 94120-6914

*Liz Claiborne, Inc.
1441 Broadway
New York, NY 10018
(212) 354-4900

*Microsoft
Attn: Recruiting Dept. CA 171-0693
One Microsoft Way
Redmond, WA 98052-6399
(425) 882-8080

*Robert Mondavi Winery
P.O. Box 106
Oakville, CA 94562
(707) 963-9611

J. P. Morgan & Co., Inc.
60 Wall Street
New York, NY 10260
(212) 648-9909
www.jpmorgan.com

Northwest Mutual Life Insurance
    Company
720 East Wisconsin Avenue
Milwaukee, WI 53202
(414) 299-1677
www.northwesternmutual.com

Pro-Found Software, Inc.
500 Frank W. Burr Boulevard, 4th Floor
Teaneck, NJ 07666
(201) 928-0400

*Raychem
M/S 111/8202
300 Constitution Drive
Menlo Park, CA 94025-1164

Rosenbluth International
2401 Walnut Street
Philadelphia, PA 19109-4390
(215) 977-4000

A. E. Schwartz and Associates
P.O. Box 79228
Waverley, MA 02479-9998
(617) 926-9111
www.a.e.schwartz.com

3M
224-1W-02
3M Center
St. Paul, MN 55144-1000
(800) 328-1343

The Titan Corporation
3033 Science Park Road
San Diego, CA 92121

*Volkswagen of America, Inc.
3800 Hamlin Road
Auburn Hills, MI 48326
(313) 340-4970

*Washington Internships for Students
  of Engineering
1899 L Street NW, Suite 500
Washington, DC 20036
(202) 466-8744

*Weyerhaeuser
IT Intern Program
WTC 1942
P.O. Box 2999
Tacoma, WA 98477-2999
(253) 924-4403

Sports-Related Fields

*National Basketball Association
Intern Coordinator
645 Fifth Avenue
New York, NY 10022
(212) 826-7000

*Nike
Internship Program
One Bowerman Drive
Beaverton, OR 97005
(503) 671-6453

PGA Tour, Inc.
112 TPC Boulevard
Pointe Verde Beach, FL 32082

*Reebok
100 Technology Center Drive
Stoughton, MA 02072
(781) 341-5000

*United States Olympic Committee
Coordinator of Educational Programs
One Olympic Plaza
Colorado Springs, CO 80909-5760
(719) 632-5551, ext. 2597

Communications—Film, Audio, Video

*Academy of Television Arts and
  Sciences
5220 Lankershim Boulevard
North Hollywood, CA 91601-3109
(818) 754-2830
www.emmys.org

Archive Films, Inc.
530 West 25th Street
New York, NY 10001

Association of Independent Video and
  Filmmakers
304 Hudson Street, 6th Floor North
New York, NY 10013
(212) 807-1400

*Bertelsmann Music Group
Alternative Marketing Program
1540 Broadway, 38th Floor
New York, NY 10036

C-SPAN
400 North Capitol Street NW,
  Suite 650
Washington, DC 20001

*Forty Acres and a Mule
   Filmworks, Inc.
124 DeKalb Avenue
Brooklyn, NY 11217
(718) 624-3703

Jazbo Productions
1801 Franklin Canyon Drive
Beverly Hills, CA 90210

*Late Show with David Letterman
Internship Coordinator
1697 Broadway
New York, NY 10019

*Lucas Digital Ltd., Lucasfilm Ltd.,
   Lucasart Entertainment Company
Box 2009
San Rafael, CA 94912
(415) 662-1999

*MTV: Music Television
1515 Broadway, 22nd Floor
New York, NY 10036
(212) 258-8000

*National Public Radio
635 Massachusetts Avenue
Washington, DC 20001-3753
(202) 414-2000

*The NewsHour with Jim Lehrer
356 West 58th Street
New York, NY 10016
(212) 560-3113

*Nightline
1717 Desales Street NW, 3rd Floor
Washington, DC 20036

*Sony Music Entertainment, Inc.
550 Madison Avenue, 5th Floor
New York, NY 10022-3211

*Walt Disney Studios
Internship Program Administrator
500 South Buena Vista Street
Burbank, CA 91521-0880

Magazine, Book, and Newspaper Publishing

American Society of
   Magazine Editors
919 Third Avenue,
   22nd Floor
New York, NY 10022

Atlanta Art Papers, Inc.
P.O. Box 77348
Atlanta, GA 30357
(404) 588-1837

*Center for Investigative
   Reporting, Inc.
c/o Communications Director
500 Howard Street, Suite 206
San Francisco, CA 94105-3000
(415) 543-1200

Discovery Communications
7000 Wisconsin Avenue
Bethesda, MD 20814
(301) 986-4971

Harper's Magazine Foundation
666 Broadway
New York, NY 10012
(212) 614-6500

Alice James Books
33 Richdale Avenue
Cambridge, MA 02140

*Los Angeles Times
Editorial Internships
Times Mirror Square
Los Angeles, CA 90053
(800) 283-NEWS, ext. 74487

*Marvel Comics
387 Park Avenue South
New York, NY 10016
(212) 696-0808

*Random House, Inc.
201 East 50th Street
New York, NY 10022
(212) 572-2610

Rolling Stone
Editorial Department
1290 Avenue of the Americas
New York, NY 10104
(212) 484-1641

Smithsonian Institution Press
470 L'Enfant Plaza, Suite 7100
Washington, DC 20560
(202) 287-3738

*Wall Street Journal
200 Liberty Street
New York, NY 10281

The Washington Post
Internship Program
1150 15th Street, NW
Washington, DC 20071-5508
(202) 334-6000

John Wiley & Sons, Inc.
605 Third Avenue
New York, NY 10158
(212) 850-6000

Performing Arts

Lincoln Center for the Performing
   Arts, Inc.
70 Lincoln Center Plaza
New York, NY 10023-6583
(212) 875-5000

Wolf Trap Foundation for the
   Performing Arts
1624 Trap Road
Vienna, VA 22182
(703) 255-1900

Government, Public Policy, and Public Services

*American Enterprise Institute
1150 17th Street NW
Washington, DC 20036
(202) 862-5900

*The Brookings Institution
1775 Massachusetts Avenue NW
Washington, DC 20036-2188

*The Carter Center
One Copenhill Avenue
Atlanta, GA 30307
(404) 420-5151

*The Coro Foundation
Midwestern Center
1730 South 11th Street
St. Louis, MO 63194

*Department of State Foreign Affairs
  Fellowship Program and The
  Woodrow Wilson National
  Fellowship Foundation
Box 2437
Princeton, NJ 08543-2437
(703) 875-7490
www.state.gov

*Federal Bureau of Investigation
(202) 324-3674

*The Fund for the Feminist Minority
1600 Wilson Boulevard, Suite 801
Arlington, VA 22209
(703) 522-2214
www.feminist.org

*Inroads, Inc.
10 South Broadway, Suite 700
St. Louis, MO 63103
(314) 241-7330

*The Kennedy Center
Internship Program Manager
Washington, DC 20566
(202) 416-8800

*NASA—National Aeronautics and
  Space Administration
Higher Education Branch
Mail Code FEH
Washington, DC 20546

*Supreme Court of the United States
Judicial Internship Program, Room 5
Office of the Administrative Assistant
  to the Chief Justice
Washington, DC 20543
(202) 479-3374

*United Nations Association of the
  United States of America
485 Fifth Avenue
New York, NY 10017

U.S. Department of State
Office of Recruitment, Student
  Programs
P.O. Box 9317
Arlington, VA 22219

*Urban Fellows/Government Scholars
  Programs
City of New York
2 Washington Street, 15th Floor
New York, NY 10004
(212) 487-5698

The White House
Internship Program
Old Executive Office Building,
  Room 84
Washington, DC 20500
(202) 456-2742

Research

*American Foundation for AIDS
  Research
1828 L Street NW, Suite 802
Washington, DC 20036
(202) 331-8600

American Heart Association
7272 Greenville Avenue
Dallas, TX 75231
(800) AHA-USA1

Lucent Technologies
AT&T Bell Laboratories
101 Crawford Corner Road
P.O. Box 3030, Room 1E-231
Holmdel, NJ 07733-3030
(732) 949-3000

*National Institutes of Health
Office of Education
Building 10, Room 1C129
9000 Rockfield Pike
Bethesda, MD 20892
(301) 402-2176
www.training.nih.gov

Education

*Center for Talented Youth
CTY Summer Programs Employment
The Johns Hopkins University
3400 North Charles Street
Baltimore, MD 21218
(410) 516-0191
www.jho.edu/gifted/

*Crow Canyon Archaeological Center
23390 County Road K
Cortez, CO 81321

Horizon for Youth
121 Lakeview Street
Sharon, MA 02067
(781) 828-7550
www.hfy.org

Interlocken
RR 2, Box 165
Hillsboro Upper Village, NH 03244
(603) 478-3166
www.interlock.org

Manice Education Center
P.O. Box 953
North Adams, MA 01247

National Foundation for the
    Improvement of Education
1201 16th Street NW
Washington, DC 20036
(202) 822-7840

*Sponsors for Educational Opportunity
23 Gramercy Park South
New York, NY 10003
(212) 979-2040

*Summerbridge National
361 Oak Street
San Francisco, CA 94102
(415) 865-2970

Westwood Hills Nature Center
8300 West Franklin Avenue
St. Louis Park, MN 55426
(612) 924-2544

Environmental Organizations

*Aspen Center for Environmental
    Studies
Summer Naturalist Intern Program
P.O. Box 8777
Aspen, CO 81612
(303) 925-5756

*Chicago Zoological Society—
    Brookfield Zoo
3300 South Golf Road
Brookfield, IL 60513
(708) 485-0263

*Environmental Careers Organization
286 Congress Street
Boston, MA 02210-1009
(617) 426-4375

*Environmental Protection Agency
NNEMS National Program Manager
US EPA (1707)
401 M Street SW
Washington, DC 20460
(202) 260-4965

*National Audubon Society
Government Affairs Internship Program
666 Pennsylvania Avenue SE
Washington, DC 20003
(202) 547-9009

National Tropical Botanical Garden
P.O. Box 340
Lawai, Kauai, HI 96765

National Wildlife Federation
1400 16th Street, NW
Washington, DC 20036-2266
(202) 797-6800
www.nwf.org

Renew America
1400 16th Street NW, Suite 710
Washington, DC 20036

Surfrider Foundation
122 South El Camino Real, #67
San Clemente, CA 92672
(800) 743-SURF

Volunteers for Outdoor Colorado
1410 Grant Street, B-105
Denver, CO 80203

Art Auctioneers, Museums, Libraries

*Butterfield & Butterfield
220 San Bruno Avenue
San Francisco, CA 94103
(415) 861-7500

*The Hermitage—Home of
   Andrew Jackson
4580 Rachel's Lane
Hermitage, TN 37076-1331
(615) 889-2841

*The Library of Congress
Junior Fellows Program Coordinator
Librarian Services LM642
101 Independence Avenue
Washington, DC 20540-8400
(202) 707-5330

*The Metropolitan Museum of Art
Attn: Education Dept.,
   Internship Program
1000 Fifth Avenue
New York, NY 10028-0198
(212) 570-3710
www.metmuseum.org

*Smithsonian Institution
Office of Museum Programs
Arts & Industries Building
Suite 2235, MRC 427
Washington, DC 20560
(202) 357-3102

*Sotheby's (auction house)
1334 York Avenue
New York, NY 10021
(212) 606-7000

*Whitney Museum of American Art
Internship Program, Personnel Office
945 Madison Avenue
New York, NY 10021

Appendix 2

Books for
Further Reference

Choosing a Career

The Harvard Guide to Careers, Harvard University Press, 1987. This book provides career guidance by providing information on scores of selected fields, including advertising, banking, and government.

How to Get Your Dream Job Using the Web, Coriolis Group Books, 1997. Find jobs that are posted only on the Internet.

How the Real World Really Works: Graduating Into the Rest of Your Life, Berkley Books, 1997. Basic survival tactics for job interviews, networking, and real life.

Jobs '98, Simon & Schuster, 1994. Job leads galore.

The Jobs Rated Almanac, Pharos Books, 1988. 250 jobs are listed and ranked here by salary, working conditions, stress level, travel opportunities, growth potential, physical demands, benefits, and job security. Data was obtained from the federal government: the Bureau of Labor Statistics, the Department of Commerce, and the Census Bureau.

Jobs Worldwide, Impact, 1996. Information on the international job market and how to make connections.

Jobsmarts: 50 Top Careers, Harper Perennial, 1997. Want a job but not sure where to start? Start with the basics and do some research.

The New York Times Career Planner, Random House, 1987. This book offers general advice for recent college graduates on how to choose a career. It helps you select a career that matches your talents. It also enables you to integrate the dream of your future with the reality of the job market by furnishing you with information you need to plan ahead. The book examines 101 opportunities for interesting professions and jobs.

100 Best Careers for the 21st Century, Macmillan, 1996. How are jobs, opportunities, and pay different than they were 10 years ago? This book will help you determine which are the hottest jobs going.

The Only Job Hunting Guide You'll Ever Need, Simon & Schuster, 1989. An encyclopedia of job wealth.

The Right Job, Penguin Books, 1993. Robert O. Snelling, the director of one of the nation's largest employment services, shares his strategy on how to scour the job market for a career that best suits your skills and interests. It moves you to consider all your options and then helps you narrow them down.

The Right Move: How to Find the Perfect Job, Ballantine Books, 1988. Michael Zey, management and career consultant, takes you through the steps of finding the perfect job. He offers information on the tangibles, such as perks and benefits, and the intangibles, such as politics and pressure. His focus is helping you find the right position. The book doesn't just list companies, it looks inside them and examines their character.

Wanted: Liberal Arts Graduates, Doubleday Books, 1987. This book helps liberal arts graduates find work in business and the arts. It includes an index of major companies looking for liberal arts graduates.

What Color Is Your Parachute?, Ten Speed Press, 1997. This whimsical book emphasizes self-assessment as the primary tool in choosing a career. Several self-assessment exercises are included. Updated editions are published every year. It is a fun book to read even if you aren't in the market.

Jobs in Specific Fields

The American Almanac of Jobs and Salaries, Avon, 1993. Provides information about entry-level to top-level positions. Includes information about where to look for jobs and special advice for specific fields.

America's 50 Fastest Growing Jobs, JST, 1994. Covers labor-market trends and provides growth projections for over 500 major jobs, by industry. The data is based on U.S. Department of Labor publications.

Finding the Work You Love: A Woman's Career Guide, Resource Publications, 1994. Designed to help women in all stages of career planning find work that uses their skills.

Hot Jobs, HarperCollins, 1994. Gives practical advice on finding jobs in the "glamour industries"—film, advertising and publicity, fashion, television, radio, publishing, the art world, and music.

Jobs for English Majors and Other Smart People, Peterson's Guides, 1986. Use your creativity in a job designed for you.

150 Best Companies for Liberal Arts Graduates, Wiley, 1992. Practical advice on how liberal arts majors can land jobs in the corporate, governmental, and nonprofit arenas, with tips from liberal arts graduates.

Job Issues for Minorities

Best Companies for Minorities: Employers Across America Who Recruit, Train, and Promote Minorities, Plume, 1993. Includes profiles of Fortune 500 and other large companies that genuinely promote diversity in their employment practices, offer career advancement, and put money in minority charities, scholarships, and training programs.

Job Strategies for People with Disabilities, Peterson's Guides, 1992. Strategies for how to overcome disabilities on the job, and job-search tactics that will help land you the job.

Experience Abroad/Travel

Abroad and Beyond, Cambridge University Press, 1988. Two university professors investigate numerous foreign study programs here and abroad. This is a good book to read to help you decide if you want to study abroad. Information is provided on costs, contacts, and preparation.

Great Jobs Abroad, McGraw-Hill, 1997. Over 1000 companies abroad—even government.

Jobs Worldwide, Impact, 1996. Help finding jobs in the international market.

Overseas Summer Jobs, Peterson's Guide, 1997. A country-by-country breakdown of job opportunities.

Taking Off, Simon & Schuster, 1989. This book offers extraordinary ways to spend your first year out of college. It explains how a productive "year off" makes you more interesting, and therefore more employable. Information is provided on teaching English in China; living on an Israeli kibbutz; helping the homeless; working in a Central American refugee camp; saving endangered wildlife.

Work Your Way Around the World, Peterson's Guides, 1998.

Internships

America's Top Ten Internships, Princeton Review, 1998. Thorough coverage of internships for college students, graduates, and high school students.

I'll Work for Free: A Short-Term Strategy for a Long-Term Payoff, Holt, 1994. Discusses how to make contacts, get experience, and get your foot in the door.

Intern Jobs—Where They Are, How to Get Them, Addison-Wesley, 1993.

The Internship Bible, Random House, 1995. Tons of internship listings in different career fields; expert advice.

Succeeding on the Job

The Achievement Factors, Dodd, Mead, 1987. What sets successful people apart from the rest of the pack? Interviews conducted with Nobel laureate Francis Crick, U.S. Supreme Court Justice Sandra Day O'Connor, composer Steve Allen, and actor Jack Lemmon show how very different people clear hurdles to success.

Getting Things Done When You Are Not in Charge, Simon & Schuster, 1993. Empowering yourself in your career.

Guerrilla Marketing, Houghton Mifflin Co., 1989. New strategies are outlined here for winning big profits for small businesses. Pleasurable and informative reading.

How to Sell Your Ideas, McGraw-Hill, 1984. Persuasion seen as an art. Teaches techniques in shepherding an idea through all the obstacles so that it comes alive in people's minds. The book makes you aware of the subtle yet powerful forces that undermine persuasion and how to deal with them. Learn how to negotiate so that all parties are satisfied.

The Portable MBA in Management, Wiley, 1995. Skills and strategies for leading any organization to success.

Taking Charge of Your Own Career, Workman Publishing, 1995. Shows you how to be your own career counselor.

What They Don't Teach You at Harvard Business School, Bantam Books, 1984. This engaging book teaches "street smarts": the ability to make active, positive use of your instinct, insight, and perceptions. It emphasizes the importance of reading people and how to use that knowledge to get what you want. Learn here how to apply "people sense" in business to get things done. Contains key chapters on reading other people and yourself.

Work with Passion, New World Library, 1984. How to do what you love for a living.

Graduate Schools

Getting into Graduate Business Schools Today, Macmillan, 1998. An inside scoop on admission into top schools.

Getting What You Came For: The Smart Student's Guide to Earning a Master's or a Ph.D., Noonday, 1992. Robert Peters offers advice on getting into and through graduate school, both in the liberal arts and the scientific disciplines.

The Official Guide to MBA Programs, Graduate Management Admissions Council, 1994. Information on MBA programs.

The Real Guide to Grad School, Linguafranca, 1997. Filled with interviews of professors, students, and admission counselors.

Academic Advice

College: The Undergraduate Experience in America, Harper & Row, 1988. The results of a three-year study done by the Carnegie Foundation on thirty public and private colleges. It reveals how colleges meet the needs of both the individual and the community and advises potential students to consider both when making college decisions.

Cultural Literacy: What Every American Needs to Know, Random House, 1988. An entertaining and informative book, a collection of facts about American culture. It emphasizes the importance of a strong core curriculum.

Sourcebook: 10 Steps in Writing the Research Paper, Barron's, 1994. A step-by-step guide to the entire writing process—from topic selection to research to final draft.

Interviews

The Complete Job Interview Handbook, Harper Perennial, 1994. Preparation, follow-up instructions, and everything in between.

Job Interviews for Dummies, IDG Books Worldwide, 1996.

Knock 'Em Dead, Bob Adams Inc., 1994. The best interview comes from preparation. This book gives great answers to tough interview questions. Over 100 winning responses for many interview situations.

Sweaty Palms: The Neglected Art of Being Interviewed, Ten Speed Press, 1992. Richard Nelson Bolles calls this "the best book I know on interviewing." Most books show you how to *get* an interview. This one focuses on how to *conduct yourself* during an interview. It helps you deal with the butterflies that come with the fear of the unknown. The book also gives advice on how to dress, present yourself, relax, prepare, negotiate salaries, etc.

Résumés

Just Resumes, Wiley, 1997. Over 200 proven successful resumes.

The Overnight Resume, Ten Speed Press, 1991. Includes special sections on financial, legal, academic, medical, computer, and technical résumés. Also includes tips for applying to overseas companies.

The Perfect Cover Letter, Wiley, 1997. What a cover letter should say to you.

The Resume Makeover, Wiley, 1995. Updating your personal résumé's image.

Throw Away Your Resume, Barron's, 1995. Create a personalized job campaign, instead.

Appendix 3

Associations and Organizations for College Students

No group will satisfy everyone. Before you join an organization, think about who you are, what you'd like to do, and how the organization would complement your schoolwork and your long-term goals.

The following list will get you started, but don't stop here. If you're interested in more specialized groups, refer to *the Encyclopedia of Associations* at your local library. Look up opportunities with community groups, local branches of national organizations, and voluntary programs in your phone book. Also, check your college catalogue for programs specific to your campus.

Alternative Education

The wide array of alternative education programs available ensures that those seeking a change of pace should be able to find something interesting. If you'd like to try an alternative education program but aren't sure which one to choose, the Association for Experiential Education (AEE), 2305 Canyon Blvd., Suite 100, Boulder, CO 80302, (303) 440-8844 (www.aee.org), will help you find the program that fits your interests and abilities.

If you're currently in school, you may be able to get college credit for alternative programs. Check with your registrar before you leave.

Earthwatch
680 Mount Auburn Street, Box 9104
Waterton, MA 02471
(617) 926-8200

Offers an array of short expeditions, from coral communities in Figi to the culture of Easter Island.

National Outdoor Leadership School
288 Main Street
Lander, WY 82520
(307) 332-6973
www.NOLS.edu

Offers a variety of courses, from mountaineering in Alaska to kayaking in

Mexico. The program is designed to develop wilderness competence and leadership

The National Theater Institute
Eugene O'Neill Theater Center
305 Great Neck Road
Waterford, CT 06385

According to the institute, 80 percent of its 1,200 alumni are still in the entertainment industry. A semester includes courses in directing, playwriting, costume design, scene design, acting, and movement.

Outward Bound USA
Route 90
R2 Box 280
Garrison, CT 10524-9757
(914) 424-4000
www.outbound.org

The leader in adventure-based education. Twenty thousand people participated in 1988, so there must be something to their claim that you don't have to be Superman to complete an expedition.

Sea Education Association
P.O. Box 6
Woods Hole, MA 02543
(800) 552-3633 or (508) 540-3954
www.sea.edu

Semester at Sea
811 William Pitt Union
Pittsburgh, PA 15260
(800) 854-0195 or (412) 648-7490

Semester at Sea is conducted aboard an ocean liner that stops at exotic ports, while the Sea Education Association's semester is devoted to learning about and sailing on the sea.

Up With People
3103 North Campbell Avenue
Tucson, AZ 85719

Up With People grew from a single theater group in the mid-1960s to five musical theater groups, each one composed of student performers who take ten months to travel to up to 80 cities while living with host families.

Honor Societies and Professional Fraternities

There are hundreds of societies and fraternities that specialize in dozens of areas. Several provide honorary awards and scholarships to their most promising members, and most hold meetings and conferences. Although some groups require that an aspiring member come from a college that has its chapter, some do not. The national organization will be helpful if you'd like to be inducted into a society that's not on your campus, or if you'd like to start a chapter of your own.

Honor Societies

Alpha Lambda Delta
P.O. Box 1576
Muncie, IN 47308
(317) 282-5620

For freshmen with a 3.5 GPA or higher

Omicron Delta Kappa
Suite 118, Bradley Hall
University of Kentucky
Lexington, KY 40506-0058
(606) 257-5000

Membership in Omicron Delta Kappa, which "recognizes and encourages superior scholarship and leadership," is awarded to juniors and seniors.

Phi Beta Kappa
1785 Massachusetts Avenue NW, 4th
    Floor
Washington, DC 20009
(202) 265-3808
www.pbk.org

Phi Kappa Phi
P.O. Box 16000
Louisiana State University
Baton Rouge, LA 70893
(504) 388-4917

Seniors may join Phi Kappa Phi if they are in the top 10 percent of their class; juniors if they are in the top 5 percent.

Professional Fraternities

Business

Beta Gamma Sigma
605 Old Ballas Road, Suite 200
St. Louis, MO 63141

Seniors in the upper 10 percent of their class are eligible for membership, as are juniors in the upper 5 percent.

Engineering

Tau Beta Pi
P.O. Box 8840, University Station
Knoxville, TN 37996-4800

Seniors who are in the top 20 percent of their engineering class and who are well-rounded socially and scholastically are considered by Tau Beta Pi.

History

Phi Alpha Theta
2333 Liberty Street
Allentown, PA 18104

For top undergraduates who have completed at least twelve semester hours in history.

Law

Phi Delta Phi
1750 N Street NW
Washington, DC 20036
(800) 368-5606 or (202) 628-0148
www.phideltaphi.org

For students who have attended at least one semester of law school and are in good academic standing.

Marketing and Management

Delta Epsilon Chi
Division of DECA
1908 Association Drive
Reston, VA 20191
(703) 860-5000
www.delta-hq.org

The college division of the high school–level Distribution Education Clubs of America, Inc., Delta Epsilon Chi is for students enrolled in marketing and management programs.

Scientific Research

Sigma Xi
345 Whitney Avenue
New Haven, CT 06511

Sigma Xi begins selecting promising research scientists during their junior year.

Job Clearinghouses

The following organizations provide information on internships and jobs with nonprofit organizations around the country.

Access
96 Mount Auburn Street
Cambridge, MA 02138
(617) 495-2178

Access produces a large loose-leaf-bound publication called Opportunities in Community Organizations; *it can be found at over two hundred locations around the country.*

Community Careers Resource Center
1516 P Street, NW
Washington, DC 20005

The center's main publication, Community Jobs, *is a monthly tabloid billed as "the only nationwide listing of jobs and internships."*

Membership Organizations

Many membership societies offer student memberships at reduced cost. Members are usually entitled to free newsletters and information about books, journals, meetings, and jobs in the field.

Architecture

The American Institute of Architecture
  Students
1735 New York Avenue NW
Washington, DC 20006
(202) 626-7472
www.aiasnatl.org

Biology

American Institute of Biological Science
1444 Eye Street NW, Suite 200
Washington, DC 20005
(202) 628-1500
www.aibs.org

Broadcasting

Intercollegiate Broadcasting System
  (IBS)
Box 592
Vails Gate, NY 12584-0592

Although IBS membership is reserved for college radio stations, its yearly national convention makes it an organization student broadcasters should look into.

Chemistry

The American Chemical Society
1155 16th Street NW
Washington, DC 20036
(202) 872-4480
www.acs.org

Computers

The IEEE Computer Society
1730 Massachusetts Avenue, NW
Washington, DC 20036-1903
(202) 371-0101
www.computer.org

Education

National Education Association (NEA)
Student Programs
1201 16th Street NW, Suite 320
Washington, DC 20036
(202) 822-7814

Environmental

Sierra Club
730 Polk Street
San Francisco, CA 94109
(415) 776-2211

In addition to literature and information on meetings, members receive material on group expeditions organized by the club and can participate in its political activities.

Inventions

Inventors Workshop International
3201 Corte Malpaso, Suite 304
Camarillo, CA 93010
(805) 484-9786

Evaluates members' inventions in terms of their manufacturing and marketing potential, and will advise about patents and other protection.

Mathematics

American Mathematical Society
P.O. Box 6248
Providence, RI 02940
(401) 272-9500

The Mathematical Association
of America
1529 18th Street NW
Washington, DC 20036
(202) 387-5200

Music

Music Educators National Conference
(MENC)
1902 Association Drive
Reston, VA 22091
(703) 860-4000

Physics

The American Physical Society
335 East 45th Street
New York, NY 10017
(212) 682-7341

Recreation

American Alliance for Health, Physical
Education, Recreation and Dance
(AHPERD)
1900 Association Drive
Reston, VA 22091
(703) 476-3400

An umbrella organization for several membership organizations, including the Americation Association for Leisure and Recreation, the Association for the Advancement of Health Education, the National Association for Girls and Women in Sport, the National Association for Sport and Physical Education, and the National Dance Association.

Pre-Professional Organizations

Agriculture

FFA
5632 Mount Vernon Memorial
Highway
P.O. Box 15160
Alexandria, VA 22309-0160
(703) 360-3600

According to FFA—formerly Future Farmers of America—only 8 percent of the careers in agriculture are in farming. FFA is mainly a high school organization, but interested college students may also join.

Leadership

American Humanics
4601 Madison Avenue, Suite B
Kansas City, MO 64112
(816) 561-6415

Founded to provide leaders for the Boy Scouts, American Humanics is on sixteen campuses, preparing students to work with organizations such as the Red Cross and Boys Clubs of America.

Vocational Training

Vocational Industrial Clubs of America
 (VICA)
P.O. Box 3000
Leesburg, VA 22075
(703) 777-8810

VICA operates in vocational high schools and junior colleges. Its program, a mixture of leadership, citizenship, and character development, is designed to complement vocational skill training.

Social Welfare

If you're a member of a social welfare group on your campus, or if you'd like to start one, the following organizations can provide you with resources.

Amnesty International
322 Eighth Avenue
New York, NY 10001
(212) 807-8400

Oxfam America
115 Broadway
Boston, MA 02116
(617) 482-1211

CARE
660 First Avenue
New York, NY 10016-3241
(212) 686-3110

Travel

American Institute for Foreign Study
 (AIFS)
102 Greenwich Avenue
Greenwich, CT 06830
(800) 727-AIFS or (203) 869-9090

AIFS offers semester and summer study programs at fifteen affiliated colleges and universities worldwide, including the University of Salzburg and the University of Paris.

American Youth Hostels (AYH)
P.O. Box 37613
Washington, DC 20013-7613
(202) 783-6161

In addition to operating a chain of inexpensive youth hostels, AYH offers a number of national and international hiking and biking trips, such as a 44-day bike tour through Europe.

Council of International Educational
    Exchange (CIEE)
205 East 42nd Street
New York, NY 10017
(212) 661-1414

Institute of International Education
809 United Nations Plaza
New York, NY 10017-3580
(212) 984-5413

*The council and the institute offer, support,
or publicize a staggering number of travel
programs of all sorts, from the Fulbright
Scholarship to work in Yugoslavia. Many
colleges are affiliated with these
organizations, so getting academic credit
for travel arranged through the council or
the institute should be easy.*

International Association of Students in
    Economics and Business
    Management (AIESEC)
841 Broadway, Suite 608
New York, NY 10003
(212) 979-7400

*AIESEC is a French acronym for an
international business-exchange program that
operates in 67 countries. If you're interested
in working for a foreign corporation, AIESEC
may have a place for you.*

Japan-America Student Conference
606 18th Street NW, 2nd Floor
Washington, DC 20006
(202) 223-4187

*The Japan-America Student Conference is
held in Japan in odd years and in the
United States in even ones. Forty American
students join the same number of Japanese
students for a month of study and cultural
exchange.*

YMCA International Camp Counselor
    Program/Abroad (ICCP/Abroad)
356 West 34th Street, 3rd Floor
New York, NY 10001
(212) 563-3441

*Places American camp counselors and
workers in foreign camps in over twenty
countries. Although students pay an
application fee and airfare, the camps
provide room and board.*

Volunteer Organizations

Groups such as the Red Cross, the Salvation Army, Boy Scouts/Girl Scouts, and Big Brothers/Big Sisters are not listed here, since these groups are organized locally. Call your local office for information about activities and opportunities.

General

Campus Outreach Opportunity League
   (COOL)
386 McNeal Hall
University of Minnesota
St. Paul, MN 55108
(612) 624-3018

COOL champions student involvement in community service through publications, regional and national meetings, and campus organizations. If you want to get involved in your town, COOL can help.

Literacy

Literacy Volunteers of America
5795 Widewaters Parkway
Syracuse, NY 13214-1846
(315) 445-8000

Laubach Literacy Action
1320 Jamesville Avenue, Box 131
Syracuse, NY 13210
(315) 422-9121

Push Literacy Action Now (PLAN)
1332 G Street SE
Washington, DC 20003
(202) 547-8903

Reading Is Fundamental (RIF)
600 Maryland Avenue SW, Suite 500
Washington, DC 20560
(202) 287-3220

The above organizations train volunteers to teach reading, using material and instructors provided by the group.

Appendix 4

Graduate School:
Applying and Getting In

Should You Stay or Should You Go?

It may surprise you that the median age for graduate students in business and law is now twenty-seven. That means that with a graduate degree at twenty-four, you'll be competing with people who have five years of work experience. So, to increase your odds, why not get some work experience after graduation before applying to graduate school? You can earn money, establish your independence, and then return to school with a new perspective. (Besides, many companies pay for their employees' graduate work. You could take courses at night and earn your degree over four or five years.)

The Exception to the Rule

If you want to become a professor, go directly to graduate school. Do not pass Go; do not collect $200. Academia is competitive on terms of its own, and "real world" experience does little to improve your chances.

Applications

If you plan on going straight to graduate school, you'll have to take admissions tests and fill out applications for prospective schools.

Scholarships

You may be eligible for local and national scholarships. Some highly competitive scholarships, like the Rhodes or the Fulbright, require recommendations, interviews, high grades, work experience, and athletic achievement. But there are hundreds of other grants available through your school's scholarship office. Check them out.

Entrance Exams

If you've decided to seek another degree beyond your B.A., you might have to take one of a battery of tests: the GRE, GMAT, LSAT, or MCAT, to name a few. Your performance on these tests is one of the factors weighed in the admissions process.

Once you know which field you'd like to do graduate work in, it's a good idea to consult the Graduate School Guide (School Guide Publications, 1-800-433-7771). You can purchase this book or check it out at the library. It contains a list of all the universities in the United States and indicates which degrees each offers. As with your college search years ago, you'll need to make a list, contact the schools, find out their requirements, apply, and be interviewed.

A good place to start is with the test itself, because your score will help you decide which schools you have a good chance of being admitted to.

Here's a breakdown of the various tests:

GRE: Graduate Record Examination

This test is designed to measure general analytical, quantitative, and verbal abilities, as well as knowledge and understanding of the subject matter of specific graduate fields. It is required for admission into many graduate and professional schools. There are three parts to the GRE: the General Test, the Subject Test, and the Minority Graduate Student Locater Service. The General Test consists of seven 30-minute sections. There are verbal, mathematical, and logical reasoning sections similar to those on the SAT. Scores for this section are reported on a scale of 200 to 800. The fifteen different subject tests (which are administered in biology, chemistry, computer science, economics, education, engineering, geology, history, literature, mathematics, music, physics, political science, psychology, and sociology) are intended for students who have majored in each subject in college and are now seeking an advanced degree. They last for two hours and 50 minutes each. Subject test scores are reported on a scale of 200 to 990. The General and Subject tests may be taken on two different dates. Scores are usually reported within four to six weeks. The Minority Graduate Student Locater Service is a free service that does not require taking the GRE; it matches minority students interested in pursuing graduate study with graduate schools seeking minority students. About 20,000 students and 220 schools participate annually.

The GRE is usually given five times a year, in October, December, February, April, and June. The test is administered at universities throughout the United States and Canada and in many foreign locations. Registration is due about one month before each test date. Computer software and practice tests are available. Further information, practice tests, and registration forms can be obtained by writing to GRE, Educational Testing Service, P.O. Box 6000, Princeton, NJ 08541-6000, or by calling ETS at (609) 771-7595.

GMAT: *Graduate Management Admissions Test*

Required for students applying to business schools, the GMAT contains eight 30-minute sections. Six are scored while the other two are experimental. The scored sections are as follows: two of regular math (not much harder than the SAT), data sufficiency (regular math concepts posed in more confusing formats), reading passages (three in order of difficulty), grammar (basic concepts tested in "What is wrong with this sentence?" format), and analysis of situations (logical reasoning). Scores are usually mailed out about five weeks after the test date.

The GMAT is administered four times a year, in January, March, June, and October; registration is due about a month before the test. Test centers are located throughout the United States and Canada and in many foreign locations. For further information, practice tests, and registration forms, contact ETS at the above address and phone number.

LSAT: *Law School Admissions Test*

The LSAT consists of four 35-minute scored sections, as well as a 30-minute writing sample and two unscored experimental sections. The four scored sections consist of facts and rules (contains outcome and factual questions), arguments (making distinctions between conclusions and assumptions), reading passages (very difficult—simply read for the main idea and refer back for specific questions) and games (involves diagramming problems), followed by the writing sample (this is sent to law schools, but it's rumored that they don't use it in making decisions). One distinguishing feature of the LSAT is that no points are subtracted for errors, so lucky guesses can raise your score. Scores are reported within four to six weeks and are on a scale of 10 to 48.

The LSAT is given four times a year, in February, June, September or October, and December; be advised that most law schools require that the LSAT be taken by December to qualify for admission the following fall. Again, there are test centers throughout the United States and in some foreign countries. For more information, call (215) 968-1001; for an application, call (215) 968-1188.

MCAT: *Medical College Admissions Test*

The MCAT is designed to test a student's knowledge and understanding of the biology, chemistry, and physics designated as prerequisite to the study of medicine. This material is usually that covered in first-year college science courses. The test also evaluates basic analytical ability in solving medically relevant problems. The day-long—8:30 to 6:00—MCAT is divided into four sections: science knowledge (separate biology, chemistry, and physics sections), science problems (the three disciplines combined in problems), skills analysis—reading (passages followed by comprehensive questions), and skills analysis—quantitative (questions involving quantitative material). A recent addition to the test is an expository essay section. Scores are given for each of the six sections, on a scale of 1 to 15; they are reported within 45 days.

Given in April and September, the MCAT registration is usually due about a month before the test. For registration information, write to MCAT registration, ACT, P.O. Box 414, 2555 North Dubuque Road, Iowa City, IA 52243; or call (319) 337-1276.

In addition to the MCAT, there are other medical tests, designed to measure general academic ability as well as science knowledge. These include the following:

- *AHPT: Allied Health Professions Test.* Required for admission into allied health schools—those that offer programs in such fields as chiropractic, dental technology, midwifery, social work, physical therapy, and many other medical professions. Write to AHPT, The Psychological Corporation, 555 Academic Court, San Antonio, TX 78204; or call (512) 270-0396 or (512) 299-1061.
- *OAT: Optometry Admissions Test.* Required for those seeking admission into schools and colleges of optometry. For further information, write to Optometry Admissions Testing Program, 211 East Chicago Avenue, Chicago, IL 60611.
- *PCAT: Pharmacy College Admissions Test.* Required for admission to colleges of pharmacy.
- *VCAT: Veterinary College Admissions Test.* For those seeking admission into colleges of veterinary medicine.

For the PCAT and the VCAT, write to The Psychological Corporation at 555 Academic Court, San Antonio, TX 78204, or call (512) 270-0396 or (512) 299-1061.

NTE: National Teachers' Exam

The NTE tests are standardized exams that measure the academic achievements of students who wish to join, or are already admitted to, teacher education programs. There are three types of exams: Core Battery Tests, the nationwide Specialty Area Tests, and the statewide Specialty Area Tests. The first of three two-hour-long Core Battery tests is the Test of Communications Skills, which examines listening, reading, and writing skills. The second, the Test of General Knowledge, tests understanding of literature and fine arts, mathematics, science, and social studies. Finally, the Test of Professional Knowledge assesses the student's aptitude for the types of decisions required of beginning teachers. The scores for this section, however, are not added into the final score. These tests are given in the following subjects: art education, audiology, biology and general science, business education, chemistry and physics, early childhood education, education in the elementary school, education of the mentally retarded, educational administration, English language and literature, French, German, home economics, industrial arts, introduction to the teaching of reading, library media specialist, mathematics, music education, physical education, school guidance and counseling, social studies, Spanish, special education, speech communication and speech-language pathology. There are also state-sponsored Specialty Area Tests in other subjects not covered in the nationwide tests. A single score is reported for each test; for the Core Battery Test there are three scores, on a scale of 600 to 695. Specialty Area scores are reported on a scale of 250 to 999. Scores are usually mailed out within four to six weeks.

Core Battery Tests are usually administered in October, March, and June, while Specialty Area Tests are given in November, March, and July. Registration closes about one month before each test date. The Core Battery and Specialty Area Tests are taken on different days; you may take one, two, or three of the Core tests on the same day and up to two Specialty Area Tests during a special double session given once a year. For further information, write to NTE Programs, Educational Testing Service, CN 6050, Princeton, NJ 08541-6050, or call (609) 771-7395.

Test Preparation Services

Whether you like them or not, standardized tests are an important part of the graduate school admissions game. They provide an efficient way for admissions officers to discriminate among hundreds of faceless applicants. Fortunately, studying for these tests can improve your scores tremendously.

Many organizations, on and off campus, offer courses that include subject reviews and practice tests as well as strategies to help students "beat" each test. Some test-takers swear by these methods, while others hesitate to invest so much money in preparing for the exams. (The classes can run upwards of $500.) Below is a description of two of the most popular courses offered nationwide.

Stanley Kaplan

The Kaplan course is for the student who thrives on self-paced study. Students are given review materials to study at home on their own time. They also have the use of the Kaplan Study Center. The center is filled with people taking practice tests, listening to audiotapes, and questioning tutors. You can come and go as you please.

Princeton Review

How is the Princeton Review different? First of all, the course caters to the student who desires a structured classroom setting. Pupils who display similar weaknesses are grouped together. During weekly lectures, techniques and concepts are taught. Workshops may be attended for further practice. Private tutoring is also available.

What Else Determines Admission?

Test scores, college grade-point average, activities, work experience, recommendations, and essays are all factors in the selection process.

Let's be realistic. No applicant is strong in all areas. As you complete your application packet, emphasize your strengths and minimize your weaknesses (don't deny them). Begin your applications early and make sure that you give recommenders plenty of time (at least one month). Remember, things always take longer than planned . . . especially things of quality.

Appendix 5

Continuing Your Education Once You Graduate

Graduated does not mean educated.
Harry Edwards, The Struggle That Must Be

The real university is a state of mind.
Robert M. Pirsig, Zen and the Art of Motorcycle Maintenance

If a well-rounded college education is a combination of academic work and real-world experience, then the best education outside of college comes both on the job and off.

Chances are that once you graduate, you will, at one time or another, be transferred to another city. Keeping yourself busy and meeting new people will become a primary concern. The following suggestions should help.

Taking Classes

"Now that I'm out of school officially, I can concentrate better on the details when I take classes at night," says Scott Freuner, who tries to take courses as much as he can. "I'm in retail and I don't get to stretch my mind academically at work. So in the evenings I take subjects like creative writing or Western civilization. It's fun, it keeps me alert, and because I'm motivated to learn, I'm remembering more than I did in college."

Many people continue their education formally by enrolling in one class every semester. Some may even earn their master's degree through evening courses over a period of years. Others may take classes that don't apply to a degree. A class on Chaucer or immigrants in urban America will help you to remember that there is a world outside your nine-to-five job. It will challenge your mind in ways that are different from your challenges on the job. The contrast is key.

Try taking courses outside a college or university, such as ballroom or salsa dancing, Chinese cooking, or pottery-making. Seminars are typically sponsored in every city. You may want to take a Saturday course in public speaking or how to use software. Even if your company will not pay, you may want to participate.

Museum and Library Lectures

"Once a month on Tuesday nights, a friend and I go to a yearlong series of lectures at our local library," says Hank Sands, an architect. "Last month the lecture was by a professor on the tropical rain forests, about which I knew little before I attended. After the talk, I went and checked out a book the lecturer recommended. I may never be an expert on any of these subjects, but over time I'll know a little about a lot of things."

Most museums and libraries offer free or affordable lecture series on topics ranging from extraterrestrials to creative writing to the life cycle of vampire bats. The lectures are given by professionals in the field. Usually the people in the audience are interesting too.

Weekend Seminars

"My weekend seminar on management training was more like a mini-vacation," says Adele Hayward, who manages an employment agency for temporary personnel. "We broke into several different groups and discussed key issues in management: how to hire the best people, how to keep them motivated, how to give people constructive criticism. I met many interesting people, including someone who made me a job offer two weeks later."

There are seminars every weekend on topics ranging from wine tasting to finance and accounting. Some of the seminars are in retreat areas in the mountains and are both educational and recreational.

Book or Writing Clubs

In every city there are informal groups where books or writing are discussed. This is a great way to make friends. You may want to form your own reading/dinner clubs to discuss classics you never read or current literature.

"My book club is like an extended family," says Margaret Maillor, a freelance photographer, who formed a club with her friends three years ago. "We've read everything from *The Origin of Species* to *The Bonfire of the Vanities*. It's been fascinating to learn different things about your friends through their interpretations of each book. We all refrain from being judgmental. Sometimes that's hard. We get into some pretty rigorous debates at times."

Outdoor Clubs

These clubs offer a variety of activities, such as hiking, canoeing, camping, sailing, and skiing. Sometimes weekend group trips are available to your favorite mountain or resort.

Pat Sullivan's membership in the Audubon Society led her to a career. Because of her affection for waterfowl, Pat often joined the Society for excursions to rookeries along the Atlantic coast. On one of these trips she met a researcher from a prestigious midwestern zoo. After they had spent the weekend together, she offered Pat a job. Six months later Pat was in Cincinnati conducting ornithological research.

Computer Groups

If you have a computer with the proper modem, you can hook it up to your telephone and exchange information and play games with other computer buffs across the country. You may also want to try your hand at co-authoring a software program.

Free Concerts

Most cities feature free concerts or plays in the summer. You can pack a picnic and a blanket and relax while listening to Verdi's *Aïda* and gazing up at the stars. If your city doesn't have a series of park concerts, check the churches and synagogues. They often feature classical music concerts.

"Summer wouldn't be summer without concerts at Wolftrap," says Richard Harrin, a congressional aide in Washington. "Music under the stars, a picnic on the grass, and wine with your friends is one of the best ways to spend a Saturday night. It's a close second to a night at the ball game."

Appendix 6

The World of Work: A Sampler

	Job Requirements											Work Environment		Occupational Characteristics			
	1. Leadership/persuasion	2. Helping/instructing others	3. Problem-solving/creativity	4. Initiative	5. Work as part of a team	6. Frequent public contact	7. Manual dexterity	8. Physical stamina	9. Hazardous	10. Outdoors	11. Confined	12. Geographically concentrated	13. Part-time	14. Earnings	15. Employment growth	16. Number of new jobs, 1984–95 (in thousands)	17. Entry requirements
Executive, Administrative, & Managerial Occupations																	
Managers & Administrators																	
Bank officers & managers	•	•	•	•	•					•				H	H	119	H
Health services managers	•	•	•	•	•									H	H	147	H
Hotel managers & assistants	•	•	•	•	•									L	H	21	M
School principals & assistant principals	•	•	•	•	•									H	L	12	H
Management Support Occupations																	
Accountants & auditors	•	•	•	•	•					•				H	H	307	H
Construction & building inspectors		•	•	•		•			•					M	L	4	M
Inspectors & compliance officers, except construction		•	•	•		•			•					H	L	10	M
Personnel, Training & Labor Relations Specialists	•	•	•	•	•									H	M	34	H
Purchasing agents	•	•	•	•										H	M	36	H
Underwriters			•	•										H	H	17	H
Wholesale & retail buyers	•	•	•	•										M	M	28	H

Engineers, Surveyors, & Architects

Architects	•	•	•									H	H	25	H
Surveyors			•	•	•	•	•					M	M	6	M
Engineers															
Aerospace engineers		•						•				H	H	14	H
Chemical engineers		•	•									H	H	13	H
Civil engineers		•	•									H	H	46	H
Electrical & electronics engineers		•	•									H	H	206	H
Industrial engineers		•	•									H	H	37	H
Mechanical engineers		•	•									H	H	81	H
Metallurgical, ceramics, & materials engineers		•	•									H	H	4	H
Mining engineers		•	•									H	L	2	H
Nuclear engineers		•	•									H	L	1	H
Petroleum engineers		•	•								•	H	M	4	H

[1] Estimates not available.
[2] Less than 500.
[3] Vary, depending on job.

L = Lowest   M = Middle   H = Highest

From *Occupational Outlook Quarterly*, Vol. 30. No. 3 (fall 1986)

Natural Scientists & Mathematicians

Column key:

Job Requirements: 1. Leadership/persuasion · 2. Helping/instructing others · 3. Problem-solving/creativity · 4. Initiative · 5. Work as part of a team · 6. Frequent public contact · 7. Manual dexterity · 8. Physical stamina · 9. Hazardous

Work Environment: 10. Outdoors · 11. Confined · 12. Geographically concentrated · 13. Part-time

Occupational Characteristics: 14. Earnings · 15. Employment growth · 16. Number of new jobs, 1984–95 (in thousands) · 17. Entry requirements

Occupation	1	2	3	4	5	6	7	8	9	10	11	12	13	14	15	16	17
Computer & Mathematical Occupations																	
Actuaries		•	•								•			H	H	4	H
Computer systems analysts	•	•	•	•						•				H	H	212	H
Mathematicians		•	•											H	M	4	H
Statisticians		•	•											H	M	4	H
Physical Scientists																	
Chemists		•	•											H	M	9	H
Geologists & geophysicists		•	•	•					•		•			H	M	7	H
Meteorologists		•	•	•										H	M	1	H
Physicists & astronomers	•	•	•											H	L	2	H
Life Scientists																	
Agricultural scientists		•	•										[1]	M		3	H
Biological scientists		•	•											H	M	10	H
Foresters & conservation scientists	•	•	•	•			•	•	•					H	L	2	H

Social Scientists, Social Workers, Religious Workers, & Lawyers

Lawyers	•				•	•	•	•	H	H	174	H
Social Scientists & Urban Planners												
Economists				•					H	M	7	H
Psychologists			•	•	•	•			H	H	21	H
Sociologists			•	•	•	•			H	L	²	H
Urban & regional planners	•		•	•	•	•			H	L	2	H
Social & Recreation Workers												
Social workers	•		•	•	•	•			M	H	75	H
Recreation workers	•		•	•	•	•	•		L	H	26	M
Religious workers												
Protestant ministers	•		•	•	•	•			L	¹	¹	H
Rabbis	•		•	•	•	•			H	¹	¹	H
Roman Catholic priests	•		•	•	•	•			L	¹	¹	H

Teachers, Counselors, Librarians, & Archivists

Kindergarten & elementary school teachers	•		•	•	•	•	•		M	H	281	H
Secondary school teachers	•		•	•	•	•	•		M	L	48	H
Adult & vocational education teachers	•		•	•	•	•	•	•	M	M	48	H
College & university faculty	•		•	•	•	•	•		H	L	-77	H
Counselors	•		•	•	•	•			M	M	29	H
Librarians	•		•	•	•	•			M	L	16	H
Archivists & curators			•	•	•				M	L	1	H

¹ Estimates not available.

² Less than 500.

³ Vary, depending on job.

Health Diagnosing & Treating Practitioners

	1. Leadership/persuasion	2. Helping/instructing others	3. Problem-solving/creativity	4. Initiative	5. Work as part of a team	6. Frequent public contact	7. Manual dexterity	8. Physical stamina	9. Hazardous	10. Outdoors	11. Confined	12. Geographically concentrated	13. Part-time	14. Earnings	15. Employment growth	16. Number of new jobs, 1984–95 (in thousands)	17. Entry requirements
Chiropractors	•	•	•	•	•	•								H	H	9	H
Dentists	•	•	•	•	•	•								H	H	39	H
Optometrists	•	•	•	•	•	•								H	H	8	H
Physicians	•	•	•	•	•	•						•		H	H	109	H
Podiatrists	•	•	•	•	•	•								H	H	4	H
Veterinarians	•	•	•	•	•	•		•		•				H	H	9	H

Registered Nurses, Pharmacists, Dietitians, Therapists, & Physician Assistants

	1. Leadership/persuasion	2. Helping/instructing others	3. Problem-solving/creativity	4. Initiative	5. Work as part of a team	6. Frequent public contact	7. Manual dexterity	8. Physical stamina	9. Hazardous	10. Outdoors	11. Confined	12. Geographically concentrated	13. Part-time	14. Earnings	15. Employment growth	16. Number of new jobs, 1984–95 (in thousands)	17. Entry requirements
Dietitians & nutritionists	•	•	•	•	•	•								M	H	12	H
Occupational therapists	•	•	•	•	•	•	•						•		H	8	H
Pharmacists	•	•	•	•	•	•								H	L	15	H
Physical therapists	•	•	•	•	•	•	•							M	H	25	H
Physician assistants	•	•	•	•	•	•								M	H	10	M

Recreational therapists	•	•	•	•	•	•	•	•		•				M	H	4	M
Registered nurses	•	•	•	•	•	•	•	•	•				•	M	H	452	M
Respiratory therapists	•	•	•	•	•	•	•							M	H	11	L
Speech pathologists & audiologists	•	•	•	•	•	•								M	M	8	H
Health Technologists & Technicians																	
Clinical laboratory technologists & technicians			•		•		•				•			L	L	18	[3]
Dental hygienists		•			•	•	•	•					•	L	H	22	M
Dispensing opticians		•	•	•	•	•	•							M	H	10	M
Electrocardiograph technicians		•	•		•	•	•							[1]	M	3	M
Electroenceph. technologists & technicians		•	•		•	•	•							[1]	H	1	M
Emergency medical technicians	•	•	•	•	•	•	•	•	•	•				L	L	3	M
Licensed practical nurses		•			•	•	•	•	•				•	L	M	106	M
Medical record technicians					•						•			L	H	10	M
Radiologic technologists		•			•	•	•		•					L	H	27	M
Surgical technicians		•			•	•	•							L	M	5	M

[1] Estimates not available.
[2] Less than 500.
[3] Vary, depending on job.

Writers, Artists, & Entertainers

	Job Requirements										Work Environment			Occupational Characteristics			
	1. Leadership/persuasion	2. Helping/instructing others	3. Problem-solving/creativity	4. Initiative	5. Work as part of a team	6. Frequent public contact	7. Manual dexterity	8. Physical stamina	9. Hazardous	10. Outdoors	11. Confined	12. Geographically concentrated	13. Part-time	14. Earnings	15. Employment growth	16. Number of new jobs, 1984–95 (in thousands)	17. Entry requirements
Communications Occupations																	
Public relations specialists	•		•	•	•									H	H	30	H
Radio & TV announcers & newscasters		•	•	•						•				L	M	6	H
Reporters & correspondents			•	•	•							•	¹		M	13	H
Writers & editors	•		•	•						•		•	¹		H	54	H
Visual Arts Occupations																	
Designers			•	•		•								H	H	46	H
Graphic & fine artists			•	•		•	•								H	60	M
Photographers & camera operators			•	•		•	•					•		M	H	29	M
Performing Arts Occupations																	
Actors, directors & producers			•	•	•	•	•				•	•		L	H	11	M
Dancers & choreographers			•	•	•	•	•				•	•		L	H	2	M
Musicians			•	•	•	•	•				•	•		L	M	26	M

Technologists & Technicians, Except Health

Engineering & Science Technicians

Occupation																	
Drafters						•			•						M	M	39	M
Electrical & electronics technicians	•		•	•	•	•			•						M	H	202	M
Engineering technicians	•		•	•	•	•			•						M	H	90	M
Science technicians	•		•	•	•	•			•						M	M	40	M

Other Technicians

Occupation																	
Air traffic controllers	•		•	•	•	•			•						H	L	[2]	H
Broadcast technicians	•		•	•	•				•		•				M	H	5	M
Computer programmers			•	•							•				H	H	245	H
Legal assistants			[3]	[3]							•				M	H	51	L
Library technicians	•		•	•	•	•						•			L	L	4	L
Tool programmers, numerical control			•	•	•	•				•					M	H	3	M

Marketing & Sale Occupations

Occupation																	
Cashiers	•		•	•	•	•			•			•			L	H	566	L
Insurance sales workers	•		•	•	•	•						•			M	L	34	M
Manufacturers' sales workers	•		•	•	•	•									H	L	51	H
Real estate agents & brokers	•		•	•	•	•		•				•			M	M	52	M
Retail sales workers	•		•	•	•	•						•			L	M	583	L
Securities & financial services sales workers	•		•	•	•	•						•			H	H	32	H
Travel agents	•		•	•	•	•									[1]	H	32	M
Wholesale trade sales workers	•		•	•	•	•									M	H	369	M

[1] Estimates not available.
[2] Less than 500.
[3] Vary, depending on job.

Administrative Support Occupations, Including Clerical

Occupation	1. Leadership/persuasion	2. Helping/instructing others	3. Problem-solving/creativity	4. Initiative	5. Work as part of a team	6. Frequent public contact	7. Manual dexterity	8. Physical stamina	9. Hazardous	10. Outdoors	11. Confined	12. Geographically concentrated	13. Part-time	14. Earnings	15. Employment growth	16. Number of new jobs, 1984-95 (in thousands)	17. Entry requirements
Bank tellers				•	•					•			•	L	L	24	L
Bookkeepers & accounting clerks		•		•						•			•	L	L	118	L
Computer & peripheral equipment operators			•	•		•				•				L	H	143	M
Data entry keyers				•	•	•	•			•				L	L	10	L
Mail carriers									•					M	L	8	L
Postal clerks				•						•				M	L	-27	L
Receptionists & information clerks	•			•	•	•				•			•	L	M	83	L
Reservation & transportation ticket agents & travel clerks	•	•	•	•	•	•				•				M	L	7	L
Secretaries				•		•								L	L	268	L
Statistical clerks				•						•				L	L	-12	L
Stenographers				•		•								L	L	-96	L
Teacher aides	•	•	•	•	•	•	•			•			•	L	M	88	L
Telephone operators	•			•	•	•								L	M	89	L
Traffic, shipping & receiving clerks		•	•	•										L	L	61	L
Typists				•		•				•			•	L	L	11	L

Service Occupations

Protective Service Occupations

Occupation																	
Correction officers				•							•	M	H	45	L
Firefighting occupations	•		•	•	•					•	M	M	48	L
Guards	•	•		•	•	•	•		•	L	H	188	L
Police & detectives	•	•		•	•	•	•		M	M	66	L

Food & Bev. Preparation & Serv. Occupations

Occupation																	
Bartenders			•	•	•		•		L	H	112	M
Chefs & cooks except short order	•	•	•	•	•	•	•	•	L	H	210	M
Waiters & waitresses	•	•	•	•	•	•	•		L	H	424	L

Health Service Occupations

Occupation																	
Dental assistants	•	•	•	•	•	•		L	H	48	L
Medical assistants	•	•	•	•	•			L	H	79	L
Nursing aides	•	•	•	•	•	•		L	H	348	L
Psychiatric aides	•	•	•	•				L	L	5	L

Cleaning Service Occupations

Occupation																	
Janitors & cleaners	•	•			L	M	433	L

Personal Service Occupations

Occupation																	
Barbers	•	•	•	•	•	•		L	L	4	M
Childcare workers	•	•	•	•	•	•	•		L	L	55	L
Cosmetologists & related workers	•	•	•	•	•	•	•		L	H	150	M
Flight attendants	•	•	•	•	•	•	•		M	H	13	L

Agricultural, Forestry & Fishing Occupations

Occupation																	
Farm operators & managers	•	•	•	•			•		M	L	-62	L

[1] Estimates not available.
[2] Less than 500.
[3] Vary, depending on job.

Mechanics & Repairers

	Job Requirements											Work Environ-ment		Occupational Characteristics			
	1. Leadership/persuasion	2. Helping/instructing others	3. Problem-solving/creativity	4. Initiative	5. Work as part of a team	6. Frequent public contact	7. Manual dexterity	8. Physical stamina	9. Hazardous	10. Outdoors	11. Confined	12. Geographically concentrated	13. Part-time	14. Earnings	15. Employment growth	16. Number of new jobs, 1984–95 (in thousands)	17. Entry requirements
Vehicle & Mobile Equip. Mechanics & Repairers																	
Aircraft mechanics & engine specialists		•		•			•	•	•		•			H	M	18	M
Automotive & motorcycle mechanics		•			•		•	•		•				M	H	185	M
Automotive body repairers		•					•	•		•				M	M	32	M
Diesel mechanics		•			•		•	•	•					M	H	48	M
Farm equipment mechanics		•					•	•		•				**M**	**L**	**2**	**M**
Mobile heavy equipment mechanics		•			•		•	•		•				M	M	12	M
Electrical & Electronic Equipment Repairers																	
Commercial & electronic equipment repairers		•	•		•	•								L	M	8	M
Communications equipment mechanics		•	•		•	•								M	L	3	M
Computer service technicians		•	•		•	•								M	H	28	M
Electronic home entertainment equip. repairers		•	•		•	•						•		M	M	7	M
Home appliance & power tool repairers		•	•		•	•								L	M	9	M
Line installers & cable splicers				•		•	•	•	•					M	M	24	L

Occupation																	
Telephone installers & repairers						•	•						M	L	-19	L
Other Mechanics & Repairers																
General maintenance mechanics	•						•					M	M	137	M
Heating, air-cond. & refrig. mechanics	•						•	•				M	M	29	M
Industrial machinery repairs	•						•	•		•		M	L	34	M
Millwrights	•						•	•				H	L	6	M
Musical instrument repairers & tuners							•					L	L	1	M
Office machine & cash register servicers	•	•					•					M	H	16	M
Vending machine servicers & repairers	•	•					•					1	M	5	M

Construction & Extractive Occupations

Construction Occupations

Occupation																	
Bricklayers & stonemasons	•				•			•	•			M	M	15	M
Carpenters	•				•	•		•	•			M	M	101	M
Carpet installers	•				•		•	•	•			M	M	11	M
Concrete masons & terrazzo workers	•				•			•	•			M	M	17	M
Drywall workers & lathers	•				•			•	•			M	M	11	M
Electricians	•				•			•	•			H	M	88	M
Glaziers	•				•			•	•			M	H	8	M
Insulation workers	•				•			•	•			M	M	7	M
Painters & paperhangers	•				•		•	•	•			M	L	17	M
Plasterers	•			•	•				•			M	L	1	M
Plumbers & pipefitters	•				•			•	•			H	M	61	M
Roofers	•				•			•	•			L	M	16	M

[1] Estimates not available.
[2] Less than 500.
[3] Vary, depending on job.

Construction & Extractive Occupations (continued)

	Job Requirements											Work Environment		Occupational Characteristics			
	1. Leadership/persuasion	2. Helping/instructing others	3. Problem-solving/creativity	4. Initiative	5. Work as part of a team	6. Frequent public contact	7. Manual dexterity	8. Physical stamina	9. Hazardous	10. Outdoors	11. Confined	12. Geographically concentrated	13. Part-time	14. Earnings	15. Employment growth	16. Number of new jobs, 1984–95 (in thousands)	17. Entry requirements
Sheet-metal workers		•		•			•	•						M	M	16	M
Structural & reinforcing metal workers		•		•			•	•	•					H	M	16	M
Tilesetters		•					•							M	M	3	M
Extractive Occupations																	
Roustabouts		•		•			•	•	•	•	•			M	L	2	L
Production Occupations																	
Precision Production Occupations																	
Blue-collar worker supervisors	•	•	•	•	•	•	•	•						M	L	85	M
Boilermakers				•			•	•	•					M	L	4	H
Bookbinding workers		•				•	•	•						L	M	14	M
Butchers & meatcutters						•	•	•	•	•				L	L	-9	M
Compositors & typesetters					•	•	•							L	M	14	M
Dental laboratory technicians						•	•	•						L	M	10	M
Jewelers	•	•	•	•	•	•	•	•			•			L	L	3	M

Machine Operators, Tenders & Setup Workers, Fabricators, Transportation and related occupations rating chart.

Occupation			Change (thousands)	
Lithographic & photoengraving workers	H	M	13	M
Machinists	M	L	37	M
Photographic process workers	L	H	14	L
Shoe & leather workers & repairers	L	L	-8	M
Tool-and-die makers	H	L	16	M
Upholsterers	L	L	6	M
Plant & System Operators				
Stationary engineers	M	L	4	M
Water & sewage treatment plant operators	L	M	10	M
Machine Operators, Tenders & Setup Workers				
Metalworking & plastic-working mach. operators		L	3	L
Numerical-control machine-tool operators	M	H	17	M
Printing press operators	M	M	26	M
Fabricators, Assemblers & Handworking Occup.				
Precision assemblers	L	M	66	L
Transportation equipment painters	M	M	9	M
Welders & cutters	M	M	41	M
Transportation & Material Moving Occupations				
Aircraft pilots	H	H	18	M
Bus drivers	M	M	77	M
Construction machinery operators	M	M	32	M
Industrial truck & tractor operators	M	L	-46	M
Truck drivers	M	M	428	M
Handlers, Equip. Cleaners, Helpers & Laborers				
Construction trades helpers	L	L	27	L

[1] Estimates not available.
[2] Less than 500.
[3] Vary, depending on job.

Acknowledgments

Since I wrote the first edition of this book a little over nine years ago, I have been able to get closer and closer to working with students directly through my job at Prentice Hall. I feel very fortunate to be able to spend all day thinking about what motivates you and what we can do to help you live up to your academic, professional, and life potential. For the first time in my life, I am actually able to live out what I have advised you all along—to be true to your inner strengths and to let all work and career points come from that center.

I have been equally blessed to work with a number of dedicated individuals on the board of Lifeskills, in Tucson, Arizona, where I grew up, in New York City, and in Denver, Colorado, where I live now. The contribution of time and money from these people has brought a world of possibilities to teenagers in the public high schools. My special thanks to Jerry Callaghan, who has been one of the primary believers and funders of this program from the very beginning.

It has been inspiring and rewarding to receive letters from those of you who read the first and second editions of this book, from the navy officer returning to college to a mother of three who asked if I had written a similar book for adults. The answer to that question is no, not until I am able to figure out various angles of thirty-something life.

Dick Bolles, author of *What Color Is Your Parachute?*, remains my life hero. I only hope that this book can accomplish half as much good as his book has for job seekers.

Elisabeth Kallick Dyssegaard is still the world's best editor. I am very appreciative of her efforts and those of all the people at Farrar, Straus and Giroux whom she has rallied behind this project.

Ingrid Damiani was my research assistant. In addition to her eye for detail and her ability to conduct and synthesize interviews, her style and personal charm motivated me each time we spoke. Ingrid has a very special way of dealing with people and an ability to understand the essence of a situation or the heart of a problem or opportunity.

My friends—Leigh, Susan, Cynthia, Julie, Anne, and Priscilla—showed tremendous support when I wrote the first edition. They have continued to encourage my writing and my love for students.

I owe my deepest appreciation to my parents. They have always taught me that no dream is too outrageous, no goal out of reach. My mom is my constant support; my dad, who died in 1991, is still a part of my daily life and thoughts.

My gratitude to the people who read this manuscript (some more than once) and gave me their suggestions on how it could be improved: Paul Alloca, Ron Avendinko, Ed Azary, Chris Barnett, Paul Bartick, Kim Caldwell-Meeks, Patti Carr, Jeff Carver, Terry Condon, Steve Dale, Jeannine Deloche, Merlene Dirielyan, Martin D'Luzansky, Cynthia Fox, Lisa Fumia, Rachel Fumia, John Isley, Linda Jacobs, Gary June, Joanne Karpe, David Lambert, Diane Lasky, Priscilla McGeehon, Karen McMillan, Darren Palmet, Vince Perez, Jon Perkins, Joyce Perkins, Jennifer Plane, Elizabeth Prince, Adrian Ramirez, Anne Riddick, Brian Sahd, Jen Salzar, Elizabeth Scarpelli, Charles Sherry, Leigh Talmage, Bud and Bonnie Therien, and Cyrus Vesser.

Finally, I want to express my gratefulness for safely progressing from the frenetic pace of my twenties, which produced this book, to the quieter, more directed life of my thirties, which has allowed me more time with my friends and family, with a greater focus on my personal mission in life: helping you to achieve all that you can be with your mind and God-given talents.

Permissions

Do You Have Advice?

If you would like to give me your comments on what you did and didn't like about the book, I would greatly appreciate it. Or, if you have a story of your own that you think would illustrate an important point, please write it down here or on a separate sheet of paper. I'll use your comments and suggestions as I revise the book for future editions.

	YES	NO
1. This book gave me a clearer focus on my college and career plans.	____	____
2. I liked the various opinions and attitudes that the book reflects.	____	____
3. This book made me feel more comfortable about starting college.	____	____

4. I would improve the book by (check one):
   Adding more examples ____
   Having fewer examples ____
   Other _____

| 5. I would recommend this book to my friends. | ____ | ____ |

6. I found out about this book by (check one):
   Seeing it in a bookstore ____
   My teacher assigned it ____
   It was a gift____

Thanks for your suggestions. Mail the form to:
   Carol Carter
   Majoring in the Rest of Your Life
   Farrar, Straus and Giroux, Inc.
   19 Union Square West
   New York, NY 10003

Your name and address: _____

_____

_____

Phone: _____

	YES	NO
Do we have permission to quote you?	____	____
Do we have permission to contact you?	____	____